W9-BDW-983

18 907061

Computer Simulation in Business Decision Making

Recent Titles from Quorum Books

Computer Simulation in Business Decision Making

A Guide for Managers, Planners, and MIS Professionals

Roy L. Nersesian

Quorum Books
New York · Westport, Connecticut · London

Library of Congress Cataloging-in-Publication Data

Nersesian, Roy L.
  Computer simulation in business decision making.

  Includes index.
  1. Decision-making—Computer simulation.
2. Corporate planning—Computer simulation. I. Title.
HD30.23.N465   1989   658.4'0352   88-32390
ISBN 0-89930-408-7 (lib. bdg. : alk. paper)

British Library Cataloguing in Publication Data is available.

Library of Congress Catalog Card Number: 88-32390
ISBN: 0-89930-408-7

First published in 1989 by Quorum Books

Greenwood Press, Inc.
88 Post Road West, Westport, Connecticut 06881

Printed in the United States of America

The paper used in this book complies with the
Permanent Paper Standard issued by the National
Information Standards Organization (Z39.48-1984).

10 9 8 7 6 5 4 3 2 1

To Maria

Contents

Introduction

Planning is expendable. Planning is a staff position, which, in these times of "mean and lean" organizations, has been severely reduced in scope or simply eliminated. In fact, the three planning positions I've held in the corporate world do not exist today. I advise my students, who are business majors, to seek line positions within the mainstream of activity of a company. I would feel guilty advising them otherwise.

Planning has not been particularly successful. The continuing jolts of future shocks becoming present reality have made a shambles of many a plan, no matter how coherent and logical these plans were when originally conceived. This has encouraged line managers to abandon planning, at least in a formal sense, and assume the responsibility themselves. Often this results in a company's reacting to change rather than anticipating change and planning accordingly.

This book is not on the virtue of a company having a planning organization. It is presumed that planning exists. The subject is how can planning be accomplished in a world of uncertainty, of change, of future shocks becoming present-day reality. Yet, let it be admitted early on that the results of the planning will be no better than the validity of the assessments incorporated in the plan. There is no promised land where planning can guarantee correct decisions.

Managers make the best decisions they can in the context of how they understand a situation at the moment the decision is made. The decision will be proven right or wrong to the degree that the unfolding of future events conforms to the assessments that were made on these events when the decision was made. It is simply a matter of choice whether a decision maker desires to have a report, or an analysis of the situation, in his hand when he makes a decision. I presume in this book that there ought to be something more to decision making than having a good gut feel of the situation.

If a planner is to aid in the decision making process, he is going to have to face certain obstacles. There will be a lack of complete data for analysis, a lack of sufficient time to perform a full analysis of the situation, and the imponderable nature of the future. A planner has some hope of dealing with the first two obstacles. It may be possible to collect more data than what is presently in hand or to allot more time to the analysis of the situation than is currently available. The last obstacle is truly intractable. There is no way to make the imponderable nature of the future ponderable.

Planners usually approach the quandary of dealing with an unknown by considering the most likely case, or a most likely series of events, with some bracketing mechanism. The bracketing mechanism is an optimistic,and a pessimistic, case or series of events. However, the degree of optimism and pessimism can vary over a wide range. A common method of analyzing the repercussions of various degrees of optimism and pessimism is to construct several scenarios around the base, or most likely, case. Equipped with the most likely case—and several other cases that bracket reasonable assessments of what may actually transpire as events unfold with the passage of time—the planner then begins the process that will lead to a recommended course of action.

This approach of assessing future outcomes is not entirely satisfactory. There is no probability distribution associated with any of the outcomes between the worst and best cases. In other words, there is no way of assessing how likely is the most likely case, or how unlikely are the optimistic and pessimistic cases. Worse yet, the model is static.

To illustrate the limitations of a static model, suppose that it is 1988 and a planner is investigating the desirability of investing in an existing oil well. The seller has indicated a price. The cost of operating the well is known within some degree of certainty. The whole exercise hinges on the assessment of the average price of oil over the remaining life of the well. The planner reads the trade journals, talks to a knowledgeable expert, and decides that $16 per barrel is the average price of crude oil over the remaining ten years of the productive life of the well. This becomes the most likely case, and the planner calculates the expected return on the investment for a price of $16 per barrel. Then he repeats the exercise and obtains the return for $24 per barrel representing the optimistic case, and $12 per barrel representing the pessimistic case.

Each of these three returns contains the explicit assumption that crude oil will be exactly $16 per barrel for ten years, or $24 per barrel for ten years, or $12 per barrel for ten years. The implicit assumption is that there is no change in the price of the oil from year to year. Furthermore, there is no probability distribution for the returns for the three prices of crude oil other than the most likely return is bracketed by the optimistic and pessimistic returns.

The reality of the situation is that we know something that is not in the model. The reality is that the price of crude will not be exactly one value for any significant duration of time, and that the costs of operating the well and the output of the well will fluctuate over the life of the well. The reality is that the well will be shut down if the price of oil falls below what it costs to operate the well, and operating costs will rise to enhance the output of the well if the price of crude oil rises to a level that justifies turning the pumps on full blast. These facts are known, yet none of them is contained in the conventional static model of analysis. All of these can be incorporated into a simulation model with less overall effort than manually calculating the return on investment for a large number of possible scenarios.

This is not to say that the result of a simulation will be any more reliable than a static conventional analysis. Both are as good as the basic assumptions. Investment mistakes can result from either method of analysis if the unfolding of events is grossly at variance with the underlying assumptions. Simulation does not provide results that guarantee correct decisions. Simulation is a planning tool that does provide, in my biased opinion, a richer harvest in the form of an expected outcome and a probability distribution for various outcomes, which can be incorporated into the making of a final decision. It is the nature of the unfolding of events after a decision has been made that determines if the decision was correct, and not the method of analysis that led to the making of the decision.

It is not difficult to construct a simulation model, as this book shows. As an added bonus, the model does not require discrete, or single, assessments of future values, which are dubious in nature because history has taught us that single values don't remain single for long periods of time. The model works off a decision maker's assessments of a range of values. This may not be any more correct than a single value assessment but certainly is a more realistic approach to assessing the imponderable nature of the future. Moreover, it is not required that the assessments remain static. For example, the decision maker's assessment of the range of the price of oil during the early life of the well may be significantly different from his assessment during the latter part of the life of the well. In fact, this is exactly his thinking on investing in an oil well during depressed times in the oil patch. He invests in an oil well in the expectation that the price of oil will increase at some point after he has made his investment, while the asking price on the well is influenced by the history of depressed oil prices and the dismal prospects of a quick turnaround.

Simulation model building does not demand knowledge of higher levels of mathematics. In fact, the key to understanding simulation is simply to understand how one would perform the calculations manually. Then it becomes a matter of having a programmer translate a human operation into something the computer can understand.

Simulation models can be groomed to fit a given situation much as a suit can be tailored to a body. This is quite the opposite of applying higher levels of mathematical modeling to analyzing business situations. Usually the business problem must be simplified to fit the structure of the mathematical model. The inherent advantage of simulation over higher levels of mathematics in problem solving is that a simulation model can be designed to fit the structure of the business problem.

This is not to say that simulation should become the only mode of analysis. A planner has a host of methodologies to address a particular problem. Each has its proper role to play. Simulation is a methodology that comes into play when other methodologies cannot address a problem adequately.

Simulation can be applied to a wide range of situations. Simulation has long been part of inventory and logistics planning, and it will be shown that those same principles can be used for personnel, production, marketing, investment, and financial planning.

This book was written for three audiences: for managers of planners, for planners, and for programmers. This was done intentionally to encourage the integration of interests and to foster mutual appreciation among the managers', planners', and the programmers' respective roles in the creation of simulation models and the interpretation of the results.

The broad objectives of each chapter are contained in an opening synopsis. The focus of each synopsis is to provide a manager of a planning organization with an appreciation of the general application of simulation to one facet of planning. Each chapter itself focuses on a particular situation that might befall a planner within the general application of simulation to the planning process. The intent is to develop a sense of how one manages the application of simulation to a particular problem. This includes the general guidance that has to be given to a programmer to permit him to set up a simulation program that is useful to the needs of a planner. One can look upon each chapter as a case study.

Simulation requires programming. It would not be in the interests of the planner to leave the programmer out of the picture. Each chapter contains an appendix for descriptive material and the applicable simulation program. The appendices are intended to aid a programmer who has not had much previous experience in setting up simulation programs.

Simulation programs consume an enormous amount of computer processing capacity. The cost to run a simulation program on a company's mainframe is prohibitively high. However, the variable cost of running an all-night simulation program on a personal computer is zero. The existence of personal computers, their low cost of acquisition, and the general ease of writing a simulation program tailored to the specific requirements of a business problem have made it possible to incorporate simulation into the planning function.

A personal computer was used to create, and run, the simulation models in this book. The simulation programs are written in the version of the BASIC language found in IBM-compatible personal computers. The graphics use the LOTUS spreadsheet software package. The purpose of the software is to augment the textual material and to demonstrate the principles of simulation model building. Readers should not interpret this choice of software as an endorsement. Rather, the choice of software should be interpreted as a historic accident. Other programming languages and other software packages may be suitable, or possibly superior, to my choice.

I am well aware that decision makers and planners are not exclusively male, although I exclusively refer to a decision maker or planner as "he." The "he" should not be construed to mean anything other than to avoid the clumsiness of having to say "he or she," or "she or he," a countless number of times.

I would like to take this opportunity to thank the staff of Quorum Books for their cooperation in transforming a manuscript into a book and to the faculty and staff of Monmouth College for their kind support in this endeavor. I would like to express a special thanks to Maria and the children, who had to endure my removing myself from their presence for long periods of time. However, in considering the alternative, one must not presume that this was too much of a sacrifice.

Computer Simulation in Business Decision Making

Breaking the Limits of Mathematical Constraints

SYNOPSIS

This chapter sets the tone of the book. The message is that a manager need not be entirely on his own if the mathematicians are unable to obtain an all-embracing solution to a management problem. The management problem under consideration here is the sequencing of jobs through a number of workshops in order to minimize the length of the workday. This is an admirable undertaking from the point of view of a manager of an establishment where jobs are completed on the basis of passing through a series of workshops.

The manager's workday is determined from the start of the first job in the first workshop to the completion of the last job in the last workshop. It is in the manager's self-interest, and in the interest of the company, to minimize the total time required to complete all the jobs through the judicious sequencing of the jobs. The mathematicians in operations research have provided the manager with a solution to this problem of minimizing the length of his workday. It is called Johnson's Rule. Unfortunately, for the manager, it may not be good enough.

Johnson's Rule imposes severe limitations as to the number of workshops through which a number of jobs can be sequenced to minimize the length of the workday. Suppose that there is a greater number of workshops than what can be handled by Johnson's Rule. What is a manager to do once the mathematical limitation of Johnson's Rule has been exceeded? There are those in operations research who maintain that the absence of an all-embracing algorithm to provide the ultimate solution means that a manager is strictly on his own. The chapter points out that the manager can at least obtain a better sequencing of jobs through simulation even if the sequencing may not be theoretically optimal. In other words, a manager need not surrender to the frustrations of the mathematicians. He can, through simulation, take effective action to minimize the length of his day for his own convenience and enhance the profitability of the company by reducing idle time in the workshops.

The March 1954 issue of the *Naval Research Logistics Quarterly* contained an article written by S. M. Johnson entitled "Optimal Two- and Three-Stage Production Schedules with Setup Times Included." Most textbooks on production management refer to this as Johnson's Rule. The three-stage production schedule is rarely discussed. Usually, Johnson's Rule is presented as a procedural methodology for sequencing jobs in a two-workshop environment with the objective of minimizing the total time to perform an assortment of jobs.

As an example, suppose that there is a furniture refinisher whose place of business consists of two workshops. The first workshop does the sanding, and the second does the varnishing. Varnishing cannot be accomplished until the sanding has been completed. There are, at the start of the day, five jobs to be accomplished. Their times in the sanding and varnishing workshops have been estimated as follows.

HOURS REQUIRED TO SAND AND VARNISH

JOB	SANDING WORKSHOP	VARNISHING WORKSHOP
1	1.50	1.25
2	2.00	3.00
3	0.50	2.00
4	2.25	1.25
5	0.75	1.25

Johnson's Rule provides the means to minimize the total time consumed in sequencing the five jobs through the sanding and varnishing workshops. The first step of Johnson's Rule is to select the job with the shortest task time. This is Job 3. As the task is sanding, Job 3 is assigned first in the sequencing of jobs. Had it been the varnishing which was the shortest task, Job 3 would have been assigned last in the sequencing of jobs.

Having assigned Job 3 as the first job to start the day, Job 3 is no longer considered in the further application of Johnson's Rule. The remaining jobs are 1, 2, 4, and 5. Of these, the shortest task to be accomplished is the sanding of Job 5. Had this been the varnishing of Job 5, it would have been assigned last, or next to last had Job 3 been assigned last. But the task is sanding. Therefore, it is assigned after Job 3. Thus the sequencing of the jobs is 3, then 5. The remaining jobs to be sequenced are 1, 2, and 4. Of these, the shortest task is a tie of 1.25 hours for varnishing Jobs 1 and 4. Johnson's Rule says that in case of a tie, select one of the jobs arbitrarily. As both of these tasks are varnishing, Job 4 is arbitrarily selected to be last in sequence. This leaves Jobs 1 and 2 left to be sequenced. The shortest task remaining is the varnishing of Job 1. This then is sequenced just before Job 4. The remaining job, by default, ends up between Jobs 5 and 1. The resulting sequence of assigning jobs to minimize the total time to perform all five jobs is 3, 5, 2, 1, and 4.

What would the workday be like if the jobs are sequenced 3, 5, 2, 1, and 4? The time to start, and the completion time, of each job through the two workshops is as follows.

```
        TIME TO START/FINISH JOB MEASURED FROM TIME 0 IN HOURS

SANDING-3      SANDING-5      SANDING-2      SANDING-1      SANDING-4
  0.00           0.50           1.25           3.25           4.75
  0.50           1.25           3.25           4.75           7.00

VARNISHING-3   VARNISHING-5   VARNISHING-2   VARNISHING-1   VARNISHING-4
  0.50           2.50           3.75           6.75           8.00
  2.50           3.75           6.75           8.00           9.25
```

Once the workday starts, the sanding workshop can start immediately working on the first job. As soon as the first job is completed, the sanding workshop can start on the next. There are no delays between jobs for the sanding workshop. The total workday for the sanding workshop is the sum of all the sanding jobs, seven hours, regardless of how the jobs are sequenced.

The varnishing workshop is a different matter. The varnishing workshop cannot start work until Job 3 is sanded as sanding must precede varnishing. After Job 3 is sanded, the workers in the varnishing shop can start working on Job 3. From this point on, the operation of the varnishing shop may be subject to delays because two conditions must be satisfied before the next job can be started. Job 5 cannot be started until the varnishing of Job 3 has been completed. But the completion of the varnishing of Job 3 does not mean that work can start on Job 5 because Job 5 must first have gone through the sanding shop. As can be seen in the prior table, there are no delays in the varnishing shop as sanding is always completed prior to the completion of the preceding varnishing task. Had this not been the case, the varnishing shop would have experienced idle time until the required sanding was finished.

It is now time to abandon Johnson's Rule. This can be easily accomplished. Johnson's Rule is limited to two, possibly three, workshops. Four workshops accomplishes the purpose of leaving a manager with no mathematical assistance. The four workshops are sanding, varnishing, etching, and finishing. All jobs must be done in sequential order. Sanding must precede varnishing. Varnishing must precede etching, and etching must precede finishing. The time duration in hours for the four operations associated with the five jobs is as follows.

JOB	SANDING TIME	VARNISHING TIME	ETCHING TIME	FINISHING TIME
1	1.50	1.25	2.50	1.25
2	2.00	3.00	1.50	1.00
3	0.50	2.00	2.50	1.00
4	2.25	1.25	3.00	0.50
5	0.75	1.25	2.25	1.25

Suppose that scheduling is done on the basis of first come, first served. That is, the scheduling is done in the order of Job 1, 2, 3, 4, and 5. The starting and finishing times of each job in the four workshops will be as follows.

TIME TO START/FINISH JOB MEASURED FROM TIME 0 IN HOURS

SANDING-1	SANDING-2	SANDING-3	SANDING-4	SANDING-5
0.00	1.50	3.50	4.00	6.25
1.50	3.50	4.00	6.25	7.00

VARNISHING-1	VARNISHING-2	VARNISHING-3	VARNISHING-4	VARNISHING-5
1.50	3.50	6.50	8.50	9.75
2.75	6.50	8.50	9.75	11.00

ETCHING-1	ETCHING-2	ETCHING-3	ETCHING-4	ETCHING-5
2.75	6.50	8.50	11.00	14.00
5.25	8.00	11.00	14.00	16.25

FINISHING-1	FINISHING-2	FINISHING-3	FINISHING-4	FINISHING-5
5.25	8.00	11.00	14.00	16.25
6.50	9.00	12.00	14.50	17.50

The total workday will be 17.50 hours long, which is starting the last job in the finishing shop (16.25 hours), plus the 1.25 hours to complete the last task in the last shop.

The derivation of the start/finish table follows a set methodology. Sanding of Job 1 starts at time zero. Job 2 sanding takes place after Job 1 has been completed. Job 1 takes 1.5 hours. The sanding of Job 2 starts at time 1.50. The sanding of Job 3 starts at time 3.50 which is two hours after the start of the sanding of Job 2. There are no delays in the sanding workshop as can be seen by observing the differences between the finishing time of one job and the starting time of the next.

The varnishing of Job 1 cannot start until sanding has been accomplished, which is time 1.50. Etching of Job 1 cannot start until the varnishing workshop has completed its work. The varnishing of Job 1 takes 1.25 hours. The etching shop cannot start work until time 2.75. And the finishing shop cannot start work until Job 1 has been through the etching shop. As the etching of Job 1 takes 2.5 hours, the workday for the finishing shop starts at time 5.25. This procedure determines the starting time of all workshops once the workday starts and the first job of the day has been selected.

Other than the sanding workshop, and the starting time of the other workshops, all other tasks are subject to delays. Consider, as an example, the scheduling of Job 3 in the finishing workshop, which, from the table, is scheduled to begin at time 11.00. The finishing of Job 3 cannot begin until the finishing of Job 2 has been completed. The finishing of Job 2 begins at time 8.00 and requires one hour of effort. The finishing shop completes Job 2 at time 9.00. However, the finishing shop cannot start the finishing of Job 3 until it has gone through the etching workshop. Job 3 entered the etching workshop at time 8.50 and requires 2.50 hours of work. Therefore, Job 3 cannot be started at time 11.00. What did the finishing shop personnel do between the completion of Job 2 at time 9.00 and the start of Job 3 at time 11.00? They rested. The differences between the completion time of the previous job and the starting time of the next reflect the inefficiency in the system with this sequencing of jobs. A review of the starting and completion times in the etching and finishing workshops shows a fair amount of idle time. The workday ends when the finishing shop starts Job 5 at time 16.25 and completes it 1.25 hours later at time 17.50.

What if you were the manager of this workshop? There is no Johnson's Rule to aid you. Given a sufficient number of clerks, you could manually schedule the jobs through every possible combination to arrive at that sequence which minimizes the length of the day. One sequence has been accomplished which establishes the methodology of determining the length of the workday. There remains only the calculational task which the clerks can perform once they have been taught the methodology. The clerks can perform the calculations for each possible sequencing of the five jobs and then select the sequence that results in the shortest day.

The unique sequencing of a group of N jobs is N!. For five jobs, the number of combinations of unique sequences is $5 \times 4 \times 3 \times 2 \times 1$, or 120 combinations, of which a few are shown as follows.

UNIQUE SEQUENCING OF FIVE JOBS

1	2	3	4	5
1	2	3	5	4
1	2	4	3	5
1	2	4	5	3
		.		
		.		
		.		
5	4	2	1	3
5	4	2	3	1
5	4	3	1	2
5	4	3	2	1

Given a sufficient number of clerks to perform the calculations, it is possible to explore different sequencing of the various jobs to reduce the idle time and cut labor costs. In other words, is there a sequence of jobs that will reduce the 17.5-hour day that resulted from the decision to schedule the work in the sequence of first come, first serve? Possibly, but not practical. Too many clerks would be required. The time saved by the clerks' examining 120 different combinations of sequencing jobs would not justify the cost. But the methodology is one of calculation: of adding and comparing. This is a programmable task that can be accomplished par excellence by a computer.

Actually, the clerks require instruction in two methodologies. One is to determine all 120 unique combinations of scheduling the five jobs. To ensure that no possible combination of sequencing the jobs is unintentionally omitted, one can instruct the clerks to start with the number 11111 and keep adding 1 until the number 55555 is obtained omitting the digits 6, 7, 8, 9, and 0. The clerks are looking at 5×5×5×5×5 combinations of numbers, or a total of 3,125 sequences. For each of these 3,125 sequences, the clerks would examine and select only those sequences where no two numbers are alike. This process will reduce the 3,125 sequences to the 120 that are unique in that every digit between 1 and 5 is represented only once.

This process does not have to be repeated. Once accomplished for a particular number of jobs, the unique sequencing of the jobs can be stored in a file. The file will contain the 120 unique sequences of the five jobs. The next time the clerks have five jobs to schedule, they can open the file which contains the 120 unique sequences and proceed from there.

After the sequencing of the number of jobs under consideration has been completed, then the length of the workday for each sequence can be calculated. If the length of the workday is shorter than the one previously calculated, the length of the day and the sequence of jobs are written on a piece of paper. The process continues until another sequence provides for a shorter day. The old record is thrown away and the new length of the workday and the sequence of jobs associated with that length of day is written down on the paper. This process continues until all the sequences have been considered. Only one result is kept during this process. After examining all the sequences, the last recorded result becomes the desired answer to the problem. Given the proper instructions, hiring the requisite number of clerks, and giving them sufficient time to complete the task, the clerks will be able to report that the shortest workday can be achieved by sequencing the jobs in the order of Job 5, 1, 3, 2, 4 resulting in a workday of 14.25 hours. The scheduling details of this sequence of assigning jobs follows.

```
       TIME TO START/FINISH JOB MEASURED FROM TIME 0 IN HOURS

SANDING-5       SANDING-1      SANDING-3      SANDING-2      SANDING-4
   0.00            0.75           2.25           2.75           4.75
   0.75            2.25           2.75           4.75           7.00

VARNISHING-5  VARNISHING-1  VARNISHING-3   VARNISHING-2  VARNISHING-4
   0.75            2.25           3.50           5.50           8.50
   2.00            3.50           5.50           8.50           9.75

ETCHING-5       ETCHING-1      ETCHING-3      ETCHING-2      ETCHING-4
   2.00            4.25           6.75           9.25          10.75
   4.25            6.75           9.25          10.75          13.75

FINISHING-5   FINISHING-1    FINISHING-3    FINISHING-2   FINISHING-4
   4.25            6.75           9.25          10.75          13.75
   5.50            8.00          10.25          11.75          14.25
```

Obviously, the number of clerks to perform this methodical and repetitive operation would be costly and time consuming. However, since the task is one of numerous calculations, a personal computer can be substituted for the clerks. Clerks require instructions and so does a computer. The major difference between clerks and a computer is that a computer requires more instructions than any clerk. Depending on his motivation and sense of responsibility, a human clerk has the potential of identifying, and perhaps correcting, an improper instruction. Not so for the computer. A computer will do exactly what it is instructed to do no matter what the consequences. The general name given to a form of instruction that must be exact in all details, and free of all error, is computer programming.

A computer program provides the explicit directions on how to determine, and store, the unique sequencing of jobs, and proceeding from there to find out the sequence of jobs that minimizes the workday. A planner would have a greater appreciation of programming if he were to bear in mind that the directions given to a computer by a programmer would not be appreciably different from the directions given to clerks to perform the same task. The major difference is that the computer represents clerks of incomparable stupidity. With that difference in mind, the planner has a fair appreciation of the programmer's task. The accompanying appendix contains the instructions for the clerks to perform the calculations to determine the unique combinations of sequencing jobs and to store the results to avoid having to repeat the exercise. The instructions to open up a correct file of unique sequencing of jobs to determine the length of the workday are also contained in the appendix. Again, these instructions are essentially no different from the ones that would be provided to human clerks.

The problem with this approach, as described up to this point, does not lie in the number of workshops. There is no limit as to the number of workshops this system can handle. The problem is the number of jobs to be sequenced. It has already been noted that there are $5 \times 5 \times 5 \times 5 \times 5$, or 3,125, combinations of the digits 1, 2, 3, 4, and 5 which have to be examined to determine $5 \times 4 \times 3 \times 2 \times 1$, or 120, unique sequences where no digit is listed more than once.

The number of combinations that have to be examined grows astronomically as the number of jobs increases. For six jobs, the number of combinations which have to be examined for uniqueness is $6 \times 6 \times 6 \times 6 \times 6 \times 6$, or 46,656, to identify the $6 \times 5 \times 4 \times 3 \times 2 \times 1$, or 720, unique sequences of six numbers where each digit is represented once. As shown in the appendix, this chore only has to be done once, and the 720 unique sequences can be stored in a file for future reference.

At some point the process has to stop. For seven jobs, there are 5,040 unique sequences to be identified from 823,543 combinations of the digits 1 through 7. For eight jobs, the corresponding numbers are 40,320 unique sequences from 16,777,216 possible combinations, and so forth.

Suppose that the manager of the workshop has a planner to assist him in scheduling jobs. If a planner were doing this process manually with the aid of the clerks, he would be forced to use random sampling techniques. Suppose that there were ten jobs to be scheduled. To obtain a random schedule of jobs to be examined, a planner might have a bag filled with ten ping-pong balls each labeled 1 through 10. A clerk would reach into the bag and take out a ping-pong ball. Suppose that the ping-pong ball has an "8" painted on it. Job 8 is now the first job to be sequenced. The clerk puts the ping-pong ball back into the bag and shakes the bag before reaching back in and taking out another ball. Suppose that it is a "6" ball. The clerk looks at the first number and notes that it is not a "6." The second job to be scheduled is Job 6, the ball is returned, the bag shaken up, and a third ball is taken out. Whatever the number on the ball, as long as it is not an 8 or 6, that becomes the third job. If the ball is an 8 or 6, the clerk is instructed to put it back in the bag, shake the bag, and draw out another ball. This process is repeated until a unique sequence of ten digits, such as 8-6-1-9-10-3-5-7-4-2 is established. Then the job sequence is used to establish the length of the workday. The process is repeated. A record is kept only of the sequence that yields the minimum length of the workday. The results of the rest are discarded.

These would be the directions a planner would provide to the clerks, and these are the exact instructions a programmer would provide to the computer as shown in the appendix. There is no difference between instructing the clerks and instructing the computer, except in the means of communication and having some evanescent hope that the clerks have sufficient intelligence to correct an erroneous instruction. The computer, however, costs much less than a horde of clerks and can perform thousands of calculations in the time it takes a clerk to reach into a bag and draw out a ping-pong ball.

A logical question is how long should the simulation program be run? Even an all-night run for ten jobs would provide a pitifully small sampling of the 3,628,800 unique sequences of the digits 1 through 10. On the other hand, one can obtain a reasonable scheduling sequence in a relatively short time. For instance, on a sample run for ten jobs, there were rapid improvements in shortening the workday during the first 200 randomly generated schedules. After that, the next improvement was on the 1,900th schedule. The next on the 3,500th, and the next minuscule improvement occurred on the 9,000th try. Watching a simulation where only the improvements are printed on the screen will demonstrate the rapidity of closing in on a reasonably acceptable scheduling sequence. In this case, running the program all night did not yield results that were materially different than running the program for two hours. Yet, even on an all-night run, depending on the computer speed, only a small percentage of all the possible unique sequencing of jobs is examined.

One might think that this avenue of approach to what is an insolvable problem might be appreciated by those involved in management science or operations research. This is hardly the case. Their search is for the Holy Algorithm, that set of rules that solves the problem of sequencing many jobs through multiple workshops with exactitude. As an operations research specialist commented to me, "All that you have done is solve a problem, you did not provide a solution."

This is precisely the point of this book. And on that day that the Holy Algorithm is provided for more than three workshops, I will abandon this chapter. But until that day, this approximation of the final solution will have to do as a substitute as the search continues for the Holy Algorithm. After all, the simulation does reduce the length of the workday for the manager, who is you or me.

Appendix to Chapter 1

This appendix provides guidance on breaking the limits of the mathematical constraints imposed by Johnson's Rule. First is setting up the methodology for calculating the length of the workday. This is followed by determining unique sequencing of jobs, the storage of the results, and the random generation of job sequences.

CALCULATING THE LENGTH OF THE WORKDAY

Let $P(I,J)$ designate the starting time of job I in workshop J. $P(1,1)$ is the starting time for the day and the starting time of the first job in the first workshop. The workshop starts work on the second job, $P(1,2)$, when the first job is completed.

$P(1,2)=P(1,1)+T(1,1)$ where $T(1,1)$ is the duration of time of the first job in the first workshop.

The starting time for the third job in the first workshop is the starting time for the second job plus the time required to complete the second job.

$P(1,3)=P(1,2)+T(2,1)$ where $T(2,1)$ is the duration of time of the second job in the first workshop.

Examining the equations can lead to a generalization where, for R number of jobs, the starting time for each job in the first workshop can be expressed in BASIC as follows.

```
1000  P(1,1)=0
1010  FOR I=2 TO R
1020  P(1,I)=P(1,I-1)+T(I-1,1)
1030  NEXT
```

One should convince oneself that substituting values of I from 2 to 5 for jobs 2 through 5, and the values of $T(I-1,1)$, which are the times of the various jobs in the first (sanding) workshop, yield the starting times listed earlier in this chapter.

The varnishing workshop cannot start the day until the sanding shop has completed sanding the first job. Let $P(2,1)$ be the starting time for the second workshop on its first job.

$P(2,1)=P(1,1)+T(1,1)$

The third workshop, the etching shop, cannot begin work until after the varnishing shop is finished with its first job because etching cannot be accomplished until after the item has been varnished.

$P(3,1)=P(2,1)+T(1,2)$ where $P(2,1)$ is the time of the start of the first job in the second workshop and $T(1,2)$ is the time duration of the first job in the second workshop. Generalizing for W number of workshops, the time to begin work in each of the sequential workshops can be expressed as follows.

```
1040   FOR I=2 to W
1050   P(I,1)=P(I-1,1)+T(1,I-1)
1060   NEXT
```

Neither the work done in the first workshop, the sanding shop, nor the start of the work in the other workshops is subject to any delay other than the completion of one preceding activity. All remaining activities are subject to a potential delay between the completion of one job and the start of the next.

```
P(1,1)                    P(1,2)
 ↑   T(1,1)                ↑   T(2,1)
 |                         |
 'Job 1 Sanding            'Job 2 Sanding


          P(2,1)                    P(2,2)
           ↑   T(1,2)                ↑   T(2,2)
           |                         |
           'Job 1 Varnishing         'Job 2 Varnishing
```

$$P(2,2)=\begin{cases} P(1,2)+T(2,1) & ? \\ P(2,1)+T(1,2) & ? \end{cases}$$

The time to start the varnishing of Job 2 is the latter time of either the completion of the sanding of Job 2 or the completion of the varnishing of Job 1. This selection of the greater of two time values holds true for every starting point within the matrix of jobs and tasks except for those jobs lying in the first row and the first task of each succeeding row. Moreover, in laying out the complete matrix and examining the nature of P(I,J), the starting time of each task, other than those P(I,J) values where either the I and the J have a value of 1, there emerges a standard procedure for the calculation of the starting times. The generalized method for calculating the starting times for R jobs and W workshops, other than the first row and the first value of each succeeding row, is as follows.

```
1070   FOR I=2 TO W
1080   FOR J=2 to R
1090   A=P(I-1,J)+T(J,I-1)
1100   B=P(I,J-1)+T(J-1,I)
1110   IF A>B THEN 1120 ELSE 1130
1120   P(I,J)=A:GOTO 1140
1130   P(I,J)=B
1140   NEXT:NEXT
```

The previous program determines two values. The variable A is the starting time of the previous task in the particular workshop plus the time required to complete the previous task. This condition has to be met before work can start on the task under consideration. The other condition is calculated as variable B. This is the starting time of the previous workshop for the particular task plus the time required to complete the work. The starting time, $P(I,J)$, of a particular task in a particular workshop is the larger of the two values A or B.

The program will provide the starting time of every job for every task. The starting time for the last task of the last job is $P(W,R)$. To this must be added the time element of doing the last job in the last workshop, $T(R,W)$, in order to obtain the length of the working day. The objective is to sequence the jobs in order to minimize the value $P(W,R)+T(R,W)$, which is the length of the workday.

SEQUENCING OF JOBS AND STORING RESULTS

Having set up the instructions to determine the length of the workday given a sequence of jobs, the next objective is to determine the sequence of assigning jobs. Suppose that there are three jobs to be sequenced. The following program examines $3\times3\times3$, or twenty-seven combinations of the numbers 1, 2, and 3 to obtain the $3\times2\times1$, or six combinations, where each number in the sequence is included once, and only once, and stores the results in a data file named "3JOB."

```
10 REM NAME OF PROGRAM IS CREATE
20 OPEN "O",#1,"3JOB"
30 K=3
40 FOR N1=1 TO K
42 N(1)=N1
45 FOR N2=1 TO K
47 N(2)=N2
50 FOR N3=1 TO K
52 N(3)=N3
70 PRINT N(1),N(2),N(3)
75 Z=0
80 FOR I=1 TO K-1
90 FOR J=I+1 TO K
100 IF N(I)=N(J) THEN 110 ELSE 120
110 Z=1
120 NEXT:NEXT
130 IF Z=1 THEN 160
135 PRINT:PRINT "WRITING INTO DATA FILE:"
140 PRINT N(1),N(2),N(3)
145 PRINT
150 WRITE #1,N(1),N(2),N(3)
155 INPUT "PRESS RETURN TO CONTINUE: ",Z$
160 NEXT:NEXT:NEXT
170 CLOSE #1
172 PRINT
```

```
175 PRINT "DUMPING CONTENTS OF CREATED FILE":PRINT
180 OPEN "I",#1,"3JOB"
190 INPUT#1,A,B,C
200 PRINT A,B,C
210 IF EOF(1) THEN 220 ELSE 190
220 CLOSE#1:END
```

Statements 40, 45, and 50, along with statement 160, create every combination of K numbers where K=3 (statement 30). These are printed on the screen (statement 70) and examined for uniqueness in statements 80–120. The indicator Z becomes 1 if any two numbers in the sequence are identical. If there are no identical numbers, Z remains at its zero value. This is interpreted to mean that the sequence is considered unique and written into the 3JOB data file in statements 135–160. At the end of selecting all unique combinations of the numbers 1, 2, and 3, the contents of the created 3JOB data file are dumped for examination. The opening, writing to and reading from the sequential data file is in conformity with the CP/M-80 and the MS-DOS operating systems.

The next task is to create the 4JOB data file which will contain the unique sequencing of four jobs. Here, 4×4×4×4, or 256 combinations of the numbers 1, 2, 3, and 4 must be examined to find the 4×3×2×1, or twenty-four unique combinations where every number in the sequence is listed only one time.

The following program to create 4JOB is very similar to the program to create 3JOB with editorial changes to statements 20, 30, 70, 140, 150, 160, 180, 190, and 200, and the addition of statements 55 and 57.

```
10 REM NAME OF PROGRAM IS CREATE
20 OPEN "O",#1,"4JOB"
30 K=4
40 FOR N1=1 TO K
42 N(1)=N1
45 FOR N2=1 TO K
47 N(2)=N2
50 FOR N3=1 TO K
52 N(3)=N3
55 FOR N4=1 TO K
57 N(4)=N4
70 PRINT N(1),N(2),N(3),N(4)
75 Z=0
80 FOR I=1 TO K-1
90 FOR J=I+1 TO K
100 IF N(I)=N(J) THEN 110 ELSE 120
110 Z=1
120 NEXT:NEXT
130 IF Z=1 THEN 160
135 PRINT:PRINT "WRITING INTO DATA FILE:"
140 PRINT N(1),N(2),N(3),N(4)
145 PRINT
150 WRITE #1,N(1),N(2),N(3),N(4)
155 INPUT "PRESS RETURN TO CONTINUE: ",Z$
```

```
160 NEXT:NEXT:NEXT:NEXT
170 CLOSE #1
172 PRINT
175 PRINT "DUMPING CONTENTS OF CREATED FILE":PRINT
180 OPEN "I",#1,"4JOB"
190 INPUT#1,A,B,C,D
200 PRINT A,B,C,D
210 IF EOF(1) THEN 220 ELSE 190
220 CLOSE#1:END
```

Similar changes can be incorporated to create the 5JOB and the 6JOB data files which contain the unique sequencing of five and six jobs.

At some point the process will have to stop. For seven jobs, there are 5,040 unique sequences requiring the examination of 823,543 possible combinations of the numbers 1 through 7. For eight jobs, the corresponding numbers are 40,320 unique sequences and 16,777,216 possible combinations of the numbers 1 through 8 which have to be examined for uniqueness. The process of obtaining every possible unique sequence has been arbitrarily stopped at six jobs. These unique sequences are contained in the data files 3JOB, 4JOB, 5JOB, and 6JOB.

SAMPLING THROUGH RANDOM GENERATED SEQUENCING OF JOBS

In the complete program listed at the end of this appendix, the problem has been expanded to handle up to ten jobs and ten workshops. The data of how long each job will take in each workshop is in the X(I,J) array, which is established in statements 50–240. READ and DATA statements could be substituted to create an internal data file. The number of jobs to be considered is a minimum of three jobs, and a maximum of ten jobs. Statement 300 assigns the three job case to statement 310. Statement 310 opens up the 3JOB data file and reads in the first line of that file and assigns it to the variables N(1), N(2), and N(3). Thus, the first time through: N(1)=1, N(2)=2, and N(3)=3.

At statements 950–980, the T(I,J) array is set up where T(1,J)=X(1,J), T(2,J)=X (2,J), and T(3,J)=X(3,J). Statements 1000–1140 are as previously described with the addition of statement 1150 which calculates the total time of the sequence. On completion of the subroutine, the program returns to statement 340 where the total time of the project is compared to Z, where Z started off with a very high value (statement 30). If the total time to complete the sequence of jobs is shorter than Z, then the total time is printed along with the sequence of jobs (statement 350). The new Z value to be beaten is established in statement 360.

If not at the end of the file, the program reverts back to statement 320 where the next line in the file is read. This will be the sequence N(1)=1, N(2)=3, and N(3)=2. The T(I,J) array will be set up in the subroutine beginning at statement 950 as T(1,J)=X(1,J), T(2,J)=X(3,J), and T(3,J)=X(2,J). If this new sequence of assigning jobs is better than the prior sequence, its total time, T, will be printed along with the sequence. The new Z value which has to be beaten is this latest value of T. If any sequence does not beat the established record, so to speak, the next line in the data file is fed into the program and analyzed. At the end of the data file, the program is directed to statement 1200 where the data file is closed and the program ended. The last printed sequence provides the shortest workday.

The technique is similar for handling four, five, and six jobs. The challenge arises on how to handle more than six jobs. No data files have been created containing every possible unique sequence of numbers for more than six jobs.

Computers are capable of generating what are called random numbers. The so-called random numbers vary in value between 0 and 1 as can be seen running the following program.

```
10   FOR I=1 TO 10
20   Y=RND(Y)
30   PRINT Y
40   NEXT
50   END
```

Run the program and examine the values. They do have an appearance of randomness. Rerun the program again and compare the results. They may be the same as before if the random number generator has not been reseeded.

Random numbers have the appearance of randomness, but they are far from random. There is nothing random about the operation of a computer. Yet the continual generation of so-called random, or pseudo-random, numbers does appear to be random in that there does not appear to be bias in one set of numbers appearing consistently more, or less, frequently than others. However, published articles suggest that there may be patterns to the sequencing of computer-generated random numbers, which, of course, should not be in a mathematically pure selection of random numbers.

Suppose that there is a desire to randomly assign the sequencing of R number of jobs. Running the following program generates a random selection of R numbers.

```
10   INPUT ''NUMBER OF JOBS: '';R
20   FOR I=1 TO 10
30   Y=RND(Y)
40   X=INT((R+1)*Y)
50   PRINT X
60   NEXT
70   INPUT ''PRESS RETURN TO CONTINUE'';Z$
80   GOTO 20
```

Since the integer function merely cuts off the decimal, and since Y is less than 1.0, the value of R is increased by 1 to make it possible to generate the integer 10. In running the program, the integer 0 appears, which is not a possible value when assigning jobs. There is also repetition of integer values. The next program is intended to create a unique sequence of the numbers 1 through 10 where no number is repeated more than once, and where every number is represented once, and where the possibility of the integers 0 and 11 has been eliminated.

```
700   R=10
710   Y=RND(Y)
720   X=INT((R+1)*Y)
```

```
725   IF X>R THEN 730 ELSE 735
730   X=R:GOTO 745
735   IF X<1 THEN 740 ELSE 745
740   X=1
745   N(1)=X
750   FOR I=2 TO R
760   Y=RND(Y)
770   X=INT((R+1*Y)
775   IF X>R THEN 780 ELSE 785
780   X=R:GOTO 795
785   IF X<1 THEN 790 ELSE 795
790   X=1
795   Z1=0
800   FOR J=1 TO I-1
810   IF X=N(J) THEN 820 ELSE 830
820   Z1=1
830   NEXT
840   IF Z1=1 THEN 760
850   N(I)=X
855   NEXT
860   PRINT N(1);N(2);N(3); N(4);N(5);N(6);
      N(7);N(8);N(9);N(10)
870   GOTO 700
```

Statements 700–745 generate a random first number for the sequence ensuring that it is not 0 or 11, or greater than 11. Statements 750–790 generate subsequent numbers, which are checked in statements 795–855 for uniqueness. The indicator Z1 remains zero only if no prior number is the same as the value for X. If this condition is satisfied, then X becomes the next sequential number (statement 850). If not, statement 840 directs the program to select another random number until uniqueness is achieved. At the end of selecting the tenth value, the results are printed in statement 860, and the whole process is repeated until a signal is received by the operator to interrupt the program.

This method of generating a unique sequence of numbers can be integrated into the work that has already been done. For seven or more jobs, randomly sequencing is programmed to occur 100,000 times. In practice, one merely stops the program when desired since the last best sequence is recorded on the screen. It is advisable to run the ten job case and watch the progress being made to reduce the length of the workday. At first, improvements come rapidly. However, the longer the program runs, the greater is the length of time between the printing of sequences which shorten the workday and the smaller will be the degree of the shortening of the workday. One cannot help but sense the feeling of diminishing returns. Running the program all night may not yield results which are materially different than running the program for an hour or two.

One might ask how long the workday would be without resorting to this program. In other words, without the use of this program, and being arbitrary in the sequencing of jobs, how long can the workday be? The worst one might do is to accidentally stumble on the sequence which maximizes the length of the workday. Two minor editing alterations change the program from one of minimizing to maximizing the length of the workday.

```
30    Z=0
870   IF T>Z THEN 880 ELSE 890
```

The point to bear in mind in this exercise is that a small bug in the program might result in unexpected, and unwanted, consequences. One must always be on guard for a program doing something it was not intended to do, which can happen when a > is inadvertently used instead of <. This is why running the program in small segments during program development to verify the results is a good practice.

Perhaps a more appropriate measure of how this program can save time in assigning the sequence of jobs is to obtain the average of random, or arbitrary, assignment of jobs. Again, only minor changes to the program are necessary. Both of these changes apply to more than six jobs. An internal data base would eliminate the need to reinput the data.

```
90    Z=0
870   Z=Z+T
880   PRINT Z/K
Delete statement 890
```

The variable Z now accumulates the time element of each randomly generated sequencing of jobs. Dividing that value by the number of sequences being analyzed yields the average time. This provides the means for measuring the effectiveness of having this program over pure arbitrary selection of the sequencing of jobs.

The program can be expanded beyond ten jobs and ten workshops. A dimension statement has to be added for N(I), and statements 20, 300, and 880 have to be modified. The complete listing of the program follows.

```
10 REM NAME OF PROGRAM IS WORKSHOP
20 DIM P(10,10):DIM T(10,10):DIM X(10,10)
30 Z=10000
40 PRINT:PRINT
50 INPUT "NUMBER OF JOBS: ";R:PRINT
60 IF R<3 THEN 70 ELSE 80
70 PRINT "JOBS MUST BE 3 OR MORE":GOTO 40
80 INPUT "NUMBER OF WORKSHOPS: ";W:PRINT
90 IF W<3 THEN 100 ELSE 200
100 PRINT "USE JOHNSON'S RULE":GOTO 80
200 FOR I=1 TO R
210 FOR J=1 TO W
220 PRINT "FOR JOB";I;"IN WORKSHOP";J
230 INPUT "HOURS TO COMPLETE: ";X(I,J)
240 PRINT:NEXT:NEXT
300 ON R GOTO 305,305,310,410,510,610,700,700,700,700
305 PRINT "NUMBER OF JOBS < 3; CHECK INPUT":GOTO 40
310 OPEN "I",#1,"3JOB"
320 INPUT #1,N(1),N(2),N(3)
330 GOSUB 950
340 IF T<Z THEN 350 ELSE 370
350 PRINT T,N(1),N(2),N(3)
360 Z=T
370 IF EOF(1) THEN 1200 ELSE 320
410 OPEN "I",#1,"4JOB"
420 INPUT #1,N(1),N(2),N(3),N(4)
430 GOSUB 950
```

```
440 IF T<Z THEN 450 ELSE 470
450 PRINT T,N(1),N(2),N(3),N(4)
460 Z=T
470 IF EOF(1) THEN 1200 ELSE 420
510 OPEN "I",#1,"5JOB"
520 INPUT #1,N(1),N(2),N(3),N(4),N(5)
530 GOSUB 950
540 IF T<Z THEN 550 ELSE 570
550 PRINT T,N(1),N(2),N(3);N(4);N(5)
560 Z=T
570 IF EOF(1) THEN 1200 ELSE 520
610 OPEN "I",#1,"6JOB"
620 INPUT #1,N(1),N(2),N(3),N(4),N(5),N(6)
630 GOSUB 950
640 IF T<Z THEN 650 ELSE 670
650 PRINT T,N(1),N(2),N(3);N(4);N(5);N(6)
660 Z=T
670 IF EOF(1) THEN 1200 ELSE 620
700 FOR K=1 TO 100000!
710 Y=RND(Y)
720 X=INT((R+1)*Y)
725 IF X>R THEN 730 ELSE 735
730 X=R:GOTO 745
735 IF X<1 THEN 740 ELSE 745
740 X=1
745 N(1)=X
750 FOR I=2 TO R
760 Y=RND(Y)
770 X=INT((R+1)*Y)
775 IF X>R THEN 780 ELSE 785
780 X=R:GOTO 795
785 IF X<1 THEN 790 ELSE 795
790 X=1
795 Z1=0
800 FOR J=1 TO I-1
810 IF X=N(J) THEN 820 ELSE 830
820 Z1=1
830 NEXT
840 IF Z1=1 THEN 760
850 N(I)=X
855 NEXT
860 GOSUB 950
870 IF T<Z THEN 880 ELSE 900
880 PRINT K;T,N(1);N(2);N(3);N(4);N(5);N(6);N(7);N(8);N(9);N(10)
890 Z=T
900 NEXT
950 FOR I=1 TO R
960 FOR J=1 TO W
970 T(I,J)=X(N(I),J)
980 NEXT:NEXT
1000 P(1,1)=0
1010 FOR I=2 TO R
1020 P(1,I)=P(1,I-1)+T(I-1,1)
1030 NEXT
1040 FOR I=2 TO W
1050 P(I,1)=P(I-1,1)+T(1,I-1)
1060 NEXT
1070 FOR I=2 TO W
1080 FOR J=2 TO R
1090 A=P(I-1,J)+T(J,I-1)
```

```
1100 B=P(I,J-1)+T(J-1,I)
1110 IF A>B THEN 1120 ELSE 1130
1120 P(I,J)=A:GOTO 1140
1130 P(I,J)=B
1140 NEXT:NEXT
1150 T=P(W,R)+T(R,W)
1160 RETURN
1200 CLOSE#1:END
```

2

A Businessman's Assessment

SYNOPSIS

Planners must deal with the future whose very nature is its inscrutability. Most means of analysis force a planner to select a single value for a key variable. Generally, businessmen are reluctant to give a single value. They are much more comfortable providing a most likely value bracketed by a reasonable limit on the range of the minimum and maximum values one can expect. Businessmen are more comfortable providing a judgment of future value in this manner because it more realistically reflects the limits of human perception on assessing future events. Using single cycle inventory management as a framework for discussion, this chapter provides the general methodology for translating a businessmen's assessment of future sales into a cumulative probability distribution, which is the key to utilizing simulation in the decision making process.

The pumpkin stand is a classic single cycle inventory problem. How many pumpkins does a pumpkin stand owner acquire in the weeks before Halloween? This is the principal business decision to be made by those in the Halloween pumpkin trade. After all, there is going to be a slight shrinkage in the value of the pumpkin inventory the day after Halloween.

The ideal, of course, is to order a sufficient number of pumpkins all of which will be sold while, at the same time, being confident that no customer will be turned away because of a lack of pumpkins. That's a tall order. But it is part and parcel of being in the pumpkin business, the Christmas tree business, or the newspaper business. For all three, there comes a day of reckoning. That day is when the $5 pumpkin is good for nothing but filling a hole in the ground, or when someone has to be paid to cart away a Christmas tree with its $50 price tag still swinging from its topmost branch, or when the 50-cent newspaper is only fit for wrapping fish. Yet, on the other hand, what pumpkin, Christmas tree, or newspaper dealer wants to be out of stock before Halloween, Christmas, or the end of the day?

This is known as the single cycle inventory problem. For purposes of discussion, consider a pumpkin stand owner: a very unusual pumpkin stand owner who keeps fairly accurate records of what he has sold in past years.

NUMBER OF OCCURRENCES	NUMBER OF PUMPKINS SOLD
2	300–400
8	400–500
4	500–600
3	600–700
2	700–800
1	800–900

His records for twenty years of selling pumpkins show that he has never sold fewer than 300 pumpkins, nor more than 900 pumpkins, and that his most likely sales is something around 500 pumpkins. There are ten occurrences of sales fewer than 500 pumpkins and ten occurrences of sales greater than 500 pumpkins. Five hundred pumpkins represents the median, in that half of the time the pumpkin dealer has sold fewer than 500 pumpkins, and half of the time he has sold more than 500 pumpkins. Although one is tempted to think in terms of the most likely sales being the average sales, the most likely sales should be interpreted as the median. That is, there is a 50 percent probability of sales being higher than the most likely sales estimate, and a 50 percent probability of sales being less than the most likely sales estimate. Moreover, the probability of sales being close to 300, or close to 900, is relatively low. The probability of sales being around 500 pumpkins is relatively high. The history of pumpkin sales can be expressed in terms of a discrete probability table by dividing the number of observations by twenty.

DISCRETE PROBABILITY	NUMBER OF PUMPKINS SOLD
10%	350
40	450
20	550
15	650
10	750
5	850

Suppose that the pumpkin stand owner is thinking in terms of stocking either 450, 650, or 850 pumpkins in preparation for the Halloween season. He sells the pumpkins for $5 each, buys them for $1, and pays a garbage man 50 cents per pumpkin to cart any unsold pumpkins to the dump. His anticipated profit prior to the start of the season for various levels of demand is as follows.

ORDER QUANTITY OF 450 PUMPKINS

DEMAND	PUMPKINS SOLD	PUMPKINS NOT SOLD	REVENUE	COST	DISPOSAL COST	PROFIT
350	350	100	$1750	$450	$50	$1250
450	450	0	2250	450	0	1800
550	450	0	2250	450	0	1800
650	450	0	2250	450	0	1800
750	450	0	2250	450	0	1800
850	450	0	2250	450	0	1800

ORDER QUANTITY OF 650 PUMPKINS

DEMAND	PUMPKINS SOLD	PUMPKINS NOT SOLD	REVENUE	COST	DISPOSAL COST	PROFIT
350	350	300	$1750	$650	$150	$ 950
450	450	200	2250	650	100	1500
550	550	100	2750	650	50	2050
650	650	0	3250	650	0	2600
750	650	0	3250	650	0	2600
850	650	0	3250	650	0	2600

ORDER QUANTITY OF 850 PUMPKINS

DEMAND	PUMPKINS SOLD	PUMPKINS NOT SOLD	REVENUE	COST	DISPOSAL COST	PROFIT
350	350	500	$1750	$850	$250	$ 650
450	450	400	2250	850	200	1200
550	550	300	2750	850	150	1750
650	650	200	3250	850	100	2300
750	750	100	3750	850	50	2850
850	850	0	4250	850	0	3400

Just looking at the profit, one would be tempted to order 850 pumpkins because that gives the highest profit. However, that profit cannot be realized unless a high level of sales is achieved. There is only about a 5 percent chance that sales will be as high as 850 pumpkins. The fact that there is only a certain probability that any particular sales level can be achieved has to be taken into account. The expected payoff is the summation of the product of the probability of a particular outcome and the amount of the outcome.

ORDER QUANTITY OF 450 PUMPKINS

DEMAND	PROBABILITY OF DEMAND	PROFIT	PROBABILITY X PROFIT
350	10%	$1250	$125
450	40	1800	720
550	20	1800	360
650	15	1800	270
750	10	1800	180
850	5	1800	90

EXPECTED PAYOFF: $1745

ORDER QUANTITY OF 650 PUMPKINS

DEMAND	PROBABILITY OF DEMAND	PROFIT	PROBABILITY X PROFIT
350	10%	$ 950	$ 95
450	40	1500	600
550	20	2050	410
650	15	2600	390
750	10	2600	260
850	5	2600	130

EXPECTED PAYOFF: $1885

ORDER QUANTITY OF 850 PUMPKINS

DEMAND	PROBABILITY OF DEMAND	PROFIT	PROBABILITY X PROFIT
350	10%	$ 650	$ 65
450	40	1200	480
550	20	1750	350
650	15	2300	345
750	10	2850	285
850	5	3400	170

EXPECTED PAYOFF: $1695

The expected payoff is $1,745 if 450 pumpkins are ordered, $1,885 if 650 pumpkins are ordered, and $1,695 if 850 pumpkins are ordered. Of the three choices, the pumpkin stand owner is best off ordering 650 pumpkins, which may not be the best choice, however. Only 3 out of 600 possibilities have been examined.

It can be mathematically demonstrated that the optimal order quantity where the expected payoff achieves its maximum value can be taken off the cumulative probability distribution at the point determined by the following equation.

$$\frac{P - C}{P + D}$$

where P is the price/unit, C is the cost/unit, and D is the disposal cost/unit.

First, there is the task of constructing the cumulative probability distribution. Once one has the discrete probabilities, the cumulative probabilities can be quickly arrived at by adding the discrete probabilities over specific ranges of pumpkin sales.

NUMBER PUMPKINS	DISCRETE PROBABILITY	CUMULATIVE PROBABILITY
300–400	10%	10%
400–500	40	50
500–600	20	70
600–700	15	85
700–800	10	95
800–900	5	100

There is a 10 percent chance that sales will fall within a range of 300–400 pumpkins. It is expected that pumpkin sales below 400 pumpkins will occur 10 percent of the time. There is a 40 percent discrete probability that sales will fall within a range of 400–500 pumpkins. The cumulative probability that pumpkin sales will be below 500 pumpkins is 50 percent. There is a 20 percent discrete probability that pumpkin sales will be between 500 and 600 pumpkins while the cumulative probability that pumpkin sales will be below 600 pumpkins is 70 percent. This interpretation of discrete versus cumulative probabilities continues through each range; until finally, the discrete probability that sales will be between 800 and 900 pumpkins is 5 percent while the cumulative probability that sales will be below 900 pumpkins is 100 percent.

Returning to the selection of the optimal order quantity, the solution states that the optimal order quantity $(P-C)/(P+D)$ is to be taken off the cumulative probability distribution. The pumpkins are sold for a price of $5 ($P=5$). The cost to acquire one pumpkin is $1 ($C=1$), and the disposal cost is 50 cents ($D=0.5$) per pumpkin.

$$(P-C)/(P+D)=(5-1)/(5+.5)=4/5.5=0.73$$

Entering the cumulative probability distribution table with a value of 73 percent for the cumulative probability yields, by visual inspection, an optimal order quantity of about 620 pumpkins. For this combination of sales price, acquisition, and disposal costs, the maximum expected payoff can be achieved by ordering about 620 pumpkins.

Suppose that the pumpkin stand owner is going to close up shop after Halloween and let any remaining pumpkins rot in situ. Now the disposal cost is zero ($D=0$).

$$(P-C)/(P+D)=(5-1)/(5+0)=4/5=0.80$$

Referring to the table containing the cumulative probability distribution with a value of 80 percent, the expected payoff can be maximized by acquiring about 670 pumpkins before the pumpkin season gets underway.

Suppose that a local bakery is willing to come down to the pumpkin stand the day after Halloween and buy all excess pumpkins for 25 cents each. For this, the disposal cost takes on a negative value to reflect the fact that someone is willing to pay 25 cents for pumpkins that could not be sold for $5 ($D=-0.25$).

$$(P-C)/(P+D)=(5-1)/(5-.25)=4/4.75=0.84$$

With his cost of disposal becoming, in effect, a partial refund on the acquisition cost, the pumpkin stand owner can afford to take on additional risk of having unsold pumpkins. By entering the cumulative probability distribution table with a value of 84 percent, the pumpkin stand owner can maximize his expected payoff by stocking about 700 pumpkins. If he could dispose of the pumpkins at the cost of acquisition—that is, $1—then the maximum expected payoff can be achieved at 900 pumpkins because there is no risk of loss for those pumpkins left behind after the day of reckoning.

One might be tempted to open a nationwide phone-in business for providing the optimal order quantity to maximize the expected payoff for purveyors of pumpkins and Christmas trees and other dated or perishable items. To advise on the optimal order quantity, the proprietors would have to be asked for a little input data.

"Sir, would you please provide us with your discrete probability distribution over a segmented range of sales figures covering much, if not all, of your history of operations? With that, sir, we can obtain the cumulative probability distribution and, from that, furnish you with the optimal order quantity which will maximize your expected payoff."

A few problems might ensue. There may be a problem of communication where the pumpkin stand owner does not understand one word of what was said. Even if he did understand, he probably wouldn't have the historic sales data recorded in sufficient detail to be of much help. Without accurate historic data, one cannot construct a discrete probability table. Without a discrete probability table, one cannot obtain the cumulative probability table. Without the cumulative probability table, one cannot obtain a solution.

However, too much effort has been expended at this point in the problem to abandon it. The questions posed to the proprietor have to be in a form to which he will readily reply. He will not readily reply to a request for a complete sales history from which a discrete probability table can be constructed. The proprietor may not have the information. Or if he has the information, he may not be willing to release it. If the pumpkin stand owner had stocked out in any year, he will have to be asked what he would have sold had he sufficient inventory. That is the nature of the information being sought—the volume of sales unimpeded by stockouts. He may not be able to answer that question.

Another problem associated with asking for historic information is that it might not be relevant. Historic sales are of interest only if the pumpkin stand owner is confident that history is repeating itself. Since it can be readily demonstrated that history is seldom that cooperative, historic records of pumpkin sales are of little use. What is important is the pumpkin stand owner's feelings about the future volume of sales. These feelings certainly are grounded in his past experience in selling pumpkins, but they are also influenced by trends which affect the future volume of sales. Such trends would include the growth of multiple pumpkin households, new housing developments near the pumpkin stand, and the number of competitive pumpkin stands.

Actually the lack of accurate historic information, and a lack of a solid foundation in mathematics on the part of the pumpkin stand owner, are not insurmountable problems. The approach to be undertaken must take into account that the pumpkin stand owner does not understand the world of mathematics nor does he look backward in time. Rather than ask questions in the language of the mathematician, ask for required information in a language that the businessman understands. Rather than ask for historic data, focus on the most important issue facing the pumpkin stand owner: the future volume of business.

"Sir, what would be the largest number of pumpkins you expect to sell next Halloween?"

"About 900."

"And the least?"

"About 300."

"Sir, if next Halloween could be repeated many times, and I asked you to select a sales figure which you feel that half of the time sales would be above this figure and half of the time sales would be below this figure, what would that figure be?"

"You mean my average sales?"

This is the unfortunate invitation for a discussion on the difference between the mean and the median. One may well end up with the mean, but it is the median that is desired.

"About 500 pumpkins."

This businessman's assessment of future pumpkin sales can be translated into a cumulative probability curve several different ways. One such method is described in this chapter's appendix which can construct a family of cumulative probability curves from a businessman's assessments of the most likely value bracketed by minimum and maximum values. Three representative cumulative probability curves with different scaling factors are shown in Exhibit 2.1.

The question then becomes which curve? Or more apropos, which scaling factor? The answer lies in the nature of the response of the pumpkin stand owner to the following inquiry.

"Would you expect sales close to 300, or close to 900, to be relatively rare events?"

Most of the time, and for most applications of businessmen's assessments to

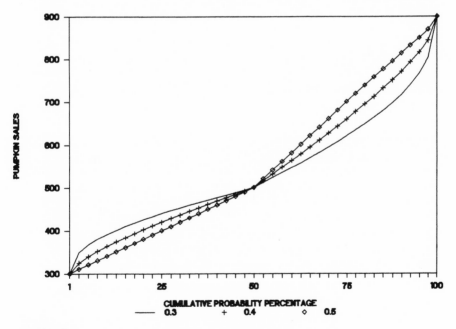

Exhibit 2.1.
Cumulative Probability Curves (various scaling factors)

simulation, the answer is going to be "yes." The three illustrated curves are three responses to the question of how "rare" is rare. All three have in common the same median of 500 pumpkins, which is the 50 percent cumulative probability point. All three curves have the same minimum sales volume of 300 pumpkins. The 1 percent cumulative probability point can, for now, be interpreted as the 0 percent cumulative probability point. All three curves have the same maximum, or 100 percent cumulative probability point, of 900 pumpkins. The difference between this pumpkin stand owner and others is that his sales history is known. This provides an assessment as to the probability of sales near the extremity points. As previously noted, the probability of sales being below 400 pumpkins is 10 percent whereas the probability of sales above 800 pumpkins is 5 percent.

In examining the three curves under consideration, the one with a scaling factor of 0.3 is the best choice. For this curve, the probability of sales being between 300 and 400 pumpkins is 12 percent. The probability of sales being between 800 and 900 pumpkins is 3 percent. This cumulative probability curve is the closest of the three curves to the historical record.

The curves were created by the computer program described in the accompanying appendix. The program is an example of the ability of the computer to generate cumulative probability curves. It is not offered as the "final solution" to generating cumulative probability curves, but to demonstrate that cumulative probability curves can be generated by a computer. A modification is necessary to better create cumulative probability curves whose scaling factor is less than 0.3.

The scaling factor of 0.5 generates a straight line which means that the discrete probability for equal increments of pumpkin sales is the same on either side of the median. The probability of sales being in narrow ranges around 300, 350, and 400 pumpkins is the same as is the probability of sales being in narrow ranges around 600, 800, or 900 pumpkins. A scaling factor of more than 0.5 means that the discrete probability of sales being in a narrow range around 900 pumpkins is higher than the discrete probability of sales being in a narrow range around 800, 700, or 600 pumpkins. Similarly, a scaling factor of more than 0.5 means that sales being in a narrow range around 300 pumpkins has a higher probability of occurring than sales in the same range around 400 or 500 pumpkins. This would be a very unusual situation for the extremities to have a higher probability of occurrence than the median. Very special circumstances would have to apply for using scaling factors of more than 0.5. In fact, it would be quite unusual to use a scaling factor of 0.5 because that implies the probability of sales being near the minimum and maximum points, or the extremities, is the same as sales near the median.

The program in the appendix creates "nicer" looking cumulative curves for scaling factor values of 0.8 and 0.9. One possible modification is to "flip" these cumulative probability curves around the straight line segments connecting the 0, 50, and 100 percent probability points to cover situations which call for scaling factors of less than 0.3.

The selection of the cumulative probability curve with a scaling factor of 0.3 was permitted by the knowledge of the pumpkin stand owner's historic discrete probability of selling less than 400 pumpkins and selling more than 800 pumpkins. How does one select the appropriate scaling factor if the pumpkin stand owner can only provide the two extreme points and the median? The answer to the question is in the nature of his response to how rare is a rare event. The rare event is the chance of sales being as low as 300 pumpkins or as high as 900 pumpkins.

"Sir, if I were to ask you how many times you would expect to see sales very close to 300 pumpkins, or 900 pumpkins, in a hundred Halloweens, what would be your response?"

"Never."

"You mean that sales actually being very close to 300 pumpkins, or 900 pumpkins, would be extremely rare events—something you may never see in your lifetime?"

"Yup."

Suppose that the actual distribution of pumpkin sales is a normal distribution. With sales that average 500 pumpkins, and for sales of 300 pumpkins to hardly ever occur, one could consider that the extreme of 300 pumpkins is three standard deviations away from the mean. The difference between 500 and 300 pumpkins divided by 3 yields an estimate of the standard deviation of 67 pumpkins. For a mean of 500 pumpkins, and a standard deviation of 67 pumpkins, the probability of sales being between 300 and 400 pumpkins corresponds to a normal deviate of 1.5.

$$\text{NORMAL DEVIATE} = \frac{\text{LOWER VALUE} - \text{MEAN}}{\text{STANDARD DEVIATION}} = \frac{400 - 500}{67} = -1.5$$

This is a lower tail situation with the area in the tail of a normal curve representing sales between 300 and 400 pumpkins, where the mean is 500 pumpkins and the standard deviation is 67 pumpkins. The area in the tail under these circumstances is .07. This means that the probability of sales being between 300 and 400 pumpkins is about 7 percent.

The distribution under consideration is skewed. Repeating the same calculation on the basis that the difference between 500 and 900 pumpkins represents three standard deviations, the resulting standard deviation is 133. The normal deviate, which corresponds to sales being greater than 800 pumpkins, is as follows.

$$\text{NORMAL DEVIATE} = \frac{\text{UPPER VALUE} - \text{MEAN}}{\text{STANDARD DEVIATION}} = \frac{800 - 500}{133} = 2.25$$

The probability of sales being greater than 800 pumpkins would be the area in the upper tail of a normal curve for a normal deviate of 2.25, which represents an area in the tail of .01, or 1 percent. Thus it seems reasonable that the appropriate scaling factor to use when the pumpkin stand owner feels that the extreme values of 300 and 900 are highly unlikely events would call for a scaling factor of something of the order of 0.20 or 0.25. To use the computer program in the accompanying appendix, one may have to resort to a five point distribution as a substitute for a cumulative probability curve with a scaling factor below 0.3. It may also be feasible to modify the program along lines previously suggested to better create cumulative distribution curves with scaling factor values of less than 0.3.

The pumpkin stand owner may feel this is a bit too extreme. If he feels that there is a small chance that sales could fall in a range of values near 300 pumpkins, then the difference between 300 and 500 pumpkins represents two, not three, standard deviations. This increases the estimated standard deviation from 67 to 100 pumpkins.

$$\text{NORMAL DEVIATE} = \frac{\text{LOWER VALUE} - \text{MEAN}}{\text{STANDARD DEVIATION}} = \frac{400 - 500}{100} = -1.0$$

The area in the tail of a normal curve representing the probability of sales being between 300 and 400 pumpkins, where the mean is 500 pumpkins and the standard deviation is 100 pumpkins, is about 16 percent. This can be represented by a scaling factor of just over 0.30.

Repeating this for the upper end of sales between 800 and 900 pumpkins, where the estimate of the standard deviation is now 200 pumpkins, follows.

$$\text{NORMAL DEVIATE} = \frac{\text{UPPER VALUE} - \text{MEAN}}{\text{STANDARD DEVIATION}} = \frac{800 - 500}{200} = 1.5$$

Under these circumstances, the probability of sales being over 800 pumpkins is about 7 percent. This also suits the selection of a scaling factor of just over 0.30.

One can sense from this that the choice of scaling factor is really based on a businessman's assessments as to how rare are the occurrences near the extreme points. If he does not expect to witness the occurrence of happenings near the extreme points in his lifetime, then a scaling factor of something less than 0.3 is appropriate. If he views the narrow range of values near the extreme points as having some low, but finite, probability of actually occurring during his lifetime, then a scaling factor of 0.30–0.35 may be more appropriate. One more repetition should provide sufficient guidance as to the selection of the appropriate scaling factor.

Suppose that the pumpkin stand owner feels that there is a reasonable chance that sales could be as low as 300 and as high as 900 pumpkins. These events may be unusual, but something which may well occur during his career in the pumpkin stand business. This would imply that the difference between sales of 300 pumpkins and 500 pumpkins represents about 1.6 standard deviations. The estimated standard deviation takes on a value of 125 pumpkins. The probability of sales being less than 400 pumpkins is calculated below.

$$\text{NORMAL DEVIATE} = \frac{\text{LOWER VALUE} - \text{MEAN}}{\text{STANDARD DEVIATION}} = \frac{400 - 500}{125} = -0.8$$

The probability of sales being less than 400 when the mean is 500 pumpkins and the standard deviation is 125 pumpkins is 21 percent. The probability for sales being above 800 pumpkins with a mean of 500 and a standard deviation of 250 follows.

$$\text{NORMAL DEVIATE} = \frac{\text{UPPER VALUE} - \text{MEAN}}{\text{STANDARD DEVIATION}} = \frac{800 - 500}{250} = 1.2$$

The probability of sales being greater than 800 under these circumstances is 12 percent. Both of these resuls are consistent with the use of a scaling factor of 0.4.

One is tempted in viewing these results to conclude that a scaling factor of around 0.4 is appropriate when the sales near the extreme points are expected to actually occur from time to time. For those situations where the actual occurrence of sales near the extreme points is, in a businessman's assessment, to be relatively unlikely events, then the appropriate scaling factor appears to be about 0.3.

There is another way to handle the situation where the businessman provides extreme points whose occurrence can best be described as miraculous. It is simply not to fret over how to create a cumulative probability curve whose scaling factor is less than 0.3. One can modify the questions such that the businessman provides assessments of the extreme points where there is some possibility of occurence for values near the extreme points. Reducing the range between the maximum and minimum assessments is another way of increasing the scaling factor.

A general approach of assessing the appropriate scaling factor has been set forth. The computer program contained in the accompanying appendix can generate the required cumulative probability curve once a businessman has given his assessment of the median and the extreme points, and the likelihood of the occurrence of values near the extreme points. Equipped with a cumulative probability curve, and with the answers to the questions concerning the sales price, and the costs to acquire and dispose of the item under consideration, one is in a position to advise on the optimal ordering quantity for single cycle inventories.

One is also in a position to open up a nationwide phone-in service to provide the optimal ordering quantity for single cycle inventories. Opening up such a business will be left to others. What is of importance is the generation of the cumulative probability curve. The cumulative probability curve described herein is one small step away from being transformed to a simulator. The simulator is the very heart of incorporating simulation in the decision making process.

Appendix to Chapter 2

GENERATION OF CUMULATIVE PROBABILITY DISTRIBUTION CURVES

Let $y(x)$ be the cumulative probability function and x be the independent variable representing a businessman's assessments. The general shape of a cumulative probability distribution curve can take the form:

$$y(x) = 1 - e^{f(x)}$$

$$f(x) = - \left[\frac{(x - A)^N}{(B - x)^M} \right](T)$$

where A represents the minimum expectation of a businessman's assessment and B represents the maximum expectation. When the independent variable $x = A$, then $f(x) = 0$, $e^\circ = 1$ and

$$y(A) = 1 - 1 = 0$$

when $x = B$, $f(x) = -\infty$, $e^{-\infty} = 0$, and

$$y(B) = 1 - 0 = 1$$

The general shape of $y(x)$ is as follows where the cumulative probability is zero when x is equal to A and is 1, or 100 percent, when x is equal to B.

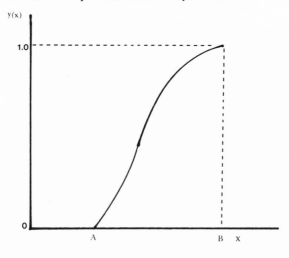

Let C represent the median. When x=C, the cumulative probability, y(C)=50% or 0.50.

$$y(x) = 1 - e^{-\left[\dfrac{(x - A)^N}{(B - x)^M}\right]^T}$$

$$0.5 = 1 - e^{-\left[\dfrac{(C - A)^N}{(B - C)^M}\right]^T}$$

$$0.5 = e^{-\left[\dfrac{(C - A)^N}{(B - C)^M}\right]^T}$$

$$\ln(0.5) = -\left[\dfrac{(C - A)^N}{(B - C)^M}\right]^T$$

$$T = -\ln(0.5)\left[\dfrac{(B - C)^M}{(C - A)^N}\right] \tag{1}$$

Let L represent the 25 percent cumulative probability point. When x=L, y(L)=0.25.

$$0.25 = 1 - e^{-\left[\dfrac{(L - A)^N}{(B - L)^M}\right]^T}$$

Taking the natural log and solving for T:

$$T = -\ln(0.75)\left[\dfrac{(B - L)^M}{(L - A)^N}\right] \tag{2}$$

Let H represent the 75 percent cumulative probability point. When x=H, y(H)=0.75 and, again solving for T:

$$T = -\ln(0.25)\left[\dfrac{(B - H)^M}{(H - A)^N}\right] \tag{3}$$

Equating (1) and (2):

$$-\ln(0.5)\left[\dfrac{(B - C)^M}{(C - A)^N}\right] = -\ln(0.75)\left[\dfrac{(B - L)^M}{(L - A)^N}\right]$$

$$\ln(0.5)\dfrac{(B - C)^M}{(B - L)^M} = \ln(0.75)\dfrac{(C - A)^N}{(L - A)^N}$$

$$\text{Let } K1 = \dfrac{\ln(0.5)}{\ln(0.75)}$$

$$K1\left(\dfrac{B - C}{B - L}\right)^M = \left(\dfrac{C - A}{L - A}\right)^N$$

$$\ln K1 + M\ln\left(\dfrac{B - C}{B - L}\right) = N\ln\left(\dfrac{C - A}{L - A}\right)$$

$$\text{Let } L1 = \ln K1,\ L2 = \ln\left(\dfrac{B - C}{B - L}\right),\ L3 = \ln\left(\dfrac{C - A}{L - A}\right)$$

$$L1 + L2M = L3N \tag{4}$$

Repeating the process by equating (2) and (3):

$$- \ln(0.75) \left[\frac{(B - L)^M}{(L - A)^N} \right] = - \ln(0.25) \left[\frac{(B - H)^M}{(H - A)^N} \right]$$

$$\ln(0.75) \, \frac{(B - L)^M}{(B - H)^M} = \ln(0.25) \, \frac{(L - A)^N}{(H - A)^N}$$

$$\text{Let K2} = \frac{\ln(0.75)}{\ln(0.25)}$$

$$K2 \left(\frac{B - L}{B - H} \right)^M = \left(\frac{L - A}{H - A} \right)^N$$

$$\ln K2 + M\ln \left(\frac{B - L}{B - H} \right) = N\ln \left(\frac{L - A}{H - A} \right)$$

$$\text{Let L4} = \ln K2, \, \text{L5} = \ln \left(\frac{B - L}{B - H} \right), \, \text{L6} = \ln \left(\frac{L - A}{H - A} \right)$$

$$L4 + L5M = L6N \tag{5}$$

Combining (4) and (5) and solving for M:

$$L1 + L2M = L3N \tag{4}$$

$$L4 + L5M = L6N \tag{5}$$

$$N = \frac{L1}{L3} + \frac{L2}{L3} M \tag{6}$$

$$N = \frac{L4}{L6} + \frac{L5}{L6} M \tag{7}$$

$$\frac{L1}{L3} + \frac{L2}{L3} M = \frac{L4}{L6} + \frac{L5}{L6} M$$

$$\left(\frac{L1}{L3} - \frac{L4}{L6} \right) = \left(\frac{L5}{L6} - \frac{L2}{L3} \right) M$$

$$M = \frac{\left(\dfrac{L1}{L3} - \dfrac{L4}{L6} \right)}{\left(\dfrac{L5}{L6} - \dfrac{L2}{L3} \right)} \tag{8}$$

Substituting equation (8) into either equations (6) or (7) results in a solution for N. The variable T has been solved in equation (1) once the variables M and N are determined. All that remains in determining M and N is to define the 25 percent cumulative probability point, L, and the 75 percent cumulative probability point, H, in terms of a scaling factor Z.

$$L = C - Z(C - A)$$

$$H = C + Z(B - C)$$

With the inputs of the 0, 50, and 100 cumulative probability percentile points, and the scaling factor, a cumulative probability curve can be generated where the y axis represents the cumulative probability and the x axis represents the businessman's assessments. The y and x axes must be switched to obtain the output as presented in the chapter.

The computer program listed at the end of this appendix generated the curves in Exhibit 2.1. The program can be incorporated either as a subroutine for generating cumulative distributions in simulation models or be a standalone program. The program, as written, is a standalone. Changing END to RETURN in statement 8840 would convert it to a subroutine.

The program can create up to eight cumulative distributions or change an existing distribution. These distributions are stored in separate sequential data files under the names CUM1 to CUM8. More files could be added, if desired.

The most common cumulative distribution will be a three-point distribution. The program creates first a "standard" distribution around a minimum value of 0, a median of 500, and a maximum of 1,000 (statement 8100). The scaling factor is entered in statements 8150–8170. The model does not work well with scaling factors of less than 0.3. The maximum scaling factor of 0.9 was arbitrarily selected. Deletion of statement 8170 would remove these restrictions. Statement 8180 uses the scaling factor to define the values for L and H at the 25 and 75 cumulative probability percentile points. The mathematics previously described are accomplished in statements 8190–8310. The actual 0, 50, and 100 percentile points are entered in statements 8330–8400 where the x axis is stretched or compressed similar to an accordian to make the cumulative probability curve fit the independent variable. In statements 8540–8590, the y and x axes are switched as presented in this chapter.

Statements 8600–8650 are simply an internal check to ensure that the cumulative probability curve always gains in value (from 0 to 100 percent) as the independent variable increases from the minimum to the maximum value. This could be omitted if desired. Statements 8650–8690 permit on screen viewing of the results in 5 percent increments. The filing of the data, if so desired, is accomplished in statements 8700–8830.

The results can be viewed in the LOTUS system by first entering the operating systems mode and renaming the sequential data files CUMx to CUMx.PRN. The universal command REN*. *.PRN is useful when the disk contains only the program CUMDIST.BAS and the sequential data files. In the LOTUS environment, any or all of the data files can be read into the spreadsheet using the File Import Number command. Suppose that column A contained the thousand values C(1) to C(1000). Another column can contain +A1, +A50, +A100, etc., which permits plotting in 5 percent increments. This is what was used to construct the curves in Exhibit 2.1 shown in Chapter 2. After viewing the graphical results, the data file names must be changed back to their original format to permit their incorporation into a simulation program. The universal command REN *.PRN*. may be useful in accomplishing this.

The five-point distribution is applicable when the 0, 25, 50, 75, and 100 percentile points are known. Statement 8130 locks in a scaling factor of 0.5. This means that the resulting cumulative distribution is straight line segments connecting each of the five points entered in statements 8410–8530.

The best way to appreciate this program is to run it under a variety of different assumptions and view the results either on screen or graphically. This is just one methodology to construct cumulative probability curves. Others may work better, or this one may be improved. The program is offered as a first step in bringing simulation onstream as an aid in the decision making process.

```
10 REM NAME OF PROGRAM IS CUMDIST
20 DIM X(1000):DIM Y(1000):DIM C(8,1000)
8000 REM SUBROUTINE FOR GENERATING CUMULATIVE DISTRIBUTIONS
8010 PRINT:PRINT
8020 PRINT "CHANGE EXISTING CUMULATIVE DISTRIBUTION: 1"
8030 PRINT "GENERATE CUMULATIVE DISTRIBUTIONS:        2":PRINT
8040 INPUT Z:ON Z GOTO 8050,8060
8050 INPUT "ENTER CUM DIST TO BE CHANGED (1-8): ";D2:D1=D2:GOTO 8070
8060 INPUT "ENTER NUMBER CUM DIST TO BE GENERATED: ";D2:D1=1
8070 FOR D=D1 TO D2
8080 PRINT:PRINT "NUMBER DATA INPUT POINTS"
8090 INPUT "3 POINT-3   5 POINT-5: ";Q1:PRINT
8100 A=0:C=500:B=1000
8110 IF Q1=5 THEN 8130
8120 IF Q1=3 THEN 8140 ELSE 8080
8130 Z=.5:GOTO 8180
8140 PRINT:PRINT
8150 PRINT "SELECT SCALING FACTOR BETWEEN 0.3 AND 0.9"
8160 INPUT "SCALING FACTOR: ";Z:PRINT
8170 IF Z<.3 THEN 8140:IF Z>.9 THEN 8140
8180 L=C-Z*(C-A):H=C+Z*(B-C)
8190 K1=LOG(.5)/LOG(.75):K2=LOG(.75)/LOG(.25)
8200 L1=LOG(K1):L4=LOG(K2)
8210 L2=LOG((B-C)/(B-L)):L3=LOG((C-A)/(L-A))
8220 L5=LOG((B-L)/(B-H)):L6=LOG((L-A)/(H-A))
8230 M=(L1/L3-L4/L6)/(L5/L6-L2/L3)
8240 N=(L1/L3)+(L2/L3)*M
8250 T1=(B-C)^M:T2=(C-A)^N:T=-LOG(.5)*T1/T2
8260 X(1)=A:K=(B-A)/1000
8270 FOR I=2 TO 1000:X(I)=X(I-1)+K:NEXT
8280 Y(1000)=1:Y(1)=0
8290 FOR I=2 TO 999
8300 Z1=(X(I)-A)^N:Z2=(B-X(I))^M
8310 Y(I)=1-EXP(-T*Z1/Z2):NEXT
8320 IF Q1=3 THEN 8330 ELSE 8410
8330 INPUT "  0 PERCENTILE POINT: ";A1
8340 INPUT " 50 PERCENTILE POINT: ";A2
8350 IF A2<=A1 THEN 8340
8360 X(1)=A1:FOR I=2 TO 500:X(I)=X(I-1)+(A2-A1)/500:NEXT
8370 INPUT "100 PERCENTILE POINT: ";A3:PRINT
8380 IF A3<=A2 THEN 8370
8390 FOR I=501 TO 1000:X(I)=X(I-1)+(A3-A2)/500:NEXT
8400 A5=A3:GOTO 8540
8410 INPUT "  0 PERCENTILE POINT: ";A1
8420 INPUT " 25 PERCENTILE POINT: ";A2
8430 IF A2<=A1 THEN 8420
8440 X(1)=A1:FOR I=2 TO 250:X(I)=X(I-1)+(A2-A1)/250:NEXT
8450 INPUT " 50 PERCENTILE POINT: ";A3
8460 IF A3<=A2 THEN 8450
8470 FOR I=251 TO 500:X(I)=X(I-1)+(A3-A2)/250:NEXT
8480 INPUT " 75 PERCENTILE POINT: ";A4
8490 IF A4<=A3 THEN 8480
8500 FOR I=501 TO 750:X(I)=X(I-1)+(A4-A3)/250:NEXT
8510 INPUT "100 PERCENTILE POINT: ";A5
8520 IF A5<=A4 THEN 8510
8530 FOR I=751 TO 1000:X(I)=X(I-1)+(A5-A4)/250:NEXT
8540 C(D,1)=A1:C(D,1000)=A5:K=1
8550 FOR I=2 TO 999
8560 FOR J=K TO 1000
8570 IF 1000*Y(J)<I THEN 8590
8580 C(D,I)=X(J):K=J:J=1000
8590 NEXT:NEXT
```

```
8600 FOR I=10 TO 1000 STEP 10
8610 IF C(D,I)<C(D,I-10) THEN 8620 ELSE 8630
8620 K=1
8630 NEXT
8640 IF K=1 THEN 8650 ELSE 8660
8650 PRINT:PRINT "IMPROPER CUMULATIVE DISTRIBUTION":PRINT
8660 INPUT "ONSCREEN PRINTOUT   YES-1   NO-2: ";Z:PRINT
8670 IF Z=1 THEN 8680 ELSE 8700
8680 PRINT "CUM PROB","VALUE":PRINT 1,C(D,1)
8690 FOR I=50 TO 1000 STEP 50:PRINT I/10,C(D,I):NEXT
8700 PRINT:INPUT "FILE DATA   YES-1   NO-2: ";Z
8710 ON Z GOTO 8720,8080
8720 ON D GOTO 8730,8740,8750,8760,8770,8780,8790,8800
8730 OPEN "O",#1,"CUM1":GOTO 8810
8740 OPEN "O",#1,"CUM2":GOTO 8810
8750 OPEN "O",#1,"CUM3":GOTO 8810
8760 OPEN "O",#1,"CUM4":GOTO 8810
8770 OPEN "O",#1,"CUM5":GOTO 8810
8780 OPEN "O",#1,"CUM6":GOTO 8810
8790 OPEN "O",#1,"CUM7":GOTO 8810
8800 OPEN "O",#1,"CUM8":GOTO 8810
8810 FOR I=1 TO 1000
8820 WRITE #1,C(D,I)
8830 NEXT:CLOSE#1
8840 NEXT:END
```

3

Inventory Planning

SYNOPSIS

This chapter is the first application of simulation to an aspect of business planning. The multiple cycle inventory problem is one of the classical applications of simulation to business decision making. Simulating the fluctuations of demand and lead time provides information that can aid in determining key decision points in inventory management. For an item in inventory, the key decisions are how many to order and when to place the order. Inappropriate decision points in inventory control can result either in excessive stockout costs or in excessive inventory carrying costs.

Simulation is a means to determine the optimal selection of how many and when to order, which minimizes total costs. The chapter begins by translating a cumulative probability curve for demand into a demand simulator. The demand simulator, coupled with a lead time simulator, are incorporated into a simulation to help determine decision points in inventory planning.

One purpose of the chapter is to acquaint the reader with the use of simulation in inventory control planning. Another purpose is to show the translation process of developing a simulation from a normal conversation where the details of a simulation are tailored to the specifics of the situation. This demonstrates how simulation can be molded to fit the peculiarities of the circumstances.

The Halloween pumpkin sales cumulative probability curve from the previous chapter is presented here with the simple change of title from Halloween pumpkins to daily sales volume of an item or product. The item or product is presumed to be finished goods where demand fluctuates and cannot be forecasted on a day-to-day basis with any degree of accuracy. Over long periods of time, aggregate demand for the product can be obtained for production purposes. But on a daily basis, there is no way to predict how many customers will walk through the door, or how many orders will come in the mail. The only guidance is the businessman's assessments that sales on any given day are not expected to be less than 300 units nor more than 900 units per day. Half of the time, sales will be above 500 units per day, and half of the time sales will be below 500 units per day. Moreover, about 10 percent of the daily sales between 300 and 900 units will fall in the range between 300 and 400 units. Similarly, about 5 percent of the

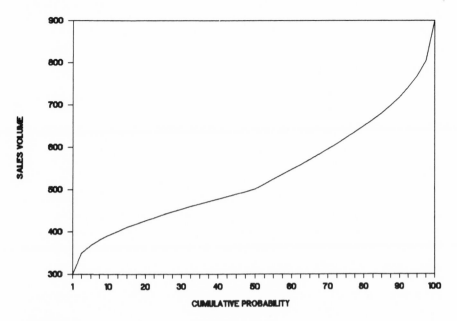

Exhibit 3.1.
Cumulative Probability Curve (scaling factor 0.3)

daily sales between 300 and 900 units will fall in the range of 800 to 900 units. The curve no longer represents annual Halloween pumpkin sales but daily sales of some product. Otherwise, the problem is the same.

The cumulative probabilities, expressed in terms of a percentage, for various sales volumes, rounded to the nearest whole number, are taken from the sequential data file used to generate the cumulative probability curve in Exhibit 3.1.

CUMULATIVE PROBABILITY	SALES VOLUME	CUMULATIVE PROBABILITY	SALES VOLUME	CUMULATIVE PROBABILITY	SALES VOLUME
1	300	41	480	81	655
2	345	42	482	82	661
3	353	43	484	83	668
4	361	44	486	84	674
5	367	45	489	85	680
6	373	46	491	86	688
7	378	47	493	87	695
8	383	48	496	88	702
9	388	49	498	89	710
10	392	50	500	90	718
11	395	51	505	91	727
12	400	52	510	92	736
13	404	53	515	93	745

CUMULATIVE PROBABILITY	SALES VOLUME	CUMULATIVE PROBABILITY	SALES VOLUME	CUMULATIVE PROBABILITY	SALES VOLUME
14	407	54	519	94	756
15	410	55	524	95	767
16	414	56	528	96	780
17	417	57	532	97	795
18	420	58	537	98	813
19	423	59	542	99	836
				100	900
20	426	60	547		
21	429	61	552		
22	432	62	556		
23	435	63	560		
24	438	64	565		
25	440	65	570		
26	443	66	575		
27	446	67	580		
28	448	68	585		
29	451	69	590		
30	453	70	595		
31	456	71	600		
32	458	72	605		
33	461	73	610		
34	463	74	616		
35	466	75	621		
36	468	76	626		
37	470	77	632		
38	473	78	637		
39	475	79	643		
40	477	80	647		

The 1 percent cumulative percentile point can, for now, be thought to represent the zero percentile point for a sales volume of 300. The 50 percentile point represents a sales volume of 500, and the 100 percentile point represents a sales volume of 900 units. There are no sales less than 300 units nor sales more than 900 units. Fifty percent of sales are above, and 50 percent of sales are below the median of 500 units. The 25 percentile point is 440 units. This means that 30 percent of the difference in sales between 300 and 500 units occur between 400 and 500 units, which corresponds to a scaling factor of 0.3. Similarly, 30 percent of the difference in sales between 500 and 900 units occur between the 50 percentile point of 500 and the 75 percentile point of 620 units.

In Chapter 1, a clerk was busily employed reaching into a bag of ten ping-pong balls, each labeled one through ten, to obtain a random sequence of jobs. Suppose that the bag is bigger and contains one hundred ping-pong balls, each labeled one through one hundred. Suppose that the clerk has been assigned the task of determining demand for the product over the next thirty days. He constructs a column of 1 to 30 representing the thirty-day assignment. For each day, he reaches into the bag and pulls out a ping-pong ball. He records the number of the ping-pong ball, puts it back in the bag, shakes the bag, and repeats the process partially filling out the following table.

DAY	NUMBER ON BALL	DAILY DEMAND	DAY	NUMBER ON BALL	DAILY DEMAND
1	81		16	95	
2	24		17	4	
3	30		18	89	
4	31		19	66	
5	51		20	55	
6	5		21	81	
7	78		22	90	
8	49		23	85	
9	36		24	86	
10	98		25	50	
11	90		26	58	
12	72		27	44	
13	1		28	86	
14	96		29	3	
15	1		30	60	

To complete the process of obtaining the demand for a product over a thirty-day period, the clerk could enter the previous table linking cumulative probabilities to demand. The labels on the columns might confuse him. He might be less confused obtaining the daily demand from the demand simulator curve (Exhibit 3.2).

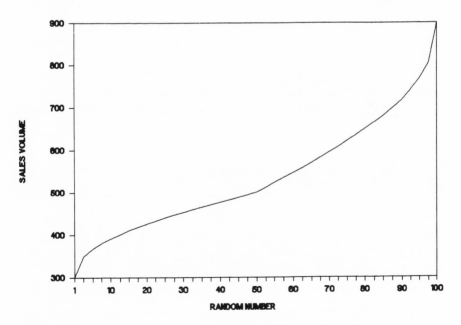

Exhibit 3.2.
Demand Simulator Curve (scaling factor 0.3)

The demand simulator curve is the previous cumulative probability distribution curve with a change in titles. What was called the cumulative probability curve is now called the demand simulator curve. What was called the cumulative probability on the x axis of the previous curve is now called the random number. Nothing else has changed. The clerk can take the number on the ball as the cumulative probability and enter the table to obtain the daily demand. Or he can enter the curve with the number on the ball as the random number and obtain the daily demand. Either way, he is now in a position to simulate demand over the next thirty days.

DAY	NUMBER ON BALL	DAILY DEMAND	DAY	NUMBER ON BALL	DAILY DEMAND
1	81	655	16	95	767
2	24	438	17	4	361
3	30	453	18	89	710
4	31	456	19	66	575
5	51	505	20	55	524
6	5	367	21	81	655
7	78	637	22	90	718
8	49	498	23	85	680
9	36	468	24	86	688
10	98	813	25	50	500
11	90	718	26	58	537
12	72	605	27	44	486
13	1	300	28	86	688
14	96	780	29	3	353
15	1	300	30	60	547

If the clerk continued this process over a sufficiently long period of time, and if the daily demand were analyzed statistically, one should come to the following conclusions:

1. Demand is never less than 300 units per day.
2. Demand is never more than 900 units per day.
3. Half of the time demand is less than 500 units per day, and consequently, half of the time demand is more than 500 units per day. Therefore, the median is 500 units per day.
4. Between the minimum point of 300 units per day, and the median of 500 units per day, daily demand is split in the ratio of 70 to 30 between the range of 300 and 400 units per day and between the range of 400 to 500 units per day.
5. Between the median of 500 units per day, and the maximum of 900 units per day, daily demand is split in the ratio of 30 to 70 between the range of 500 and 700 units per day and between the range of 700 and 900 units per day.

In other words, the demand simulator simulates actual demand. The simulation program contained in Chapter 2 works on the basis of a bag which holds not

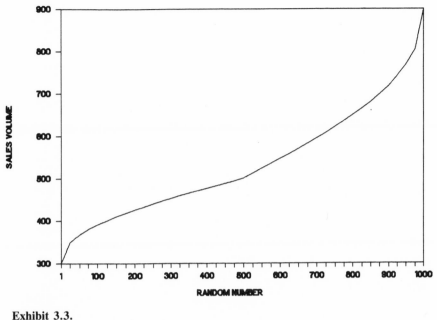

Exhibit 3.3.
Demand Simulator

100, but 1,000 ping-pong balls. The title "Demand Simulator Curve" from the previous figure can be retitled simply the "Demand Simulator" (see Exhibit 3.3) because that is exactly the function being performed. And the random numbers have been expanded from 100 to 1,000.

Naturally, the clerk will never be hired. Random numbers will be drawn, so to speak, by the computer using its random number generator. Questions have been raised whether a computer's random number generator truly creates random numbers. This is a fair question because nothing that a computer does can be considered random including generating random numbers. This can be easily demonstrated on a computer which does not automatically "seed" itself when generating random numbers. Instruct the computer to provide three random numbers between 1 and 100, and one might obtain 81, 24, 30. Start the program over again and one will again obtain the sequence 81, 24, 30. Obviously, the computer is not generating random numbers randomly but using a special set of instructions which generates the same sequence of random, or more accurately, pseudo-random numbers. "Seeding" means that the starting point for generating random numbers begins at a different point in the fixed sequence of numbers each time a simulation is run. One way to seed is to have the start point in a sequence of numbers keyed to the time of day that the simulation is run.

Random numbers should have no bias where one number appears consistently more, or less, than another. One way to check for bias is to generate 10,000 random numbers between 1 and 100 and count each time an individual number appears. Each individual number should appear about one hundred times. Some individual numbers will appear less and some will appear more than one hundred times. Seldom will an individual number appear exactly one hundred times. This exercise can be repeated for 20,000 selections of random numbers and an inspection made for individual numbers which appear less than 200 times and more than 200 times. The exercise can then be repeated for 30,000 selections, 40,000 selections, etc. There would be evidence of bias if any individual number was consistently below, or above, the expected number of appearances.

Much more subtle to detect is the generation of sequences of random numbers. Does the sequence 22, 55, 2, and 4 appear more often than one would expect from a mathematically pure random selection of numbers? Some writings on this subject suggest that there may be sequencing patterns in computer-generated random numbers which would not be present in a mathematically pure selection of random numbers.

For purposes of simulating business problems, it might be advisable to keep an open mind as to how random are computer-generated random numbers. Some comfort should be taken in that there is little evidence of bias. There is a possibility of sequential patterns appearing in a series of random numbers. Such patterns, even if proven to exist, would not materially affect the nature of the outcomes in the applications of simulation to business decisions. The nature of the variance inherent in the businessman's assessments of a situation has a much more pronounced effect on the results of a simulation than the possible existence of sequential patterns in the generation of random numbers.

Once a demand simulator is developed, the next step would be to create a lead time simulator. Lead time is that time interval between giving an order to a supplier until the time of delivery. Suppose that the businessman's assessment, drawn from experience, is that the minimum time between calling in an order and receiving a delivery is three days. Half the time deliveries take less than five days, and half the time they take more than five days. However, deliveries have taken as long as fifteen days.

This is a highly skewed distribution. The businessman will have to be asked questions to determine the 75 cumulative percentile point.

"Let us focus only on those deliveries which take longer than five days."

"Alright."

"Between deliveries which take five days, and deliveries which take as long as fifteen days, if you were to divide these deliveries into two categories of equal size, what would be the dividing point?"

"About seven days."

"You're telling me that three-quarters of all deliveries take place in seven days or less after you made a call for a delivery."

"That's right. And the killer are those times when deliveries take ten, twelve, or as long as fifteen days to arrive."

"And that occurs about one-quarter of the time when you reorder? One time in four?"

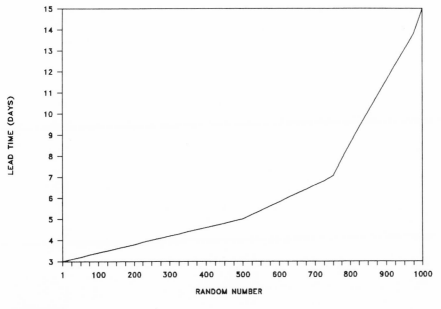

Exhibit 3.4.
Lead Time Simulator

"Yes."

The lead time simulator using the five-point distribution (three days, four days, five days, seven days, and fifteen days for the 1, 25, 50, 75, and 100 cumulative probability points respectively) is shown in Exhibit 3.4.

The clerk need only reach into a bag filled with 1,000 ping-pong balls labeled 1 through 1,000 and obtain the lead time off the lead time simulator rounding the lead time to the nearest whole number. The clerk does not have to have a formal simulator to determine lead time. He could work off a table of values. He reaches into the bag and pulls out a ping-pong ball. He can then refer to the following table to determine the lead time.

NUMBER ON BALL	LEAD TIME IN DAYS
1–124	3
125–375	4
376–561	5
562–685	6
686–764	7
765–796	8

NUMBER ON BALL	LEAD TIME IN DAYS
797–830	9
831–863	10
864–897	11
898–932	12
933–966	13
967–994	14
995–1000	15

The table was constructed by first affixing .PRN to the sequential data file on the cumulative distribution for lead time. Then the file was entered into the LOTUS spreadsheet using the /FIN command (Command Files Import Numbers). Lead time is rounded to the nearest whole integer. Whether the clerk is supplied with a table, or a curve, depends on the simplicity of the situation. For simple applications such as there being a 50 percent chance of a variable taking on one value and a 50 percent chance of it having another value, a table should be used. For this particular application, it may be easier for the clerk to read the curve than to construct a table.

The clerk, however, needs more instructions than those already provided.

"I would like you to run a problem for me."

"What is the nature of the problem?"

"I have already developed a simulator for determining daily demand for a particular product and the lead time from the time that I placed an order to the time of delivery. My problem is to determine how much I should order when I phone the supplier and the point at which I make that call. How many I should order is the order quantity, and the level of inventory which triggers a phone call to the supplier is the reorder point."

"So I guess you are going to give me different order quantities and different reordering points?"

"Yes, and you are going to figure out the different costs for each of these combinations, and I'll use my judgment to select the combination that gives me the lowest total cost."

"Right, that's your job. I'm here simply to perform all your calculations. But I am going to need some instructions."

"I guess you'll have to know how long to run each simulation?"

"Yes, that would be nice to know."

"I'm not sure. Let's just say many years. Maybe as many as one hundred years. I'll make up my mind before you start the calculations."

"You are giving me demand on a daily basis, and I hear you talking about years. I need guidance to translate years to days, or I'll be doing the calculations for one hundred days while you are thinking that I'm doing it for one hundred years."

"Okay. All you have to do is multiply the number of years I give you by 365. So one hundred years would become 36,500 days."

"That's what I need to know. And if you ever again mention years, I'll remember that all I have to do to translate it to days is to multiply by 365."

"That's good. But there is a complicating factor. We sell only on weekdays. We are closed on weekends. There is no demand for a product on weekends when the doors are locked shut."

"I think I need guidance as to how to tell whether it is a weekday or a weekend."

"Mondays, Tuesdays, Wednesdays, Thursdays, and Fridays are weekdays and Saturdays and Sundays are weekends."

"You may find this hard to believe, but I have trouble understanding that. Could we do this using numbers rather than words?"

"For you to tell if a day falls on a weekend or not, you are going to need a special counter. During the entire 36,500-day sequence, if we were doing a hundred year simulation, you'll have to keep adding 1 to the counter. When the counter value exceeds 7, it automatically becomes 1 again. When the counter has a value of 1 through 5, another variable will have a value of 1. This variable will be multiplied by the daily demand. Thus the daily demand remains unchanged for five days a week. When the counter has a value of 6 or 7, the variable will take on a value of 0, which, when multiplied by the daily demand, will reduce the demand to zero, signifying a weekend. Do you understand these instructions?"

"Yes, I do."

"And if I ever say the words *weekday* in the future, you'll know what to do without my having to repeat this whole routine again, right?"

"Yes, now that you have given me detailed instructions of what you mean by weekday and weekend, I will be able to recall them whenever I hear them again."

"Tell me how you understand the situation at this point."

"You will give me a reorder point and an order quantity to examine for some number of years which I will translate to days. You have given me a bag with 1,000 ping-pong balls which permits me to randomly select numbers between 1 and 1,000. By referring to the demand simulator, I can get daily demand. Throughout this period, I am now able to identify whether it is a weekday or a weekend by a 1 or a 0 value which I will assign to a variable. Multiplying this variable by the daily demand will designate the day of the week. And you have provided me with a lead time simulator. I am lost as to what to do now."

"At the start of each day, determine demand from the demand simulator and subtract demand from the previous day's inventory."

"You better give me an inventory at the very start of this process."

"Make it the ordering quantity that we are analyzing."

"After I subtract the daily demand from the previous day's inventory, what should I do next?"

"First, you better check if the resulting inventory is a negative number."

"And if it is, what do you want me to do?"

"I have had some discussions with our materials manager concerning the matter of backorders and lost sales . . . "

"Your discussions are of little use unless you can give me some precise instructions."

"For the particular product we are modeling, he figures that we do not lose any sales on the day of the stockout. We can treat it all as a backorder if later in the day a shipment comes in. When a shipment comes in, we can honor all backorders still on the books."

"Your instructions are still a bit vague."

"On the day of a negative inventory, the full amount becomes a backorder for day one. You will have to take a negative of a negative value. Backorders have to be positive numbers."

"That's precise enough. Now what do you want me to do?"

"Well, we want to age any previous backorders by one day and apply the following rules. If a backorder is two days old, 25 percent of it will be considered lost sales. The lost sales accumulator should be increased by the amount of the lost sales, and the backorders, which are two days old, will have to be reduced by the amount of the lost sales."

"Can do."

"Again, based on my conversations with the materials manager, based on his experience . . . "

"I don't care about your conversations, just give me the instructions I need."

"For the remaining backorders which are three days old, half of them are to be considered lost sales. So you will have to take half of the backorders which are three days old and add them to lost sales and reduce the number of backorders which are three days old to half their original amount."

"And backorders which are four days old?"

"Well, based on our talks, if we can't honor orders in four days, we might as well consider them lost sales. So take whatever backorders there are that are four days old and consider them lost sales. After increasing lost sales by all backorders which are four days old, set the four-day-old backorders to zero. And while you are at it, set the inventory to zero because, physically, there is no such thing as a negative inventory."

"Right. What should I do if the inventory is positive rather than negative?"

"Regardless if the inventory is negative or positive, I want to check to see if we are below the reordering point."

"Suppose we are not below the reordering point?"

"Well, for now just add the end-of-day inventory to an accumulator to keep track of the total and proceed to the next day."

"Suppose I am below the reordering point, what should I do?"

"First you better see if an order has already been placed during this inventory cycle. If an order has already been placed, check to see if it has come in by looking at your calendar containing the lead time for the arrival of the next shipment. If the order has not come in, check off another day on the calendar, add the inventory to the accumulator keeping track of the inventory, and proceed to the next day.''

"And if the order has come in?''

"Increase the inventory by the amount of the shipment and honor all existing backorders. Set the backorder counters to zero. Check, just in case, that the inventory is positive. If it isn't because backorders exceeded the amount of the shipment, increase the lost sales by the amount of the negative inventory, and set the inventory to zero. Then add the day's ending inventory to the inventory accumulator and proceed to the next day. And also make sure that the mechanism which prevented reordering more than once during an inventory cycle is reset to permit reordering on the next cycle.''

"Let's cover the situation where the inventory falls under the reordering point for the first time.''

"Make sure your calendar for the next shipment day has been erased of all previous information. Then reach into the bag with the ping-pong balls, take one out, and note the number. Refer then to the lead day simulator and pick off the lead time and round it to the nearest whole number and mark it on your calendar. Make sure you start looking at the calendar from its beginning day, do something about not reordering again during this inventory cycle, and keep track of the number of orders you are making. Again, make sure you are keeping track of the amount of inventory at the end of the day before proceeding to the next day.''

"And at the end of all of the days of the simulation?''

"Record in a notebook the reorder point and order quantity, or shipment size, we have been analyzing along with the daily average inventory level, and the average annual number of orders, the average annual number of backorders, and lost sales. Then proceed on to the next reorder point and shipment size I have given you and repeat the calculations. Make sure you record the results at the end of each combination of reorder point and ordering quantity which I have given you.''

"That ought to keep me busy.''

"Not for one as fast with calculations as you are.''

"Then what?''

"When you are finished with every combination of reordering point and order quantity that I have given you, then I will provide you with the economic values to obtain a total cost figure for inventory carrying costs, ordering costs, and the punitive charges for backorders and lost sales. Then using your stored results for each combination of reorder point and shipment size, you can give me the total cost of each combination. Then I can work off the total cost to obtain an assessment of the optimal reordering point and the shipment size. That's my job. Your job is to give me the figures. How long will it take you to get them?''

"If you use some judgment on the number of combinations I have to analyze, you'll have the results in the morning. If you don't use much judgment, you may never see the results."

This conversation is similar to instructions that may be given to a fifth-generation computer. These computers are being designed to respond verbally to the instructions provided by a human voice. Since these computers are not yet available, the clerk must be spoken to in a language he understands. Fortunately, we need not speak in machine language. User friendly languages are available such as BASIC and others. The appendix for this chapter contains the program which is nothing more than a translation of the previous conversation into a language that the computer understands.

The key to understanding the role of the computer is that everything must be reduced to an arithmetic calculation. The computer can also perform simple comparative operations: Are two numbers the same, or is one larger in value, or smaller in value, than the other? And to complete the picture, computers can store and retrieve information.

Computers sometimes appear to have intelligence such as when they play a game of chess and beat a master chess player. One ought not forget that the master chess player is not playing against a computer, but against the programmer who gave the computer its instructions in terms of simple rules of arithmetic for calculating numbers and simple rules of logic for comparing two numbers.

Using simulation to help in determining key decision points concerning inventory management requires that an economic analysis be done on the cost of ordering a product, carrying it as inventory, the potential loss of a customer's goodwill in having to backorder an item, and the real loss associated with a customer taking his business elsewhere.

The ordering cost is generally arrived at by taking the entire cost of having a purchasing department and dividing it by the annual number of processed orders. Sometimes, however, there is confusion over the fixed and variable costs of a purchasing department. For instance, if a policy is adopted which reduces the number of orders processed, and there is no reduction in the size of the purchasing department, all that occurs is an increase in the cost of ordering since the same annual cost must be covered by a smaller number of orders. Looking at this situation in another way, the savings in reducing the workload by one order may be just the savings for one telephone call, which is far different than what is included in the derivation of the ordering cost. These points have to be borne in mind because the ordering quantity determines the number of orders to be processed. The larger the ordering quantity, the fewer orders that have to be processed. The inherent assumption is that the incremental cost of one more order, or the incremental savings of one less order, is the same as the overall cost of placing an order.

The inventory carrying cost is more difficult to assess than the ordering cost. Some think in terms of the financing cost being the carrying cost of an inventory. This is just one portion of the carrying costs. An inventory requires a warehouse.

A warehouse represents a capital cost and an operating cost in terms of utilities, maintenance and repair, taxes, equipment, and personnel. An inventory has to be insured. An inventory is exposed to the risks of technological obsolescence, deterioration with age, and pilferage. Studies have shown that the appropriate annual carrying cost often is in the range of 20 to 30 percent of the value of the average inventory. This is about double the financing cost.

If arriving at the inventory carrying cost appears to be a little fuzzy, it is nothing compared to the fuzziness of arriving at the punitive charges to be applied against backorders and lost sales. To illustrate the problem of determining punitive charges for backorders and lost sales, consider a person purchasing a six pack of a particular brand of beer. If a customer visits his usual liquor store, and the store is out of his favorite brand of beer, his reaction may be to come back another day for the six pack because he still has some bottles left in his refrigerator. If this poses little in the way of additional effort on the customer's part, the cost of the backorder may be close to zero. If the customer feels inconvenienced in having to come back for the beer, there should be a higher punitive charge applied against the backorder.

If there is no beer left in the house and the customer goes to another liquor store, the backorder is immediately transformed into a lost sale. The appropriate punitive charge may be the loss of gross margin on the six pack. That is true if all that the customer buys at a competitive store is a six pack of beer. If the customer stocks up on other items while at the liquor store, then the appropriate punitive charge would be the loss of gross margin on the six pack and anything else that he has purchased. The customer may be sufficiently irritated over the liquor store not having his favorite brand of beer such that he transfers all his business to another store. Then the appropriate punitive charge would be the loss of gross margin on the six pack plus the gross margin on all future sales of six packs, and the gross margin on anything else the customer would be purchasing at the other store for the rest of his life.

The very fuzziness concerning discrete values for the punitive charges associated with backorders and lost sales means that discrete values should not be assigned. The model could have been built incorporating a punitive charge backorder simulator and a punitive charge lost sale simulator. In fact, it would be easier to treat backorders and lost sales in this fashion rather than try to determine discrete punitive charges.

Nevertheless, the model demands that the various charges be assessed a value. Charges have to be applied against the number of orders, the average inventory level, and against backorders and lost sales. These charges have to be reexamined from time to time to ensure they reflect changing conditions. One may object to having to perform such an analysis, but simulation, and analytic methods in general, require that costs be quantified. All analytic methods introduce an element of discipline of thought into the management process. Without giving thought to the costs associated with inventory management, it would be difficult to manage inventory in any systematic way.

Once these costs have been assessed, the physical outcomes of various combinations of reordering points and shipment sizes, or order quantities, can be compared on an economic basis. The simulation does not provide the final solution. It provides the data from which a solution can be determined. Usually the outcomes are plotted (see Exhibit 3.5).

The bands indicate the variance in the results—that is, the results of a simulation do not necessarily plot along a nice smooth curve. The reorder point and the order quantity that generate the lowest total cost would be selected as the optimal choice. A precise point may not be the answer. Area I in Exhibit 3.5 shows a range of shipment sizes (order quantities), where the total cost remains essen-

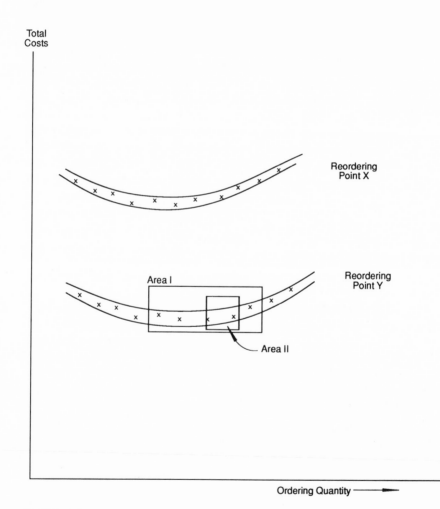

Exhibit 3.5.
Cost Curves—Reordering Point/Ordering Quantity Combinations

tially unchanged at a minimal level for the simulations under consideration. The flatness of this area is caused by the decrease in punitive charges for backorders and lost sales being compensated by the increase in inventory carrying costs of ordering larger sized shipments. In other words, the additional cost in inventory carrying charges by having larger order quantities is compensated by savings in having less dissatisfied customers because of fewer occurrences of backorders and lost sales. Since, in effect, there is no net cost being incurred in having larger sized shipments, one might as well select the order quantity at the right side of Area I denoted as Area II. By so doing, one can enhance service by minimizing backorders and lost sales at effectively no additional cost.

No price discounts for larger sized order quantities have been built into the model. Price discounts can be incorporated in the model by adjusting total costs to include the procurement cost of the item.

Depending on the circumstances, the usual optimal choice lies in the area where there is some small degree of backordering and lost sales. Most suppliers are averse to stockouts and maintain safety stocks of such proportions that stockouts are virtually impossible. Stockouts from time to time do have beneficial effects. The amount of potential loss from technical obsolescence and deterioration through aging is lessened by having a stockout now and then. A stockout occurring about the time a new computer model is introduced means that there will be less in losses as price slashing becomes necessary to liquidate the technologically obsolescent model. A stockout also helps to minimize an inventory deteriorating to the point where it is no longer fit for sale. Yellowed-with-age Mother's Day cards don't sell as well as the pristine white variety. Stocking out of Mother's Day cards prevents having to dispose of yellowed cards.

Sometimes retailers seem to believe that a stockout means the loss of a customer forever. Customers don't stop purchasing from a hardware store for the rest of their lives because the half-inch screw is stocked out once in six months—particularly when a five-eighths inch screw is an adequate substitute. Naturally, frequent stockouts would adversely affect the perception of service and, therefore, customer loyalty. On the other hand, an infrequent stockout does have beneficial effects such as enhancing the profitability of a business by reducing overall inventory costs.

Lacking both analytic tools to handle a given situation, and wishing not to have to think about punitive charges for backorders and lost sales, many managers rely on heuristic rules for determining the reorder point.

One heuristic rule is to reorder at a point which represents the highest possible demand during the longest possible lead time. The highest demand for the item under consideration is 900 units per day, and the longest lead time is fifteen days. Applying this heuristic rule to this scenario, the reordering point is 13,500 units. When the inventory reaches a level of 13,500 units, the inventory control manager calls the supplier for another shipment. Even if the supplier takes fifteen days to deliver the shipment, and even if demand is at the highest possible level for fifteen consecutive days (a combination of events which has an incredibly small chance of happening), there would be no stockout. No stockouts sounds fine to the customers, but a merchant will pay a heavy price for this policy in the form of inventory carrying charges. As previously mentioned, the charges are not just financial. More warehouse space has to be acquired, and every now and then, a portion of the inventory is thrown away because it has become either technologically obsolete or has deteriorated to the point of being unfit for sale.

Another heuristic rule might be to reorder at a point which represents 150 percent of the average demand multiplied by the average lead time. With demand varying between 300 and 900 units per day, one might assess average demand at 600 units per day. The average weighted lead time is slightly over six days. This heuristic rule establishes a reorder point of a little over 3,600 units. This is a small fraction of the first heuristic rule. Stockouts and backorders will definitely occur, but the heuristic rule does not provide any guidance on how often they will occur and how many units will be involved.

The Economic Order Quantity (EOQ) is certainly a guide to the order quantity. However, the mathematical basis of the EOQ has been violated in that demand is not constant. Nor can the usual mathematic treatment concerning the level of safety stocks be applied if demand, or lead time, variations do not have a normal distribution. Simulation makes no such demands. The distributions for demand and lead time in this chapter are non-normal distributions. Conventional mathematical formulations would be rather complex to handle the transformation of backorders to lost sales as was described. There is no problem in fitting the simulation to the characteristics of a given situation as long as the situation can be described in terms of simple arithmetic calculations and simple rules of logic.

One can criticize the use of simulation for determining inventory control points as too much trouble and rely on heuristic rules. The problem with heuristic rules is the sheer number of heuristic rules. Which one do you select? Usually the one that avoids stockouts—the one that usually means higher total costs in the form of inventory carrying costs. The return on utilizing simulation in helping to make decisions in inventory control has to be in the form of savings in reduced levels of inventories. This means a greater probability for some degree of stockouts. Simulation provides the data that will permit a manager to judge the frequency and the magnitude of the stockouts if he decides to adopt inventory decision points which generate savings in overall costs. The economic benefits of simulation cannot be achieved unless the manager has made up his mind to live with some risk of stockouts.

Appendix to Chapter 3

SIMULATION PROGRAM FOR INVENTORY PLANNING

It is presumed that the simulator for daily demand and lead time has been generated separately and stored in the sequential files CUM1 and CUM2, respectively. Had these files been viewed in the LOTUS environment, the .PRN suffix would have to be removed first.

```
10 REM NAME OF PROGRAM IS INV
20 DIM D(1000):DIM L(1000):DIM W(20)
30 OPEN "I",#1,"CUM1"
40 FOR I=1 TO 1000
50 INPUT #1,D
60 D(I)=INT(D+.5)
70 NEXT
80 CLOSE #1
90 OPEN "I",#1,"CUM2"
100 FOR I=1 TO 1000
110 INPUT #1,L
120 L(I)=INT(L+.5)
130 NEXT
140 CLOSE #1
150 PRINT "I","D(I)","L(I)"
160 PRINT "1",D(1),L(1)
170 FOR I=50 TO 1000 STEP 50
180 PRINT I,D(I),L(I)
190 NEXT
```

The program opens up the CUM1 and CUM2 files and transfers the contents to the arrays D(I) and L(I) respectively rounding the contents of the file to the nearest whole number. The arrays for demand and lead time are printed on the screen in 5 percent intervals for visual inspection.

```
200  OPEN ''O'',#1,''INVF''
```

The INVF sequential data file will record the results of each run.

```
210 PRINT:INPUT "YEARS OF SIMULATION: ";Y
220 PRINT:PRINT "REORDER POINT":PRINT
230 INPUT "START: ";Q1
240 INPUT "END:   ";Q2
```

```
250 INPUT "STEP:   ";Q3
260 PRINT:PRINT "ORDER QUANTITY":PRINT
270 INPUT "START: ";Q4
280 INPUT "END:   ";Q5
290 INPUT "STEP:   ";Q6
300 FOR R=Q1 TO Q2 STEP Q3
310 FOR Q=Q4 TO Q5 STEP Q6
```

The simulation will run for Y years. The reorder point will start at Q1 and proceed to Q2 in steps, or increments, of Q3. For each reorder point, the order quantity will start at Q4 and proceed to Q5 in steps, or increments, of Q6. This sequence of running the simulation for all order quantities for a given reorder point was selected in the fore-knowledge that the results of the simulation will be analyzed in terms of order quantities for given reordering points.

```
320  FOR I=1 TO 4:B(I)=0:NEXT
330  FOR I=1 TO 20:W(I)=0:NEXT
```

The array B(I) ages the backorders. Backorders are reduced to zero over a four-day period by their conversion to lost sales. The array W(I) is the calendar for determining the arrival time of the next shipment. All these values are set to zero at the start of a run to avoid contamination of results from the previous run.

```
340  V=Q:Y1=365*Y:N=0:K=0:S=0:B=0:R1=0:V1=0
```

The initial inventory V is the Q under consideration. The days of the simulation is 365 times the number of selected years. N is the indicator indicating whether an order has been placed when the inventory V is below the reordering point R. K is the indicator indicating whether it is a weekday. S is the counter which accumulates the total number of lost sales throughout the simulation. B is the counter, or accumulator, for the total number of backorders which are honored when a shipment arrives. R1 is the accumulator for the total number of orders placed during the simulation. V1 is the accumulator for the daily inventory throughout the simulation. All counters and accumulators are set to zero at the start of the simulation to eliminate any data from previous runs.

```
350  FOR I=1 TO Y1
360  K=K+1
370  IF K>7 THEN 380 ELSE 390
380  K=1
390  ON K GOTO 400,400,400,400,400,410,410
400  K1=1:GOTO 420
410  K1=0
420  X=INT(1000*RND(X)+.5)
430  IF X<1 THEN 420
440  D=K1*D(X)
```

For all the days of the simulation, the counter K will proceed from 1 through 7 and repeat itself again. For values of K between 1 and 5, K1 has a value of 1. For values of K of 6 and 7, K1 is assigned a value of 0. Statement 420 is equivalent to reaching into a bag of 1,000 ping-pong balls. There is a small chance of obtaining a zero. If that happens, another ping-pong ball is drawn. Statements 420 and 430 generate random numbers between 1 and 1,000. Statement 440 determines the daily demand taking into consideration that the place of business is closed on the weekends.

```
450   V=V-D
```

Except for the first day, V is the ending inventory of the previous day. The inventory is reduced by the amount of the daily demand.

```
460   IF V<0 THEN 470 ELSE 600
```

The only way to enter statement 470 is for the inventory to have a negative value.

```
480   B(4)=B(3):B(3)=B(2):B(2)=B(1)
```

This is the aging process of backorders. B(4) represents backorders which are four days old. B(3) represents backorders which are three days old. B(4) takes on the value contained in B(3). B(3) takes on the value contained in B(2). Note that the order of aging is crucial. The value contained in B(3) must be transferred to B(4) before B(3) assumes the value contained in B(2). Otherwise the information contained in B(3) is lost.

```
490   B(1)=-V
```

The value assigned to B(1) is the negative of a negative number in order for B(1) to have a positive value.

```
500   S2=.25*B(2):B(2)=B(2)-S2
510   S3=.50*B(3):B(3)=B(3)-S3
520   S4=B(4):B(4)=0:S=S+S2+S3+S4:V=0
```

Twenty-five percent of two-day-old backorders, 50 percent of three-day-old backorders and all four-day-old backorders become lost sales. The new backorders are adjusted for that portion which has become lost sales. S is the accumulator for all lost sales during the course of the simulation. V is set to zero because there cannot be a negative inventory in a physical sense. The negative V has been accounted for in terms of backorders and lost sales. The aging of the backorders, and closing the business on weekends, are examples of fitting the simulation to the nature of the problem.

```
600   IF V<=R THEN 610 ELSE 730
```

After the daily demand has been taken away from the inventory, the question is asked whether the new inventory is below the reorder point. The only way to enter statement 610 is that the inventory is below, or equal to, the reorder point.

```
610   IF N=0 THEN 620 ELSE 660
```

An inventory control manager places one order during an inventory cycle. If some precaution is not built into the program, an order will be placed every day during the lead time because the inventory is below the reordering point. To model the behavior of an inventory control manager, some mechanism has to be incorporated in the program to prevent multiple orders. The only way to enter statement 620 is on the first day in an inventory cycle when the inventory has fallen below, or is equal to, the reorder point. After the order has been placed, the indicator N is assigned a value other than zero which prevents multiple orders. When the shipment does arrive, N is reassigned a value of zero to permit a reordering when the inventory is once again below the reordering point.

```
620   FOR J=1 TO 20:W(J)=0:NEXT
630   X=INT(1000*RND(X)+.5)
640   IF X<1 THEN 630
650   W(L(X))=1:J=0:R1=R1+1:N=1:GOTO 730
```

Any previous data in the calendar for lead time is first erased. The array "mailbox" corresponding to the randomly determined lead time is set equal to 1 while the other "mailboxes" have a value of 0. The counter J is the means to count off the days to the arrival of the shipment. R1 is the counter which accumulates the total number of orders placed during the simulation. Setting the value of N to anything other than zero is the means to identify that an order has been placed during this inventory cycle.

```
660   J=J+1
```

The only way to enter statement 660 is for the inventory to be less than the reorder point and for an order to have already been placed. J will increase from an initial value of zero in increments of one.

```
670   IF W(J)=1 THEN 680 ELSE 730
```

On the day after an order is placed, "mailbox" W(1) is examined to see if a shipment has arrived. A "0" in the "mailbox" means that the shipment has not arrived while a "1" means it has arrived. The next day, "mailbox" W(2) is examined. And each succeeding day, "mailboxes" W(3), W(4), W(5), etc. are looked into until that day when the contents of the "mailbox" indicates that a shipment has finally arrived.

```
680   V=V+Q-B(1)-B(2)-B(3)-B(4)
690   B=B+B(1)+B(2)+B(3)+B(4)
700   FOR J1=1 TO 5:B(J1)=0:NEXT:N=0
```

The only way to enter statement 680 is the day a shipment arrives. The inventory is increased by the size of the shipment and reduced by the number of backorders on the books. The counter B accumulates the total number of backorders which are filled. Backorders, which have not been filled, have already been accounted for as lost sales in the accumulator S. The calendar for backorders is then set to zero in preparation for the next inventory cycle. The indicator N is also set to zero to permit reordering during the next inventory cycle.

```
710  IF V<0 THEN 720 ELSE 730
720  S=S-V:B=B+V:V=0
```

There is a possibility that the number of backorders exceeds the shipment size. This will result in a negative inventory which is detected in statement 710. If the inventory has a negative value, statement 720 converts all unfilled backorders to lost sales. The lost sales accumulator is increased by the negative of the negative inventory. The backorder accumulator has to be reduced by the number of backorders which were actually not filled, and the inventory is set equal to zero. Leaving out statements 710 and 720 will result in a bug in the program which can cause the simulation to run with negative inventories. During program development, judiciously placed PRINT statements can ferret out these bugs if they happen to occur while the programmer is watching the screen. Another and perhaps more effective way of ensuring the program isn't running on negative inventories is to place a statement to stop the program if the inventory has a negative value at an inappropriate point such as the start of a day.

```
730  V1=V1+V
740  NEXT
```

All paths end in statement 730 where the V1 accumulates the daily inventory at the end of the day. Statement 740 closes the loop to repeat the process for each day of the simulation.

```
750  V1=V1/Y1:R1=R1/Y:B=B/Y:S=S/Y
760  WRITE#1,R,Q,V1,R1,B,S
770  NEXT:NEXT:CLOSE#1
```

At the end of the Y1 days of the simulation representing Y years, the accumulator containing the total inventory is divided by the total number of days to obtain the average daily inventory. The remaining accumulators are divided by the number of years to obtain the annual averages for the number of orders placed and the number of backorders and lost sales. This information, along with the reorder point and order quantity under scrutiny, is written in a sequential data file called INVF. The process is repeated for every order quantity associated with each reordering point and then repeated for every reordering point under consideration. The INVF data file is closed when all simulations have been completed.

```
800 PRINT
810 INPUT "VALUE OF SINGLE UNIT OF PRODUCT: ";U
820 INPUT "CARRYING COST AS % OF VALUE:     ";H:H=H/100
830 INPUT "ORDERING COST PER ORDER:         ";C
840 INPUT "BACKORDER PUNITIVE CHARGE:       ";P1
850 INPUT "LOST SALE PUNITIVE CHARGE:       ";P2
860 LPRINT:LPRINT
870 LPRINT "RESULTS OF THE SIMULATION IN ANNUAL COSTS":LPRINT
880 LPRINT "REORDER" TAB(10) " ORDER" TAB(20) "CARRYING";
890 LPRINT TAB(30) "ORDERING" TAB(40) "BACKORDER" TAB(50);
900 LPRINT "LOSTSALE" TAB(60) "TOTAL"
910 LPRINT " POINT" TAB(10) "QUANTITY" TAB(20) "  COST";
920 LPRINT TAB(30) "  COST" TAB(40) "  COST" TAB(50);
```

```
 930 LPRINT "  COST" TAB(60) " COST":LPRINT
 940 OPEN "I",#1,"INVF"
 950 INPUT #1,R,Q,V1,R1,B,S
 960 T1=INT(V1*H*U):T2=INT(C*R1):T3=INT(B*P1):T4=INT(S*P2)
 970 T5=T1+T2+T3+T4
 980 LPRINT R TAB(10) Q TAB(20) T1 TAB(30) T2 TAB(40);
 990 LPRINT T3 TAB(50) T4 TAB(60) T5
1000 IF EOF(1) THEN 1010 ELSE 950
1010 CLOSE #1:END
```

The economic inputs are entered, and costs are calculated and printed on a line printer in whole numbers. For record purposes, the economic input values should also be printed on the line printer. Note that the simulation does not have to be rerun if there is a change in the economic inputs because the physical aspects of the simulation (the average inventory, number of orders, backorders, and lost sales) contained in the INVF file remain unchanged. If the economic situation has changed, directing the program to start at statement 800 will redo the economic calculations. Separate data files should be set up for different products. The analysis to obtain the optimal selection of the reordering point and ordering quantity has already been described earlier.

4

Logistics Planning

SYNOPSIS

Logistics encompasses all facets of the movement of raw materials and components to manufacturing and processing plants and the movement of finished goods from these plants to consumers. The organization and control of the movement and storage of raw materials into a manufacturing or processing plant is called materials management while the same functions being performed on finished goods is called physical distribution management. Logistics includes inventory control, modes of external transport including applicable rules and regulations, warehousing, and storage facilities. Materials handling, or internal transportation of raw materials, components, and finished goods within a manufacturing or processing plant, is part of logistics. The cost of logistics in the form of resources and personnel dedicated to the transport and storage of goods and materials is an appreciable portion of the total cost of manufactured goods.

The application of simulation to logistics planning will be illustrated through design considerations for a crude oil transshipment terminal. The question to be addressed is the size of the transshipment terminal to accommodate the internal company's need for steady delivery of crude oil to the transshipment terminal and to accommodate the external customers' needs for seasonal deliveries of crude oil. The model will be built on value tables rather than on simulator curves. Value tables can be used when the number of values to be assigned to a variable are relatively few.

This chapter also demonstrates the relative ease of fitting simulation to a situation—not unlike fitting a glove to the shape of the hand. But the fitting required the simulator model builder to interview three different departments of the same company. No one individual possessed both the overview of the situation and the details necessary for the design of the model. The combined opinions, and experience, of executives in the three departments had to be integrated into the simulation.

During the late 1960s, Very Large Crude Carriers (VLCCs) made their debut on the world tanker scene. These vessels were capable of carrying four to five times the cargo carried in what were then called supertankers. These former supertankers are now called medium-sized tankers or, from the point of view of the transshipment terminal, shuttle tankers. The underlying reason for the development of VLCCs was their inherent economy to carry crude oil long distances at a low cost of transport. This, in turn, was in response to the growing dependency of the United States on imported crude oil. Having more or less exhausted the capacity of nearby sources of imported crude oil, notably Venezuela at that time, oil companies in the United States were looking far afield for supplies of oil. Nothing is more far afield than Saudi Arabia and other Middle East oil exporters. As these exporters were becoming more prominent as suppliers of U.S. import needs, there was an ever-growing incentive to find a means of transport to reduce the cost of transportation.

Although the Middle East had the deep water ports necessary to handle VLCCs, the United States did not have ports with sufficient depth of water to accommodate these vessels. Dredging was prohibitively expensive. A more feasible solution was the construction of a transshipment terminal in the deep water ports of the Caribbean islands. The economics of scale of the VLCCs could be utilized on the long distance voyage from the Middle East to the Caribbean transshipment terminal. The final leg of the movement of crude oil from the transshipment terminal into the relatively shallow ports of the United States would be by shuttle tankers—the supertankers of yesterday.

The integrative nature of logistics can be seen by the programmer of the simulation model having to interview three different management groups. The executives of the transshipment terminal had an overview of the entire project. The marine department possessed the specialized knowledge for scheduling the VLCCs, and the marketing department was cognizant of customers' needs. Each group had to be interviewed by the planning department's simulation model builder for him to understand the project in its entirety and to obtain the necessary data for modeling the particulars of the project.

During the interviews with several oil company executives, the model builder noted the following major points concerning the criteria of performance for the logistics system connecting the Middle East oil fields with refineries located along the U.S. Gulf Coast.

The transshipment terminal will be supplied by six VLCCs on a year-round basis. VLCCs are costly investments, and their economy of scale can only be achieved through continuous employment. Furthermore, the supply contracts with the Middle East supplier call for regular liftings by the VLCCs year-round.

The customers' demand for imported crude oil into the United States is seasonal. The seasonal peak runs from about October through February when refinery output expands to satisfy heating oil demand. The slack season is from March to July. The slack season is particularly pronounced because refinery operators tend to liquidate any remaining inventories from the previous winter peak season. This means that, from the point of view of the transshipment terminal, cargo sales slump from March to May as domestic refinery operators reduce their crude inventories to normal summer levels. The slump actually extends far into the summer because the domestic refinery operators tend to rely more on domestic

U.S. sources of crude oil during the summer than during the winter. The import oil market picks up in late summer as refinery operators begin to expand their inventory levels in anticipation of the upcoming winter heating season.

The scheduling of the VLCCs is an important matter in the minds of management because the financial performance of the system is ultimately based on the delivery of crude oil by these vessels. Revenue is basically a throughput fee on crude oil passing through the terminal. If the transshipment terminal is not large enough to accommodate offloading a VLCC, the vessel must wait until there is sufficient empty capacity to be offloaded. The gross revenue of the terminal is adversely affected while the vessel waits. In fact, any idle time, no matter what the cause, adversely affects the financial performance of the transshipment terminal.

The scheduling of the shuttle vessels is not important in that the oil company sells oil from the transshipment terminal as a supply point. Sometimes the oil company pays for the shipping costs on the final leg of the voyage, and other times the customers pay depending on the conditions of sale. The important point is that there is a large available supply of shuttle tankers in the Caribbean. Their numbers are such that chartering arrangements can be made on relatively short notice, if necessary, to move cargoes. The critical point is not the number of vessels available to move the cargoes, but the number of cargoes that can be sold from the transshipment terminal. Of particular concern are the sales of cargoes during the summer. Sales of cargoes during the winter pose no potential problem. In fact, it is a management objective that winter sales be of such a magnitude to "empty the tanks at least once a year."

The building of a berth for the VLCCs is expensive. Only one berth is planned. The inner harbor to the transshipment terminal has a number of berths for the shuttle vessels. Considering the number of berths for shuttle vessels in the inner harbor, and considering that two more shuttle vessels could be loaded from the VLCC berth when that berth is empty, there is no expected shortage of berths for the shuttle vessels. However, there is some question whether one berth will be sufficient to offload the VLCCs.

These were the considerations expressed by upper level management in interviews with the designer of the simulator model. Although the viewpoints of upper level management tend to be general in nature, some of their concerns can be quite specific. A meeting was then arranged with the marine department concerning the scheduling of the VLCCs because more details were needed. Experienced personnel in the marine department made the following observations.

The round-trip steaming time at rated speed assuming moderate weather is fifty-four days. However, delays can result when the weather is not moderate. These weather delays are seasonal varying with the month. There is sufficient data in ship voyage reports to assess weather delays on the Middle East to Caribbean trade.

Discharging the crude oil cargo at the transshipment terminal cannot proceed unless the berth is available and there is sufficient empty space in the transshipment terminal to take on the cargo. Once discharge is completed, the rescheduling of the VLCC will be in accordance with the following table.

	DAYS TO LOAD	DAYS TO DISCHARGE	RANGE OF DELAY DAYS DUE TO: CONGESTION LOAD PORT	WEATHER DELAYS
January	2	2	2 – 8	4 – 9
February	2	2	2 – 6	4 – 8
March	2	2	1 – 5	3 – 8
April	2	2	0 – 3	2 – 6
May	2	2	0 – 1	1 – 4
June	2	2	0 – 1	0 – 3
July	2	2	0 – 1	0 – 3
August	2	2	0 – 3	0 – 3
September	2	2	1 – 4	1 – 4
October	2	2	2 – 5	2 – 6
November	2	2	2 – 7	3 – 7
December	2	2	2 – 8	4 – 8

The time in days from the point of beginning the discharge at the transshipment terminal to the arrival at the transshipment terminal with another full cargo to be discharged is the sum of the following factors: 2 days to discharge + 54 days at sea + 2 days to load + load port congestion + weather delays.

The procedure for calculating load port congestion, using December as a sample month, is straightforward. The minimum port congestion time is two days. It could be as long as eight days. If X is a random number which has a value between 0 and 1, then port congestion time will be $2 + X*(8-2)$. If X has a value of 0, port congestion will be two days. If X has a value of 1, port congestion will be eight days. If X is 0.5, then port congestion will be five days. The same procedure can be employed to determine the extent of weather delay days.

The scheduling of the next call at the transshipment port can be obtained by rounding the sum to the nearest whole day. This is done by adding 0.5 to the sum and taking the integer value which, in effect, discards the decimal value. If the sum of the four components is 63.423, adding 0.5 is 63.923, and taking the integer value yields sixty-three days. If the sum is 63.811, adding 0.5 brings the total to 64.311, and taking the integer value yields sixty-four days.

This general procedure for determining load port congestion and weather delays assumes equal probability for, in the case of December load port congestion, two, three, four, five, six, seven, and eight days. This is equivalent to generating a simulator curve with a scaling factor of 0.5.

There may be delays in discharging the cargo caused by insufficient empty capacity in the transshipment terminal to accommodate the cargo, or because a berth is not available if another VLCC is being discharged. These delays are accounted for by the vessel not being rescheduled until the start of discharge is permitted. These particular delays are recorded during the running of the simulation to determine system performance.

In conversations with the marine people, one other factor was discussed. VLCCs are taken out of service once per year for a fifteen-day maintenance period. Usually, drydockings for annual maintenance are scheduled sometime between the start of the slack season in March through early summer.

Conversations are then held with the marketing people responsible for sales from the transshipment terminal. They indicate that the average cargo sale is 50,000 tons of crude oil with the following seasonal pattern.

SALES IN TERMS OF 50,000 TON SHIPMENTS

	MINIMUM NUMBER OF SHIPMENTS	MAXIMUM NUMBER OF SHIPMENTS
January	20	30
February	20	30
March	5	10
April	5	10
May	5	10
June	5	10
July	5	10
August	10	15
September	20	30
October	20	30
November	20	30
December	20	30

The minimum annual number of shipments is 155, and the maximum annual number of shipments is 245. The average number of shipments is 200. Average annual delivery is 200 shipments, or 10 million tons of crude oil at 50,000 tons per shipment. There are six VLCCs in continuous employment for 350 days a year allotting 15 days per year for maintenance. For an average voyage of about 65 days, each vessel can deliver about 5.4 cargoes per year to the transshipment terminal. Each cargo is 250,000 tons of crude oil. Each vessel can deliver an annual total of about 1,350,000 tons of crude oil; six vessels can deliver 8,100,000 tons per year. Thus, on average, cargo sales exceed the delivery of crude oil, and this should satisfy management's objective that the transshipment terminal be more or less drained dry, so to speak, at least once per year. This would occur during the peak season.

Management will not arrange a sale if there is insufficient crude oil at the transshipment port. Therefore, there is no need to build in a punitive charge if the potential for cargo sales exceeds inventory levels. The system is being driven by the actual deliveries of the six VLCCs, not by potential sales from the transshipment terminal. However, cargo sales must exceed actual deliveries by the VLCCs if management's desire to stockout once per year is to be satisfied. Under the circumstances, it appears that any excess inventory of crude oil at the transshipment terminal can be liquidated by increasing cargo sales during the peak winter season.

As before, the total outgoing shipments to onshore refinery operators for any given month will be the minimum lifting plus a random number between 0 and 1 multiplied by the difference between the maximum and minimum number of liftings with the result rounded to the nearest whole number. This determination can be performed at the start of each year of a simulation with the liftings randomly distributed throughout the appropriate month, or done at the start of each particular month. If there happens to be insufficient inventory on the day of the lifting, the lifting will be cancelled with no punitive charge. This simulates the workings of a management control system which prevents the sale of a cargo if there is insufficient inventory to cover the sale.

The simulation requires a calendar to keep track of VLCC arrivals and shuttle vessel loadings. A number of types of calendars can be set up. If a simulation were to run for fifty years of 360 days per year, then a calendar consisting of 18,000 days may be in order. If each VLCC were to have its own calendar, then six calendars totaling 108,000 separate days would be required. Calendars of this size may not fit into a computer. A much smaller calendar of 360 days can be used for keeping track of all vessel arrivals. The calendar must then be recycled at the end of each year erasing previous data each time the calendar is recycled. Actually the calendar has to be larger than 360 days to take into account vessel scheduling which takes place in November and December. When this occurs, the next scheduled arrival is some time in January and February of the following year. These ship arrivals must be preserved in recycling the calendar at the end of the year.

In examining the combination of delays from weather and port congestion, the longest possible scheduling would be seventy-five days. Therefore, a calendar extension of the order of ninety days from the end of the year would be ample in ensuring that no ship arrival is lost while recycling the calendar. Changes in the data base which lengthen the round-trip voyage would necessitate expanding the calendar extension.

The calendar consists of 450 days—the normal 360-day year plus a ninety-day extension to cover what amounts to arrivals during the thirteenth, fourteenth, and fifteenth months of the year. At the start of the year, all previous data for the 360-day year is erased, and all arrivals scheduled during the extension period are assigned to the first three months of the new year. Then the extension period calendar is erased of all previous data. A value of zero for any day of the 360-day calendar means no ship arrival that day. A value of 1 means that one ship is scheduled to arrive that day. A value of 2 means two ships are arriving. As six vessels are in continuous employment, it is possible to have a value of 6 assigned to a particular day which means that six vessels are arriving at the same time. Having six vessels call all on the same day would have a low probability of occurrence. However, it is highly likely that all of the ships will begin to have similar arrival and departure schedules.

This is called bunching and has been observed in practice. Buses leaving a terminal at regular intervals end their route all in one bunch. The same is true in shipping. Two conditions help to correct bunching. One is the fact that only one ship can be discharged at a time while the others wait. This tends to spread out the next sequence of arrivals. The second factor can be more significant in spreading out the next sequence of arrivals. If the storage tanks at the transshipment terminal cannot take on all the cargoes, the VLCCs must wait until the shuttle vessels have removed sufficient cargoes to permit discharge of the larger vessels. As each one waits its turn to discharge, its schedule, in relation to the schedules of the other vessels, becomes more regular—that is, more equal spacing of time intervals between arrivals.

During the 360-day year, VLCCs experience different port and weather delays depending on the month. Moreover, crude oil sold from the transshipment port varies on a monthly basis. Therefore, there has to be a way to determine a particular month during a 360-day period. As the following illustration shows, this can be done by taking one less than the day number, dividing the result by 360, then taking the integer and adding one to the result: Number of Month=1 + Integer Value of (Day Number − 1)/30

DAY NUMBER	DAY NUMBER LESS ONE	DIVIDED BY 360	INTEGER VALUE	ONE PLUS INTEGER VALUE	RESULTING MONTH
1	0	0	0	1	January
15	14	0.50	0	1	January
30	29	0.966	0	1	January
31	30	1.000	1	2	February
59	58	1.933	1	2	February
60	59	1.966	1	2	February
61	60	2.000	2	3	March
330	329	10.966	10	11	November
331	330	11.000	11	12	December
359	358	11.933	11	12	December
360	359	11.966	11	12	December

Knowing the month of the year, one is in a position of applying seasonal factors such as weather and port delay time and cargo sales from the transshipment port to U.S. Gulf Coast refinery operators. From the point of view of sizing the transshipment terminal, the relevant factor is not the peak season for selling cargoes, which extends from September to February, but the subsequent slack season. In particular, the months following March—when onshore refinery operators are liquidating excess inventories and depending on domestic sources of crude oil—are critical in determining the size of the transshipment terminal. These are the months when it is most likely for an incoming VLCC not to be offloaded because of insufficient empty space at the terminal. If this is the case, then the vessel must wait until there is sufficient space in the terminal to offload the cargo.

One remaining detail has to be arranged. The VLCCs are taken out of service for fifteen days per year for maintenance. This is usually done during the slack season. Some sort of mechanism has to be incorporated in the model which extends the first six voyages from the beginning of the slack season in March by fifteen days. As the simulation is running on a 360-day year, and the vessels actually operate on a 365-day year, the extension for maintenance will be ten days which compensates for the five-day difference between the real and the simulated year.

The object of the simulation is twofold: One is to obtain the optimal capacity of the transshipment terminal, and the other is to judge whether one VLCC unloading berth is adequate. Both of these objectives are judged by the inability to discharge the cargo. If there is insufficient empty capacity in the transshipment terminal to hold another 250,000 tons of cargo, the vessel arrival is delayed by one day, and a counter will keep track of VLCC–Insufficient Capacity Days Lost. If there is sufficient capacity, but the berth is busy unloading another VLCC, the arrival date will be postponed by one day, and another counter will keep track of VLCC–Berth Days Lost. Precedence is given to the Insufficient Capacity Days Lost counter because a vessel cannot discharge if there is insufficient capacity regardless if a berth is available. Economic considerations as to the charge to be placed against the total capacity of the transshipment and the cost of days lost do not have to be performed at this point. The economic evaluation will be done after the simulation is run.

The simulation program is developed in the appendix to this chapter. The smallest size of the transshipment terminal from the point of view of running the program is bound by the size of the VLCC. The smallest sized terminal must be able to hold at least one VLCC cargo, which is 250,000 tons. The largest sized terminal to be considered is one where there are no days lost because of insufficient storage space. There is no need to give this much thought. The simulation will begin at 300,000 tons and continue running with transshipment capacity increasing in increments of 200,000 tons until there are essentially no days lost from insufficient storage space.

The simulation in the appendix was run over a fifty-year period of time and the following results were obtained.

STORAGE CAPACITY IN 000 TONS	AVERAGE NUMBER ANNUAL VOYAGES	AVERAGE ANNUAL VLCC DAYS LOST INSUFFICIENT CAPACITY	AVERAGE ANNUAL VLCC DAYS LOST DISCHARGING BERTH UNAVAILABLE
300	27.0	343	0
500	27.8	291	0
700	28.5	243	1
900	29.2	203	1
1100	30.3	135	1

STORAGE CAPACITY IN 000 TONS	AVERAGE NUMBER ANNUAL VOYAGES	AVERAGE ANNUAL VLCC DAYS LOST INSUFFICIENT CAPACITY	AVERAGE ANNUAL VLCC DAYS LOST DISCHARGING BERTH UNAVAILABLE
1300	31.1	85	2
1500	31.8	50	2
1700	32.2	23	2
1900	32.4	10	2
2100	32.5	2	3
2300	32.6	0	4

The average number of annual voyages unimpeded by storage limitations is 32.6 voyages per year for the six VLCCs. This is an average of about 5.4 voyages per year per vessel. The difference between 32.6 voyages for the largest sized terminal and the 27 voyages for the smallest sized terminal is roughly the equivalent of losing the services of one vessel. What that means is that, on average throughout the year, there is always one VLCC present at the terminal unable to discharge because of a shortage of empty capacity. This is reinforced by the 343 VLCC–Days Lost Insufficient Capacity, which is equivalent to losing the services of one vessel. The fact that the vessels are making about 5.4 voyages per year is of comfort that the model is working (although this should not be interpreted as proof of its correctness).

As the terminal capacity increases, the ship days lost from insufficient capacity declines. There is always sufficient capacity to take on another cargo of crude oil when the transshipment terminal has a capacity of 2.3 million tons. The days lost because a vessel cannot offload because another VLCC is in the unloading berth is zero for smaller sized terminals because insufficient storage space is preventing the unloading of the vessel. Whether the berth is available is not important. For larger sized terminals where there is sufficient storage space, the number of days when one vessel is in the berth being offloaded while another vessel is awaiting to be offloaded increases. However, at no point does it become a meaningful number.

The simulation provides the physical performance of terminals of varying sizes. The final decision as to the optimal size of the transshipment terminal results when economic factors are applied to the physical performance of the system. Changing the economic factors does not require rerunning the simulation because the physical performance of the system remains the same. All that has to be adjusted when economic factors change is the economic analysis of the results of a simulation.

In talking to top level management, the performance of the VLCCs was considered critical. Suppose that the transshipment terminal works off a through-put charge of 25 cents per barrel. With seven barrels to a ton of crude, and 250,000 tons to a shipment, the revenue lost for non-delivery of a cargo is $437,500. A vessel can deliver a maximum of about 5.4 cargoes, assuming no delays at the transshipment terminal, and operates an average of 350 days a year. Taking into consideration the cost of a non-delivery of a cargo multiplied by the number of cargoes which can be delivered per year, and divided by the number of days in a year, a day lost at the transshipment terminal will cost the company about $6,750 per day in lost revenues. In addition, the cost of capital invested in the ship, and the cost of operation, is $20,000 per day. The total cost of each day lost because of insufficient capacity to offload a vessel, or berth unavailability, is $26,750 per day.

On the other hand, the larger the terminal, the larger the investment. Suppose that the operating and capital charges for a terminal is $7 per ton of capacity per year. The previous table can now be translated from physical attributes to economic values upon which a decision can be made.

STORAGE CAPACITY IN 000 TONS	ANNUAL COST STORAGE CAPACITY IN 000 DLRS AT $7/TON	AVERAGE ANNUAL VLCC DAYS LOST ALL REASONS	ANNUAL COST DAYS LOST AT $26,750/DAY	TOTAL ANNUAL COSTS 000 DLRS
300	$2,100	343	$9,175	$11,275
500	3,500	291	7,784	11,284
700	4,900	244	6,527	11,427
900	6,300	204	5,457	11,757
1100	7,700	136	3,638	11,338
1300	9,100	87	2,327	11,427
1500	10,500	52	1,391	11,891
1700	11,900	25	669	12,569
1900	13,300	12	321	13,621
2100	14,700	5	134	14,834
2300	16,100	4	107	16,207

The operational people sitting around a table discussing the size of the proposed terminal would tend to focus on the days lost column and support the largest sized terminal. They would tend to have difficulty accepting a situation where 100, 200, or 300 ship days are lost per year because of insufficient storage at the terminal whose operations are their responsibility. They would, by nature, feel that they would be blamed for this undesirable situation.

The financial people might be tempted to look at the smallest possible terminal because this represents the minimum capital investment. Their job is to raise capital, and the smaller the project, the easier their task.

Those in a more neutral position, such as planners or upper management, might look at the total cost column and conclude that it doesn't matter what size the terminal is, up to about 1.3 million to 1.5 million tons of capacity, because the total annual costs are about the same regardless of the size of the terminal. As the terminal size increases, the number of ship days lost caused by insufficient capacity in the terminal to offload the vessels, declines. The additional cost of a larger terminal is offset by savings in fewer ship days lost.

Hopefully, no decision would be reached. For the system to perform smoothly as presently conceived, a huge investment is needed in tanks at the transshipment terminal. For example, 1.5 million tons of onshore tankage is equal to the total capacity of the offshore fleet. In essence, two fleets are being built—one to move the cargo at sea, and the other to store it on land. This is a consequence of the severe nature of the slack season on cargo sales. Management may well decide that it might be better to build a smaller transshipment terminal, take the money that would have been invested in building a larger terminal, and purchase a refinery in the U.S. Gulf Coast area. The refinery's crude oil intake from March through July would be from the transshipment terminal. The net effect of this is to reduce the severity of the slump in sales and the need for such a large amount of storage capacity.

In analyzing the strategy of obtaining an interest in a U.S. Gulf Coast refinery to enhance the summer throughput of the transshipment terminal, the same simulation program can be run with simply a higher level of minimum sales during the slack season to determine the optimal size of the transshipment terminal. Or the model can be scrapped and a new one constructed to reflect the operations of a VLCC–transshipment terminal–shuttle tanker–refinery system.

The real value of simulation, and analytic methods in general, is that they tend to focus the discussion during the managerial decision making process. Seldom do the economics of a situation dictate a decision. However, without an economic analysis, the discussion of a situation lacks a focal point and becomes too general to make a hard decision on other than platitudes and gut feelings. With an economic analysis, the discussion can concentrate on the results of the analysis and can deal with specifics.

Meetings, in general, do not end with a decision. The usual result of a meeting is to perform another analysis. The appropriate course of action, based on the simulation just performed, is to deal with the issue of the severity of the summer slump. An analysis of the simulation did not lead to a decision as to the optimal size of the transshipment terminal. It led to a conclusion that the system isn't going to function well as presently conceived. Too much tank capacity has to be built to keep the VLCCs operating on a regular schedule. It is problematic whether this might have been realized without the simulation.

However, after a few of these meetings, and after a few sessions of going back to the drawing board, the underpinnings of a decision will begin to emerge whose nature goes beyond platitudes and gut feelings. This is the true contribution of simulation to management decision making.

Appendix to Chapter 4

TRANSSHIPMENT TERMINAL SIMULATION MODEL

The program in this appendix is tailored for the situation described in this chapter. The V array is the 450-day calendar for the VLCCs. The S array is the calendar for cargo sales from the transshipment terminal. The C array is the internal data base for the monthly minimum and maximum cargo sales. The L array and the W array are the internal data bases for the monthly load port congestion and the monthly weather delays, respectively. Statements 30–80 assign the data to the appropriate arrays. The number of years for running the simulation is entered in statement 90. S is the variable for designating the size of the storage capacity at the transshipment terminal, and its stepping sequence is established in statement 100. Before a new storage capacity is analyzed, counters containing data from the previous run are restored to a zero value.

N is the counter that keeps track of the number of voyage discharges; D for the number of ship days lost because of insufficient empty storage capacity to unload a vessel; and B for the number of ship days lost because of the berth serving another vessel. B1 and B2 record the status of the berth on a two-day schedule, and V is the inventory. The initial inventory at the start of the simulation is zero because a VLCC will be assigned to arrive on the first day of the simulation.

Statement 120 starts the multiyear simulation. At the start of the first year, the simulation is directed to statements 170–190 where the calendars are set to zero values and the initial schedule of arrivals is established for the six VLCCs on the basis of an arrival on the first day and every ten days thereafter.

A zero value in the V array means that no ship has arrived that day, and a zero value in the S array means that no cargo shipment is to be made that day. For any other year of the simulation, the first 360 days of the V array and the entire S array is set to zero. The 90-day extension of the old V array is transferred to the beginning 90-day period of the new V array before its contents are set to zero.

Beginning in statement 200, the cargoes sold from the transshipment terminal are determined and assigned to days throughout the entire year. The number of cargoes for a particular month is established in statement 210 and rounded to the nearest whole number in statement 220. Statements 230–270 assign a day of the month for shipping the cargo from the transshipment terminal. Statement 245 is necessary because it is possible to obtain a zero day from statement 240.

Statement 290 is the start of simulating 360 days of operation. Q is the number of ten-day delays to simulate drydocking the VLCC for its annual maintenance. Each year, six such ten-day delays are to be incorporated in the scheduling of the VLCCs. The counter is returned to a zero value at the start of each year.

The true heart of the simulation begins with statement 300. The instructions in verbal format are as follows: For each day of a 360-day year, transfer the status of the berth from old day-two to new day-one and make the berth available for use on the new day-two. Reduce the inventory in the transshipment terminal by 50 (50,000) tons for each cargo sold. If, by chance, the inventory is negative, set it equal to zero. This simulates management control over sales to prevent selling more cargoes than there is inventory in the tanks. Check to see if a VLCC has arrived. If not, move on to the next day.

If a VLCC has arrived as indicated by a non-zero value on the V array, check to see if there is at least 250 (250,000) tons of empty capacity in the tanks. If there is, and if the day-one berth indicator is 0, which signifies that the berth is available, then increase the inventory by 250. Set the day-one and day-two berth indicators to a value of 1, which indicates that the berth is not available to offload another VLCC either today or tomorrow. Then reschedule the VLCC based on time to discharge, time to load, normal time at sea, plus contingencies for load port congestion and weather delays. After obtaining the number of days of the next arrival, check to see whether it is after March and whether less than six drydockings have already been scheduled. If both conditions are satisfied, add another ten days to the voyage and increase the drydocking counter by one. Then make a notation on the calendar of the new arrival date, add one to the counter for the number of discharges, and see if another vessel has arrived that same day. If not, proceed to the next day.

If the V array still has a positive number after subtracting one, repeat the same procedure. First check to see if the terminal can take another cargo. If not, add one to the counter for insufficient capacity and reschedule the vessel to arrive the next day. If yes, check the status of the berth. If it is unavailable, as it will be in this case, increase the counter for days lost because of an unavailable berth by one and reschedule the vessel to arrive the next day.

Proceed with this monotonous routine until every day of every year of the simulation has been accomplished. Then print the storage capacity and the average annual values for the number of discharges, the average ship days lost for insufficient capacity at the terminal, and the average ship days lost for the berth being unavailable. Then repeat the exercise for each storage capacity under consideration.

It was fortunate for the simulator builder that no one at the management meeting reviewing the results asked whether the transshipment terminal was drained dry, so to speak, once per year. No check was incorporated in the model to ensure that this was the case. This can be performed by having a new Y array for every year of the simulation. At, or around statement 110, give Y(I) a value of 1 for each year of the simulation. At statement 330, let Y(I) be given the value of 0. At statement 510, print the sum of the array Y(I) for each year of the simulation. If the sum is near the number of years of a simulation, say fifty, for a fifty-year simulation, then the tanks were hardly ever drained dry. This will lead to an erroneous conclusion as to the optimal size of the transshipment terminal by overstating its size requirements. On the other hand, if the sum is near zero, then one can conclude that management's desires have been fulfilled.

Ethics enter the picture as to what the simulator builder should do about this situation if he discovered its existence during the course of the management meeting. A check was made in the development of the program to ensure that the average number of cargo sales did exceed the likely deliveries from the VLCCs. However, this is insufficient for the situation under analysis. Management is adamant that cargo sales in the peak winter season will empty the transshipment terminal at least once. If this doesn't occur, then the requirements for the transshipment terminal will be larger than necessary. A specific check should be incorporated in the program to ensure that this objective is being accomplished.

How should a simulator builder react if he discovered this fact during the management meeting? He may wish to say nothing because a check was made to ensure that the transshipment terminal tanks, on average, should be emptied during the course of the peak winter season. An average, however, does not mean that the tanks will be emptied each and every year. Open admission may affect the credibility of the simulator builder's work. Silence may affect the credibility of his work if someone else at the meeting raises this point. The simulator builder might consider the gamble of the model results being rejected on the basis of the marketing assessment during the summer slump season. There is a fair chance that someone might request a rerun of the model with a less severe seasonal variation in cargo sales. Then the check can be incorporated in the model with no one being the wiser. All the same, trust in simulation as an analytical technique will be diminished once it is discovered that the simulation builder is being less than forthright in his dealings with his mentors. This latter point is the most important point of all.

No computer program is built without bugs. Print statements were implanted as follows for checking out the S array.

```
202  PRINT ''MTH'';J:INPUT Z$
222  PRINT ''T '';T
262  PRINT ''L '';L
```

The rescheduling of the VLCC's was observed with:

```
415  PRINT ''K '';K
445  PRINT ''Q & K'';Q,K
```

And the general operation of the program with:

```
345  PRINT ''I V(I) V(I+1) '';I,V(I),V(I+1):INPUT Z$
```

Another check for bugs is assessing the reasonableness of the output. Are the annual number of deliveries about what one would expect for six VLCCs in continuous service? Do the ship days lost from insufficient capacity decrease as capacity increases? Can one offer a reasonable explanation as to why ship days lost from berth unavailability increase as capacity of the terminal increases?

Most bugs have disastrous effects on the output. Actually this is what one wants. The worst bugs are those whose effects on the output are more subtle to detect. Perhaps the best preventive measure for bugs of this nature is a sense of humility on the part of the programmer plus a certain dedication of purpose to check every possible routine through the liberal use of PRINT statements during program development.

```
10 REM NAME OF THIS PROGRAM IS TRANSSHIP
20 DIM V(450):DIM S(360)
25 DIM C(2,12):DIM L(2,12):DIM W(2,12)
30 FOR I= 1 TO 2
32 FOR J=1 TO 12
34 READ C(I,J)
36 DATA 20,20,5,5,5,5,5,10,20,20,20,20
38 DATA 30,30,10,10,10,10,10,15,30,30,30,30
```

```
40 NEXT:NEXT
50 FOR I=1 TO 2
52 FOR J=1 TO 12
54 READ L(I,J)
56 DATA 2,2,1,0,0,0,0,0,1,2,2,2
58 DATA 8,6,5,3,1,1,1,3,4,5,7,8
60 NEXT:NEXT
70 FOR I=1 TO 2
72 FOR J=1 TO 12
74 READ W(I,J)
76 DATA 4,4,3,2,1,0,0,0,1,2,3,4
78 DATA 9,8,8,6,4,3,3,3,4,6,7,8
80 NEXT:NEXT
90 PRINT:INPUT "YEARS FOR SIMULATION: ";Y2:PRINT
100 FOR S=300 TO 2300 STEP 200
110 N=0:D=0:B=0:B1=0:B2=0:V=0
120 FOR Y1=1 TO Y2
130 IF Y1=1 THEN 170
140 FOR I=1 TO 360:V(I)=0:S(I)=0:NEXT
150 FOR I=1 TO 90:V(I)=V(360+I):NEXT
160 FOR I=361 TO 450:V(I)=0:NEXT:GOTO 200
170 FOR I=1 TO 450:V(I)=0:NEXT
180 FOR I=1 TO 360:S(I)=0:NEXT
190 FOR I=1 TO 6:V(10*(I-1)+1)=1:NEXT
200 FOR J=1 TO 12
205 X=RND(X)
210 T=C(1,J)+X*(C(2,J)-C(1,J))
220 T=INT(T+.5)
230 FOR I=1 TO T
235 X=RND(X)
240 L=INT(X*30+.5)
245 IF L<1 THEN 235
250 L=30*(J-1)+L
260 S(L)=S(L)+1
270 NEXT:NEXT
290 Q=0
300 FOR I=1 TO 360
305 B1=B2:B2=0
310 V=V-50*S(I)
320 IF V<0 THEN 330 ELSE 340
330 V=0
340 IF V(I)=0 THEN 500
350 IF S-V<250 THEN 360 ELSE 370
360 D=D+1:V(I+1)=V(I+1)+1:V(I)=V(I)-1:GOTO 340
370 IF B1=0 THEN 380 ELSE 480
380 B1=1:B2=1:V=V+250
390 X=RND(X):Y=RND(Y):M=INT((I-1)/30)+1
400 K=58+L(1,M)+X*(L(2,M)-L(1,M))+W(1,M)+Y*(W(2,M)-W(1,M))
410 K=INT(K+.5)
420 IF M<3 THEN 450
430 IF Q=6 THEN 450
440 K=K+10:Q=Q+1
450 V(I+K)=V(I+K)+1:N=N+1:V(I)=V(I)-1
460 GOTO 340
480 V(I+1)=V(I+1)+1:B=B+1:V(I)=V(I)-1:GOTO 340
500 NEXT:NEXT
510 LPRINT S,N/Y2,D/Y2,B/Y2
520 NEXT:END
```

5

Service and Production Planning

SYNOPSIS

The service business is marked by a more or less constant rate of being able to provide a service and a highly varying rate of demand. A classic application of simulation has been in analyzing how many tollbooths should be built in a toll plaza of a major highway. The number of tollbooths will be fixed when the toll plaza is constructed. The rate of providing the service is the sum of the time elements for an automobile entering a tollbooth, and the toll keeper determining the toll, if necessary, the exchange of money, and the automobile leaving the tollbooth to allow the next automobile to enter. The service rate of a toll plaza is the average rate for automobiles passing through a tollbooth, with a relatively narrow range of variability, multiplied by the number of tollbooths.

This fairly constant rate of service certainly does not apply to the demand for the services of a toll plaza. Demand for service is measured in terms of the arrival rate of automobiles. During the morning rush hour, automobiles jam the toll plaza in one direction and then, during the evening rush hour, jam the toll plaza in the opposite direction. Arrival rates during other times of the day are a series of peaks and valleys, which are difficult to predict. A more or less constant rate of being able to provide a service for customers and a highly variable rate of customer arrivals, or demand for the service, are the hallmarks for firms in the service business. The same methodology that is used to select the optimal number of tollbooths in a toll plaza can be used to select the optimal number of teller booths in a bank or the optimal number of counter service points in a fast food restaurant.

The same techniques can be applied to production planning. The major difference between service and production planning is that the arrival rate at a work station is more predictable in the sense that the arrival of work is the output of work from a preceding work station. Although there is less variability in the arrival rate, the methodology of simulating work stations in a manufacturing environment follows the same methodology of simulating service points in a non-manufacturing environment.

The chapter deals with the descriptive aspects of setting up a simulation to determine the optimal number of eye doctors to be assigned at a new location for an eyeglass franchise. The discussion focuses on the design of the output of the simulation and ends with a discussion and an application of simulation in a production setting.

Eye Doctor is a nationwide franchise catering to servicing the eyeglass needs of office workers. Eye Doctor usually opens offices in downtown locations where there is a high population of office workers. All business is conducted on a basis of walk-ins. The time to service a customer varies between ten and twenty minutes with most eye examinations taking close to fifteen minutes. Fees are charged for customers who do not require new eyeglasses or for replacing a lens in existing eyeglasses or for buying a new set of eyeglasses. For the most part, it doesn't matter what the customer elects to do. The fee structure has been set up so that the gross margin on services rendered is much the same whatever the customer decides to do once he is examined by an eye doctor.

The central question to opening up a new franchise is the number of eye doctors to be assigned at the new location. The greater the number of eye doctors, the larger the required office space and the higher the fixed charges in salaries for the eye doctors. Too large a franchise will bankrupt the franchisee. Too small a franchise will not only create suboptimal profits, but the overall business of the office will act as a stimulus for competitive eyeglass franchises to open an office in the same general area.

The purpose of a simulation is to determine the physical performance of the eyeglass franchise for a specific number of doctors. The physical performance deals with how many customers are served, how many are turned away because of their unwillingness or waning of patience to wait for the service, and how busy the eye doctors are. The simulation is rerun with a different number of doctors to assess the same measures of performance. After the simulations are completed, an economic analysis can be performed as to the fixed costs in terms of rentals, overhead, and salaries for the different sized Eye Doctor offices. Revenue is based on the number of customers served. The optimal number of eye doctors to be assigned to a potential location is selected by analyzing the financial results of each alternative under investigation.

The principal variable in the simulation is the level of customer arrivals at a prospective location. The new location under consideration is in White Collar Office Complex, a large concentration of offices in a suburban setting. The location of Eye Doctor condemns it to this general profile of walk-ins in terms of paying customers.

HOUR OF DAY	FREQUENCY CLASSIFICATION OF WALK-INS
8AM - 9AM	MEDIUM
9AM - 10AM	LOW
10AM - 11AM	LOW
11AM - NOON	HIGH
NOON - 1PM	HIGH
1PM - 2PM	MEDIUM
2PM - 3PM	LOW
3PM - 4PM	LOW
4PM - 5PM	MEDIUM
5PM - 6PM	MEDIUM

A franchise representative, knowledgeable in the number of walk-ins at various franchise locations, investigated the potential site, conducted a survey, and provided his assessments as to the number of walk-ins for the general frequency classifications.

NUMBER OF HOURLY PAYING WALK-INS FOR GENERAL FREQUENCY CLASSIFICATION

	LOW	MEDIUM	HIGH
MINIMUM	0	1	3
MOST LIKELY	1	4	8
MAXIMUM	3	9	12

Three customer arrival simulators can now be generated. The low frequency classification can be contained in the $Q(1,J)$ array, the medium frequency classification in the $Q(2,J)$ array, and the high frequency classification in the $Q(3,J)$ array. Each of these three arrays consists of 1,000 mailboxes. After drawing a random number between 1 and 1,000, one enters the applicable mailbox and draws out a number. That number, rounded to the nearest integer, represents the number of hourly walk-in paying customers.

Having set up a simulator which applies for each of the three general frequency scenarios, the A array is set up to simulate customer arrivals during a 600-minute day. The A array consists of 600 mailboxes representing each minute of a ten-hour day. A zero in a mailbox means that no customers have arrived for that particular minute. At the start of each day, the contents of all mailboxes are set to zero. At the beginning of each day, and in sixty-minute intervals thereafter, reference is made to the following table to determine the applicable customer arrival simulator.

HOUR OF DAY	FREQUENCY OF WALK-INS	APPLICABLE ARRIVAL SIMULATOR
8AM - 9AM	MEDIUM	$Q(2,J)$
9AM - 10AM	LOW	$Q(1,J)$
10AM - 11AM	LOW	$Q(1,J)$
11AM - NOON	HIGH	$Q(3,J)$
NOON - 1PM	HIGH	$Q(3,J)$
1PM - 2PM	MEDIUM	$Q(2,J)$
2PM - 3PM	LOW	$Q(1,J)$
3PM - 4PM	LOW	$Q(1,J)$
4PM - 5PM	MEDIUM	$Q(2,J)$
5PM - 6PM	MEDIUM	$Q(2,J)$

Once the applicable customer arrival simulator has been selected for a particular hour, a random number between 1 and 1,000 is selected for J. The applicable mailbox is opened and the number contained therein is rounded to the nearest integer. The total number of arrivals is translated to a time of arrival during the next sixty minutes using the same methodology described in the previous chapter for cargo deliveries from the transshipment terminal. The only difference is that the next thirty days in the previous example has become the next sixty minutes. The end result is that the A array consists of 600 mailboxes where a zero means no customer arrivals, 1 for one customer arriving that particular minute, 2 for two customers arriving that particular minute, and so forth.

Suppose, for purposes of illustration, that the eyeglass franchise follows these guidelines in determining the size of a prospective Eye Doctor office. No more than six chairs are in an Eye Doctor office because experience has shown that walk-ins will balk at the sight of six people waiting to be served. That is, with six people waiting for the service, the prospective customer immediately walks off the premises without joining the line. Balking may, or may not, be a lost customer depending on the circumstances. If the customer comes back another time for the service, then balking cannot be considered a lost customer. If he goes elsewhere for the service, then he is a lost customer.

The chairs are labeled one through six. Customers are served on a first come, first served basis. Chair number one is filled first by the walk-ins, then chair two, chair three, and so forth in numerical order. When an eye doctor has finished with one customer, the customer in chair number one is served next. Every customer moves up one chair. Market research has found that customers are less likely to renege—that is, leave their place in line if they physically move from chair to chair.

A customer sitting in chair number one or two will not renege. Once customers realize that they are first and second in line, they remain in their chairs no matter how long the wait. However, customers assigned to chairs three through six will renege. Depending on the part of the nation, customers are willing to sit for some specified minimum length of time without considering leaving. The impatience of New Yorkers is not comparable to the patience of upstate New Yorkers. The Eye Doctor franchise organizers have all the numbers.

There is a limit of patience for even upstate New Yorkers, however. If they sit in the same chair long enough, they will get up and leave the establishment. Again, this may not necessarily mean a lost customer if they intend to return at another time. Reneging is a function of the chair number. A person in chair six will renege sooner than someone in chair three. As mentioned, once in chair one and two, customers will not renege.

For purposes of illustration, suppose that three eye doctors are being considered for assignment to this particular location of Eye Doctor. Each one will be assigned an array, $D(1,J)$, $D(2,J)$, $D(3,J)$, with each array representing every minute of a 600-minute day. A zero value in this minute calendar means that the doctor is not busy, and a 1 means that he is servicing a customer. A service time simulator will determine the time between ten and twenty minutes that each service will consume. When the service is completed, the doctor will see if there is someone in chair number one waiting to be served.

Each chair has an indicator, $C(1)$, $C(2)$, . . . $C(6)$. An indicator value of 1 means that someone is sitting in the chair. An indicator value of zero means that the chair is empty. The people working in White Collar Office Complex are not especially patient. A person in chair six will remain there for three minutes without reneging. If within three minutes he has moved to chair five, he will remain there five minutes without reneging. In chair four, reneging time is seven minutes; chair three, ten minutes. Once in chairs one and two, he will not renege. It is possible to have reneging simulators where a customer will remain seated without changing chairs for a minimum time, but not to exceed a maximum time, with some most likely in-between time. A fixed reneging time will be used in this example.

The simulation program itself must include an accounting feature to keep track of everyone entering the service. The number entering the service for each minute of the day is contained in the A array. As each minute of the day ticks away, those entering the service are kept track of by the A counter. There are four ways to account for customers once they enter the service. One, a customer notes that all chairs are filled and balks. Two, a customer sees an empty chair and sits down waiting to be served. Three, the customer sits too long in a chair and reneges his position in line. Four, the customer is served by an eye doctor. If a customer balks, the B counter will increase by one; if he reneges, the R counter will be increased by one; if he is served, the S counter will increase by one. At the end of the day, any remaining customers are assumed to be served. Thus, at the end of the simulation, the sum of the B, R, and S counters ought to equal the A counter, which is the sum of all arrivals.

For each minute of a 600-minute day, the following procedure is followed. Each doctor's array is checked for a zero. If a zero exists, chair one array is checked for occupancy $(C(1)=1)$. If this were the case, then the time of service simulator is entered to obtain the time of service. If the simulator determines that the time of service is to be twelve minutes, and if this is minute 139 of the day, and doctor number two is available, then mailboxes $D(2,139)$ through $D(2,151)$ will be set to 1 signifying that the doctor is now busy and will remain busy for the next twelve minutes. The S counter will be increased by 1 signifying another customer has been served. Chair one is now deemed empty, and the indicator value of chair two would then be transferred to chair one. The indicator value of chair three would be transferred to chair two, chair four to chair three, chair five to chair four, and chair six indicator would be set to zero indicating that it is now empty, regardless of its status beforehand. This process continues until all the doctors are busy or until all the chairs are empty, whichever occurs first.

When people switch chairs, the counters for reneging are turned back to zero for chairs three through six if they are occupied. Once a person moves up a position in a line, his internal clock measuring his patience to remain in line starts over again. Reneging cannot occur during any minute that a doctor takes on a new customer because everyone's internal clock is set back to zero.

For those minutes where the doctors are all busy at the start of the minute, which can be assessed by totaling up D(I,J) and seeing if the sum equals the number of doctors, the possibility of reneging has to be considered. Chairs one and two cannot renege. One is added to the reneging counters associated with chairs three to six. Then the counters are examined in numerical order starting with chair three. If the counter value is the critical value for the chair number, then that chair is vacated. The aggregate reneging counter, R, is increased by one to signify that a customer has reneged. The subsequent chairs move up one as before, and their individual chair reneging counters start anew. This places a limit on reneging of one per minute because of the reneging counters starting over for the higher numbered chairs.

Once the doctors' schedules have been initially checked and any potential reneging has been taken care of, the arrival array is examined for new customers entering the Eye Doctor office. Counter A is increased by the total number of arrivals. Each doctor is first examined to see if he can take a customer. If he happens to be idle, the patient walks directly in his office and the doctor is classified busy for the requisite number of minutes determined by the time of service simulator. If not, each chair is examined in the order of chair one to chair six. If a chair is empty, the new customer fills the chair and the reneging counter for that particular chair is set to zero. The reneging counter always has a value of zero if a chair is unoccupied. If all the chairs are full, then the balking counter is increased by one.

Some programming may appear a bit vague at this point, but a programmer can fill in the details. What is important to note is that the indicators, counters, and (minute) calendars are providing a detailed diary of the minute-by-minute happenings in the Eye Doctor office. Appropriate PRINT statements could create a screen display for every minute. The following series of displays shows a "simulated" three minutes starting with the end of minute 136.

```
END OF MINUTE: 136
```

```
                    1-BUSY/0-IDLE
```

	1-BUSY/0-IDLE
DOCTOR #1	1
DOCTOR #2	1
DOCTOR #3	1

	1-FULL/0-EMPTY	STATUS RENEGE COUNTER	RENEGE AT COUNTER READING
CHAIR #1	1		
CHAIR #2	1		
CHAIR #3	1	8	10

```
CHAIR #4              1                   2              7
CHAIR #5              0                   0              5
CHAIR #6              0                   0              3
```

```
TOTAL NUMBER
ARRIVALS:    478
WAITING:       4
SERVED:      325
BALKS:        23
RENEGES:     126
```

****

START OF MINUTE: 137
                    1-BUSY/0-IDLE

DOCTOR #1	1	Note: The doctors are still
DOCTOR #2	1	busy with customers
DOCTOR #3	1	during minute 137.

	1-FULL/0-EMPTY	STATUS RENEGE COUNTER	RENEGE AT COUNTER READING
CHAIR #1	1		
CHAIR #2	1		
CHAIR #3	1	9	10
CHAIR #4	1	3	7
CHAIR #5	0	0	5
CHAIR #6	0	0	3

Note: The renege counters
      for filled chairs
      are increased by one
      because there is no
      change in seating.

NUMBER OF ARRIVING CUSTOMERS: 3

END OF MINUTE: 137

                    1-BUSY/0-IDLE

DOCTOR #1	1
DOCTOR #2	1
DOCTOR #3	1

	1-FULL/0-EMPTY	STATUS RENEGE COUNTER	RENEGE AT COUNTER READING
CHAIR #1	1		
CHAIR #2	1		
CHAIR #3	1	9	10
CHAIR #4	1	3	7
CHAIR #5	1	0	5
CHAIR #6	1	0	3

Note: Chairs five and six
      are filled and there
      is one balk.

```
TOTAL NUMBER        Notes:
ARRIVALS:    481    Increased by 3 to reflect arrivals
```

```
WAITING:        6    Sum of C(1) to C(6)
SERVED:       325    No change
BALKS:         24    Increased by one
RENEGES:      126    No change
```

****

START OF MINUTE: 138

                    1-BUSY/0-IDLE

```
DOCTOR #1            1
DOCTOR #2            1
DOCTOR #3            1
```

		STATUS RENEGE	RENEGE AT COUNTER
	1-FULL/0-EMPTY	COUNTER	READING
CHAIR #1	1		
CHAIR #2	1		
CHAIR #3	1	10	10
CHAIR #4	1	4	7
CHAIR #5	1	1	5
CHAIR #6	1	1	3

> Note: Doctors still busy, one is added to each renege counter of an occupied chair.

NUMBER OF ARRIVING CUSTOMERS: 0

END OF MINUTE: 138

                    1-BUSY/0-IDLE

```
DOCTOR #1            1
DOCTOR #2            1
DOCTOR #3            1
```

		STATUS RENEGE	RENEGE AT COUNTER
	1-FULL/0-EMPTY	COUNTER	READING
CHAIR #1	1		
CHAIR #2	1		
CHAIR #3	1	0	10
CHAIR #4	1	0	7
CHAIR #5	1	0	5
CHAIR #6	0	0	3

> Note: Chair three reneges. Filled chairs move up one, renege counters turned back to zero. Chair six empty.

```
TOTAL NUMBER         Notes:
ARRIVALS:     481    No change
WAITING:        5    Sum of C(1) to C(6)
SERVED:       325    No change
BALKS:         24    No change
RENEGES:      127    Increased by one
```

****

START OF MINUTE: 139

```
                    1-BUSY/0-IDLE

DOCTOR #1               1
DOCTOR #2               0
DOCTOR #3               0
                                    Note: Two doctors have
                                          completed service
                                          on customers.

                                    STATUS      RENEGE AT
                                    RENEGE      COUNTER
                    1-FULL/0-EMPTY  COUNTER     READING

CHAIR #1                1
CHAIR #2                1
CHAIR #3                1              0           10
CHAIR #4                0              0            7
CHAIR #5                0              0            5
CHAIR #6                0              0            3
                        Note: Customers move up by two
                              positions. Renege counters
                              reset to zero.
```

NUMBER OF ARRIVING CUSTOMERS: 0

END OF MINUTE: 139

```
                    1-BUSY/0-IDLE

DOCTOR #1               1    Note: Doctors 2 and 3 busy as
DOCTOR #2               1          for the next number of
DOCTOR #3               1          minutes as determined by
                                   time of service simulator.

                                    STATUS      RENEGE AT
                                    RENEGE      COUNTER
                    1-FULL/0-EMPTY  COUNTER     READING

CHAIR #1                1
CHAIR #2                1
CHAIR #3                1              0           10
CHAIR #4                0              0            7
CHAIR #5                0              0            5
CHAIR #6                0              0            3

TOTAL NUMBER        Notes:
ARRIVALS:    481    No change
WAITING:       3    Sum of C(1) to C(6)
SERVED:      327    Increased by 2
BALKS:        24    No change
RENEGES:     127
```

****

    The presentation can be changed by printing BUSY when the doctor status is 1 and printing IDLE when the doctor status is 0. Similarly the 1 for the chair status can be printed as OCCUPIED and 0 can be printed as EMPTY. Moreover, a BALK and a RENEGE can be printed on the screen when appropriate. The new minute-by-minute presentations would appear as follows.

```
END OF MINUTE: 136

DOCTOR #1            BUSY        CHAIR #1            OCCUPIED
DOCTOR #2            BUSY        CHAIR #2            OCCUPIED
DOCTOR #3            BUSY        CHAIR #3            OCCUPIED
                                 CHAIR #4            OCCUPIED
                                 CHAIR #5            EMPTY
                                 CHAIR #6            EMPTY


TOTAL NUMBER
ARRIVALS:    478
WAITING:       4
SERVED:      325
BALKS:        23
RENEGES:     126

                 ************************************

START OF MINUTE: 137

DOCTOR #1            BUSY        CHAIR #1            OCCUPIED
DOCTOR #2            BUSY        CHAIR #2            OCCUPIED
DOCTOR #3            BUSY        CHAIR #3            OCCUPIED
                                 CHAIR #4            OCCUPIED
                                 CHAIR #5            EMPTY
                                 CHAIR #6            EMPTY

NUMBER OF ARRIVING CUSTOMERS: 3

END OF MINUTE: 137

DOCTOR #1            BUSY        CHAIR #1            OCCUPIED
DOCTOR #2            BUSY        CHAIR #2            OCCUPIED
DOCTOR #3            BUSY        CHAIR #3            OCCUPIED
                                 CHAIR #4            OCCUPIED
                                 CHAIR #5            OCCUPIED
                                 CHAIR #6            OCCUPIED

                                   ONE CUSTOMER BALKED
TOTAL NUMBER
ARRIVALS:    481
WAITING:       6
SERVED:      325
BALKS:        24
RENEGES:     126

                 ************************************

START OF MINUTE: 138

DOCTOR #1            BUSY        CHAIR #1            OCCUPIED
DOCTOR #2            BUSY        CHAIR #2            OCCUPIED
DOCTOR #3            BUSY        CHAIR #3            RENEGED
                                 CHAIR #4            OCCUPIED
```

```
                                        CHAIR #5        OCCUPIED
                                        CHAIR #6        OCCUPIED

                                 ONE CUSTOMER RENEGED

NUMBER OF ARRIVING CUSTOMERS: 0

END OF MINUTE: 138

DOCTOR #1           BUSY        CHAIR #1        OCCUPIED
DOCTOR #2           BUSY        CHAIR #2        OCCUPIED
DOCTOR #3           BUSY        CHAIR #3        OCCUPIED
                                CHAIR #4        OCCUPIED
                                CHAIR #5        OCCUPIED
                                CHAIR #6        EMPTY

TOTAL NUMBER
ARRIVALS:   481
WAITING:      5
SERVED:     325
BALKS:       24
RENEGES:    127
              ***********************************
START OF MINUTE: 139

DOCTOR #1           BUSY        CHAIR #1        OCCUPIED
DOCTOR #2           IDLE        CHAIR #2        OCCUPIED
DOCTOR #3           IDLE        CHAIR #3        OCCUPIED
                                CHAIR #4        EMPTY
                                CHAIR #5        EMPTY
                                CHAIR #6        EMPTY

NUMBER OF ARRIVING CUSTOMERS: 0

END OF MINUTE: 139

DOCTOR #1           BUSY        CHAIR #1        OCCUPIED
DOCTOR #2           BUSY        CHAIR #2        OCCUPIED
DOCTOR #3           BUSY        CHAIR #3        OCCUPIED
                                CHAIR #4        EMPTY
                                CHAIR #5        EMPTY
                                CHAIR #6        EMPTY
              TWO CUSTOMERS ENTERED DOCTORS' OFFICES
OFFICES
TOTAL NUMBER
ARRIVALS:   481
WAITING:      3
SERVED:     327
BALKS:       24
RENEGES:    127
              ***********************************
```

These screen presentations are shown for every minute of the simulation. A start-stop mechanism may have to be built into the program to permit the viewer to proceed to the next minute at his convenience. Nonetheless, viewing individual minutes of simulation would become tiresome at some point. Viewing might not become as tiresome at least as quickly if the minute-by-minute presentation was transformed to frame-by-frame instructions for a video presentation.

The layout for a video could be shown as follows:

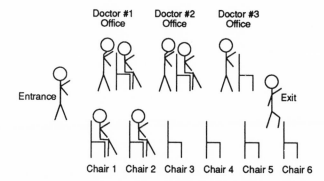

Caricature instructions for, say, stick characters, would be determined by the values assigned to the variables. For instance, a doctor who is busy would trigger the instructions of a caricature of a stick character of a doctor leaning over a stick character of a customer sitting in a chair in his office. A doctor who is idle would be pictured standing by an empty chair in his office. A chair that is empty would be pictured, appropriately, as an empty chair while an occupied chair would have a stick character of a customer sitting in a chair. The change of status of a busy doctor to an idle doctor would trigger a set of instructions for the patient to stand up, leave the doctor's office, and walk out the exit. A change of status of an idle doctor to a busy doctor with chair one occupied would trigger another set of instructions which would show a patient leaving chair one and entering the appropriate doctor's office. This, in turn, would trigger the instructions for all waiting customers to move up one chair. A reneging of a chair would trigger the imaging instructions for the movement of the occupant to the exit with some appropriate visual effects indicating that a customer has reneged.

The arrivals for that particular minute will line up at the entrance. An arriving customer can go directly to an idle doctor's office or to the first empty chair, or he can balk and walk away with more appropriate visual effects of a customer who is unwilling to get in a line of six waiting customers. The bottom of the screen can show a running tally of served customers, those waiting to be served, those who balked, and those who reneged.

If one had secret desires to become a famous producer of videos for the simulating arts, a cash register can be shown ringing up receipts when each customer starts, or finishes, being served. Checks can be flying out of a checkbook at the end of each day for the daily pay of the doctors, space rental, and other expenses of running an Eye Doctor office. The accumulated profits can be pictured as an ever-growing pile of greenbacks with a smiling franchisee taking a vacation to Hawaii, or purchasing a new Cadillac, when the pile reaches a sufficient height. Accumulated losses need not be shown in such a dramatic fashion. A church bell can ring when a customer enters a doctor's office while bongs and buzzes can announce balks and reneges. Rather than stick characters, well-dressed males and females can make up the customer lineup while the doctors look like miniature Clark Gables or Florence Nightingales. The interior of the Eye Doctor office can be furnished, and the video can be done in color. The outside of the franchise can have a large, fancy clock with passersby walking past the Eye Doctor office in numbers geared to the time of day. Music and voice commentary can accompany the video to induce a prospective franchisee to enter into an easy-to-sign, and hard-to-break, contract.

SIMULATIONS IN A MANUFACTURING ENVIRONMENT

These same principles can be applied to the simulation of a series of workshops in the production cycle of a product. Each workshop consists of a number of machines performing a certain function. The output of one workshop becomes the input of the next in a sequential mode of production. Each machine has minimum, maximum, and a most likely time element for performing the function based on the proficiency of the operators. The time element can include the normal time lost for making adjustments to the machine or resupplying the machine with whatever is consumed in its operation.

For producing a video, the article being manufactured can be pictured as a small box. If a workshop is undermanned, so to speak, with machines, the boxes will begin to pile up at the front end of the workshop. Idle workers by idle machines can carry the message that a workshop has too much capacity. An extra machine can be added to an overworked workshop and the video rerun. A whole factory can be laid out using cartoons to identify potential bottlenecks in production.

To provide an example of a simulation geared to a production setting, suppose that a factory is laid out in a sequential arrangement of Workshop A, Workshop B, Workshop C, etc. Workshop A takes the starting steps for the manufacture of a product. Suppose that Workshop A consists of four machines whose output for a single cycle of operation requires between four and ten minutes depending on the proficiency of the operator or operators. The accompanying appendix contains a program which simulates the minute-by-minute production of the four machines in Workshop A for a 480-minute workday. The output of Workshop A for an arbitrarily selected segment of time of between 250 and 280 minutes is shown as follows:

MINUTE	TOTAL OUTPUT FROM WORKSHOP A
250	1
251	0
252	0
253	0
254	1
255	3
256	0
257	0
258	0

MINUTE	TOTAL OUTPUT FROM WORKSHOP A
259	1
260	2
261	0
262	0
263	1
264	0
265	0
266	1
267	1
268	0
269	1
270	0
271	0
272	2
273	0
274	0
275	1
276	0
277	0
278	1
279	0
280	1

During this thirty-minute period, Workshop A completes the initial operation on a total of seventeen products or components. The minimum time for an operation in Workshop A is four minutes and the maximum is ten minutes. The average time is seven minutes. On average, one machine, with an operator, can accomplish 8.6 cycles of an operation in sixty minutes. Four machines can turn out thirty-four such items. Doing seventeen operations in this one arbitrarily selected half-hour period is in line with the productive capacity of the four machines.

The output, or delivery, schedule of Workshop A becomes the input, or arrival, schedule for Workshop B. The rules of logic for Workshop B are somewhat more complex than Workshop A. In Workshop A, all machines work with no delays because Workshop A is the first workshop in a manufacturing process. This is not true for Workshop B, and for the other workshops after Workshop B. The output of Workshop A is the input for Workshop B. The output of Workshop B becomes the input for Workshop C, and so forth. Workshop B cannot begin work on a product unless Workshop A has first performed its function. This holds true for all workshops in a sequential mode of production except for the first workshop.

The simulation in the appendix first checks whether there is delivery from Workshop A during a particular minute or whether there is work left over from the previous minute. If so, then a check is made to see if a machine is available in Workshop B for that particular minute. If there is an idle machine, then it is assigned a busy status which lasts between ten and eighteen minutes, and the pile of items delivered from Workshop A is reduced by one. If all the machines are busy, and there are still items being delivered from Workshop A, the unfinished items are transferred to the next minute arrivals, which can be pictured as a pile of goods accumulating in front of Workshop B. If Workshop B cannot keep up with the work coming from Workshop A, then the existence of an ever-growing pile of boxes by Workshop B signifies a bottleneck.

Suppose that a machine in Workshop B requires an average of fourteen minutes to complete its cycle of operations before a part can be passed on to Workshop C. One machine, with its operator or operators, can accomplish 4.3 operational cycles in one hour in Workshop B compared with 8.6 cycles per machine in Workshop A. There should be twice the number of machines in Workshop B than in Workshop A because each machine in Workshop B takes twice as long to perform its operation on the item being manufactured. The simulation in the appendix is designed to run for different numbers of machines. Suppose there are six machines in Workshop B. One would expect a bottleneck to develop. And one certainly does; whereas, eight machines have a much smaller, and manageable, bottleneck.

	SIX MACHINES		EIGHT MACHINES	
MINUTE	UNITS PILED UP IN FRONT OF WORKSHOP B	UNITS BEING DELIVERED TO WORKSHOP C	UNITS PILED UP IN FRONT OF WORKSHOP B	UNITS BEING DELIVERED TO WORKSHOP C
250	36	0	4	1
251	36	0	3	1
252	36	0	3	0
253	35	1	3	0
254	36	0	4	0
255	38	1	6	1
256	37	1	6	0
257	37	0	5	1
258	37	0	5	0
259	38	0	4	2
260	39	1	4	2
261	39	0	4	0
262	39	0	3	1
263	39	1	4	0
264	39	0	4	0
265	39	0	4	0
266	39	1	5	0
267	40	0	5	1
268	39	1	3	2
269	39	1	4	0
270	38	1	2	2
271	38	0	2	0
272	40	0	4	0
273	38	2	4	0
274	38	0	4	0

	SIX MACHINES		EIGHT MACHINES	
MINUTE	UNITS PILED UP IN FRONT OF WORKSHOP B	UNITS BEING DELIVERED TO WORKSHOP C	UNITS PILED UP IN FRONT OF WORKSHOP B	UNITS BEING DELIVERED TO WORKSHOP C
275	39	0	4	1
276	39	0	3	1
277	38	1	3	0
278	39	0	4	0
279	39	0	3	1
280	40	0	3	1

With six machines in Workshop B, units from Workshop A continue to pile up in ever-increasing numbers in front of Workshop B. The total number of completed operations for this particular half-hour period of time is twelve units in Workshop B—about two-thirds of what is coming from Workshop A. These twelve units become the arrival schedule for work to be accomplished in Workshop C.

With eight machines in Workshop B, the line is more balanced. There is a small pile of units outside the workshop, but its total output of eighteen units during this half-hour period is in line with the eighteen or so units coming from Workshop A. The pile outside Workshop B is small and manageable. Adding a ninth machine does eliminate the pile outside Workshop B, but output from Workshop B does not improve other than in the most marginal way. The ninth machine does little to increase overall productivity in Workshop B because the productivity potential of Workshop B is limited by the output from Workshop A. The ninth machine in Workshop B is mostly excess capacity.

Further programming steps would be necessary in the simulation in the appendix to provide the user with the sense of the magnitude of the inefficiency of excess, or idle, machine capacity. The simulation in the appendix also stops at Workshop B. But the methodology for including Workshop C would be the same in structure as that incorporated for Workshop B. Other workshops could be added to Workshop C in the same manner.

The model could be adapted to reflect downtime from unexpected breakdowns, in addition to normal downtime to adjust or resupply a consummable in the operation of a machine. Lunch breaks, whether for the whole factory at one time or staggered hours for individual workers within the workshops, could be incorporated in the model. The operators of the machine could be simulated not only to eat lunch on a fixed schedule, but also to take breaks randomly. The model could also be front-end loaded, so to speak, with delivery of needed supplies of raw materials and components from various sources including the capacity limitations of a material handling system with limits on the amount of storage facilities and number of unloading docks. The model could be back-end loaded with similar restrictions on material handling capacity, availability of warehouse space, and number of loading docks. A simulation model was built for an automobile assembly plant prior to its construction to try to identify bottlenecks in a bloodless experiment, before the fact, to avoid facing a bloody experience with bottlenecks after the fact.

Appendix to Chapter 5

SIMULATION PROGRAM FOR TWO WORKSHOPS

For the workshop simulation, statements 30–120 create the output of Workshop A which serves as input to Workshop B. The schedule for the four machines is derived individually starting at time zero. The loop starting in statement 50 ceases to determine the time of delivery of an item from one machine when the time of day for completion exceeds eight hours (480 minutes). Setting J = 1000 in statement 100 stops the looping process. Statement 70 determines the time of the next cycle of operation for a machine. The time can range between four and ten minutes. Note the existence of a separate statement (statement 60) which defines X as a random number. Writing statement 70 as: 70 A = INT(4 + RND(X)*6 + .5) may result in an unchanging random number.

Statements 130–170 print the output from Workshop A for the time segment discussed in the chapter. The selection of the number of machines in Workshop B is performed in statement 180. On the first minute of the day, the machines are set to an idle status in statement 210. For any other minute of the day, a value of 1 is subtracted from the counters M(J) which indicate how many more minutes are required to complete the current operation. A zero value means that the machine is available to start another operation. Starting at statement 270, a check is made to see if there is anything to be done. A zero value in A(I) means that there is nothing available to be worked on which has already been processed by Workshop A.

If there is work to be processed, a check must first be made to see if a machine is available. N is an indicator for machine availability. A non-zero value for N means that no machine is available. N can only be turned to a zero value if a machine is available (statements 300–310). If this is the case, the available machine is identified in statement 350, and the number of items to be worked on is reduced by one (statement 360). The counter for the machine for the time it will be busy is set for some time interval between ten and eighteen minutes (statements 370–390). The delivery of the finished item from Workshop B is stored in the B array (statement 400). If there were a Workshop C in the program, the B array would become the arrival schedule of work for Workshop C in the same fashion that the A array is the arrival schedule of work for Workshop B.

This process continues until there are no more machines available, or no more work to be processed, whichever occurs first. A key statement in the program is in statement 440. Any items from Workshop A that cannot be processed in Workshop B this minute are carried forward to the next minute. This is what determines the size of the pile outside Workshop B.

The size of the pile in front of Workshop B, and its output to Workshop C, are printed in statements 460–500.

```
10 REM NAME OF PROGRAM IS PROD
20 DIM A(500):DIM B(500)
30 FOR I=1 TO 4
40 T=0
50 FOR J=1 TO 1000
60 X=RND(X)
70 A=INT(4+X*6+.5)
80 T=T+A
90 IF T>480 THEN 100 ELSE 110
100 J=1000:GOTO 120
110 A(T)=A(T)+1
120 NEXT:NEXT
130 INPUT "PRINTOUT OF OUTPUT OF WORKSHOP A?  YES-1  NO-2: ";Z
140 ON Z GOTO 150,180
150 FOR I=250 TO 280
160 PRINT I,A(I):INPUT Z$
170 NEXT
180 PRINT:INPUT "NUMBER OF MACHINES WORKSHOP B: ";M
190 FOR I=1 TO 480
200 IF I>1 THEN 220
210 FOR J=1 TO M:M(J)=0:NEXT:GOTO 270
220 FOR J=1 TO M
230 M(J)=M(J)-1
240 IF M(J)<0 THEN 250 ELSE 260
250 M(J)=0
260 NEXT
270 IF A(I)=0 THEN 450
280 N=1
290 FOR J=1 TO M
300 IF M(J)=0 THEN 310 ELSE 320
310 N=0
320 NEXT
330 IF N=0 THEN 340 ELSE 440
340 FOR J=1 TO M
350 IF M(J)=0 THEN 360 ELSE 420
360 A(I)=A(I)-1
370 X=RND(X)
380 K=INT(10+X*8+.5)
390 M(J)=K
400 B(I+K)=B(I+K)+1
410 J=M
420 NEXT
430 GOTO 270
440 A(I+1)=A(I+1)+A(I)
450 NEXT
460 PRINT " ","INPUT","OUTPUT"
470 PRINT "MINUTE","W.S. B","W.S. B":PRINT
480 FOR I=250 TO 280
490 PRINT I,A(I),B(I):INPUT Z$
500 NEXT
510 END
```

6

Forecasting the Optimal Product Mix

SYNOPSIS

Production planning requires a sales forecast as a first step in allocating a company's resources for the manufacture of goods. Various means are available to perform a forecast. For example, forecasting can be performed by the production department or by the marketing department or as a joint effort between the two departments with one or the other having primary responsibility.

If production is doing the forecasting, the forecasting methods tend to look backward in time with less emphasis on the anticipated changes in the marketplace. On this basis, an argument can be made for forecasting to be in the hands of marketing people because their orientation is toward the future. However, if marketing is responsible for performing the forecast, there is a tendency for bias to enter into the forecast. A better forecast might integrate the efforts and information of both departments.

One criticism of conventional forecasting methods is that there is no direct reference to profit maximization. Price to sell, and cost to make, are not part of conventional forecasting. If price, cost, and manufacturing capacities could be integrated into a forecasting methodology whose orientation is profit maximization, then, presumably, the forecast will better serve the purpose of being in business. Conventional forecasts are usually oriented toward maximization of sales volume, which is far different from maximization of profits. Volume maximization and profit maximization occur hand-in-hand when the unit price does not erode as the volume of sales increases. The most elementary economics textbooks would deny this relationship, yet conventional forecasts implicitly contain this assumption. Rarely does one see a price associated with a forecast on volume.

The chapter begins with a short discussion of conventional forecasting techniques before proceeding with an alternative system of forecasting volume by focusing on the optimal product mix to maximize profits. The objectives of the two systems are not quite the same. The objective of conventional forecasting techniques is to arrive at a forecast of sales volume. In this environment, sales volume is dealt with directly with a tendency for including some sort of goal-setting mechanism in the forecast. The objective of trying to determine the optimal product mix is to maximize the profitability of the company. The volume forecast to be used by production planning is a consequence of trying to maximize profits. In this environment, sales volume becomes a means to maintain a pricing structure, not an objective to be maximized.

Planning of production cannot take place without a sales, or volume, forecast. When production is responsible for a forecast, the general tendency is to adopt one, or more, methodologies sometimes referred to as autogeneration. A good example of autogeneration is the running average. Two months ago, sales were 342 units; last month, 289 units; this month, 311. For a three-month running average forecast, add the sales for the three months, divide by three, and voilà, the forecast for next month: 314 units. Autogeneration means that the past sales self-generate the forecast. The forecast of 314 units depends entirely on past sales. There is no reference to the future in autogeneration. There is also no reference to the business cycle, no reference to the product life cycle, no reference to seasonal factors, no reference to efforts by marketing to promote sales, no reference to moves by competitive firms, and no reference to prices.

Other forms of autogeneration are weighted averages and exponential smoothing. Trend and time series analyses are usually not included in the general category of autogeneration, but a review of their methodology shows that a forecast performed by these means relies exclusively on the nature of the historic sales data. Both trend and time series analyses look backward in time to get a glimpse of the future.

Running and weighted averages and exponential smoothing are used when forecasting is limited to one unit of time—be it next week, next month, or next year. For instance, in the previous example of a three-month running average, a forecast of 314 units was obtained for next month. How about the month after that? It is difficult to obtain a multiperiod forecast by these particular methods of forecasting.

However, a multiperiod forecast can be obtained through trend and time series analyses. Trend analysis captures the long-term trend in sales. The current trend is presumed to continue into the near-term allowing one to pick off the forecast by extrapolating the trend line. The easiest way to perform trend analysis is to plot the past annual sales and draw in the "best fitting" curve. A three-year forecast based on trend analysis starting in year thirteen is shown in Exhibit 6.1.

The forecast for years thirteen, fourteen, and fifteen using trend analysis is about 515, 535, and 545 units, respectively.

Time series is a more mathematically oriented approach to fitting a curve to historical data. The "best fitting" curve attempts to follow the ebb and flow of the historical data more closely. A three-year forecast with the same historical data using time series analysis is illustrated in Exhibit 6.2.

The forecast for years thirteen, fourteen, and fifteen with time series analysis as the forecasting method is about 460, 470, and 490 units, respectively. Time series analysis presumes that the trend line along with its cyclical components

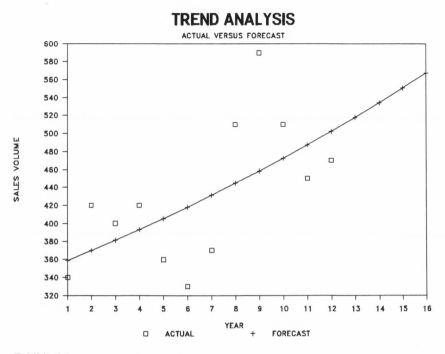

Exhibit 6.1.
Trend Analysis (actual versus forecast)

can be extrapolated into the future while trend analysis presumes that only the long-term trend can be extrapolated into the future.

Which is right? Perhaps it is better to first conclude that all forecasts are wrong before trying to select which method might be right. Forecasting is a humbling experience, as any forecaster knows but may not be anxious to admit. If the historic trend is the prologue to the future, then trend analysis will be less wrong than time series analysis. If the historic cyclical pattern is the prologue to the future, then the time series forecast will be less wrong than the trend analysis forecast. If the assumption that a forecast can be obtained by the extrapolation of a trend, with or without its cyclical components, is wrong, then both methods should be avoided.

Another, perhaps more esoteric, method of forecasting is regression analysis. This is a method of forecasting without using time directly. For instance, the conversion of homes from heating oil to natural gas may be related to the price of heating oil. The higher the price of heating oil, the greater the incentive for a homeowner to convert to natural gas. Suppose that a firm is in the business of converting homes from heating oil to natural gas. Rather than plot the historical number of conversions with time to obtain a forecast using trend or time series

TIME SERIES ANALYSIS

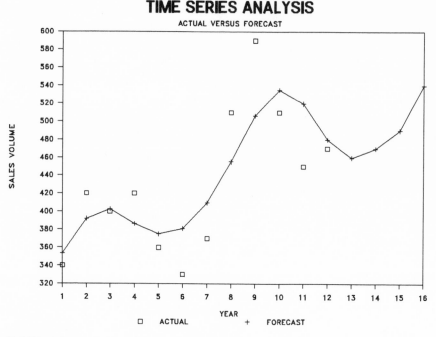

Exhibit 6.2.
Time Series Analysis (actual versus forecast)

analysis, the number of conversions can be plotted against the price of heating oil as shown in Exhibit 6.3.

When the price of heating oil was 75 cents per gallon, there were 150 conversions from oil to gas. When the price was $1.30 per gallon, there were 250 conversions. Time only links the price of heating oil in a particular heating season with the number of oil to gas conversions. Once the data points of the number of gas conversions and the price of heating oil have been plotted, time does not enter into a forecast. What is important for the number of conversions from oil to gas is not the forecast year, but the price of heating oil for the forecast year. If the data points linking the number of conversions and the price of heating oil fall fairly close around a straight line as is the case in Exhibit 6.3, then a "best fitting" straight line can be drawn through the data points. A forecast for the number of gas conversions can be easily obtained by entering the x axis at the appropriate price for heating oil for the forecast year. The forecast for the level of business one might expect can then be read off the y axis.

Time does not enter the picture when doing the forecast using regression analysis. Next year's forecast on the number of expected conversions is not based on an extrapolation of a long-term trend of 5 percent more business this

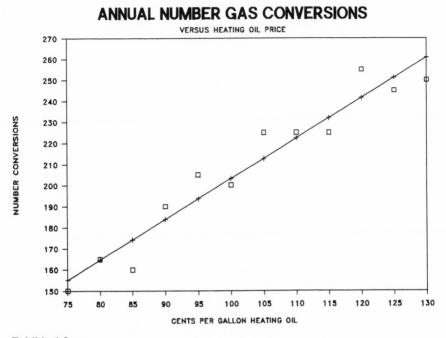

Exhibit 6.3.
Annual Number Gas Conversions (versus heating oil price)

year than the previous year. The forecast is built on something that should affect the level of conversions much more significantly than time: the price of heating oil.

Some businesses have a natural lag between something happening, which is known, and its effect on sales. For instance, suppose that a company's business is the roofing of newly built homes. The county administrative office has building permits for new homes. There is a natural lag between the issuing of a building permit for the construction of a new home and the need for the installation of a roof. Foundations are usually dug first; the roof follows some months later. A forecaster can build a regression model incorporating a lag factor between building permits and roofing sales.

Suppose that the best model has a six-month lag. Using the statistical relationship derived through regression analysis, a forecast for roofing sales for this month would be statistically linked to building permits issued six months ago. A forecast for next month's business can be obtained by substituting the number of building permits issued five months ago into the regression equation. A forecast of two months into the future can be obtained by substituting the number of building permits issued four months ago into the equation. And the number of building permits issued this month will be the independent variable for forecasting sales six months down the road. The greater the lag, the longer the forecasting period.

The degree of scatter in the data around the straight line provides a degree of confidence in the reliability of the forecast. One can ascribe a high degree of confidence to a forecast if the data points lie, or nearly all lie, on the regression line itself. However, regardless of the degree of confidence one may wish to ascribe to a forecast, the forecast is as good as the fact that the statistical relationship linking natural gas conversions to the price of heating oil, or roofing jobs to building permits, has not changed. Unfortunately, the one great weakness of regression analysis is that the statistical relationship linking two variables may well change with time. There can be no greater Achilles' heel than this in depending on regression analysis to provide a forecast.

These are the most common methods used by production in forecasting demand. All of these methods have strong roots in the past. They depend on the implicit assumption that the past is a prologue to the future—which actually may be the case from time to time.

Marketing people have an entirely different orientation than production people. While production looks to the past for guidance, marketing is facing the future. Yesterday's sales have no relevance to marketers—what counts is what is moving off the shelves today and what will move off the shelves tomorrow. Their performance may be judged on how tomorrow's sales compared with yesterday's, but that is just about the entire extent of interest in past numbers. No one in an organization is in a better position to sense the happenings of tomorrow than the marketing people. It should not be surprising that the marketing department may be responsible for a forecast, particularly when one realizes that forecasting is an ongoing activity in the setting of sales goals.

Marketing forecasts are usually judgmental and usually take the form of polling of salespeople responsible for sales within a given territory. The territory sales manager performs a forecast for each of the principle products in his territory, with or without reference to the salespeople reporting to him. The territory sales manager should know all that is happening in his territory from the sales records of his representatives augmented with written and oral reports. The territory sales managers pass their forecasts to a regional manager. The regional manager aggregates the results, throws in a little B factor for where he feels the economy is in the business cycle, a little P factor for where a particular product is in its product life cycle, and forwards the results to his superior. The next layer of managers aggregates the results from the different regional managers, throws in their own B and P factors, and forwards the results to their superiors. At some point in the collecting and forwarding of the individual forecasts, the senior executive in the marketing department will end up with the aggregate results for the entire company, which he reviews and adjusts, before passing them on to production.

The system could probably survive the B and P factor adjustments. High and low B and P factors counterbalance themselves to some extent as do overestimation and underestimation of sales by individual territory sales managers. Unfortunately, there is one other adjustment that is difficult to remove from the final forecast. Every territory sales manager realizes that his forecast will be revisited on the forecaster. If the forecast for sales in a territory is 1,000 widgets for a period of time, and actual sales are 900 widgets during that same period of time, someone will ask for an explanation. That is what a good regional sales manager is supposed to do. Knowing that, might not the territory salesperson be tempted to provide a forecast which would give him the least degree of personal pain? And how about the incentive program? How are the sales levels, which serve as markers for various forms of bonus payments, determined? Are these in any way linked to the sales forecast provided by the territory sales managers? This will bias the results of a forecast more than anything else. Even if there is no connection between a bonus plan and a forecast, how does one persuade the territory sales managers otherwise?

The problem with forecasts from the marketing department is that they are biased—call it the H, or human, factor. The H factor contaminates the polling process that is the heart of a marketing forecast because those supplying the data are thinking in terms of the repercussions of the forecast on themselves.

The problem with forecasts from the production department is that they do not take into proper consideration changes in the business environment that the marketing department senses from its continual contact with clients and customers. If the H factor could be removed from a marketing forecast, their forecast ought to be preferred over a forecast performed by the production department. One way to remove the H factor is to have marketing forecast something other than volume which could end up being translated to a volume forecast. This can be done by having marketing focus on price sensitivities for incremental changes in volume. Since it is difficult for the individual supplying the price sensitivity information to translate the data to a volume forecast, this might prove to be a means of obtaining an unbiased assessment of future sales.

Suppose that a company produces Products A, B, C, and D and sells these products through five regional sales areas (Regions I–V). Suppose that the marketing managers for these five regional sales areas are asked the following questions about each of the four products.

What would be the average price over the next twelve months if the sales volume were 10 percent below current levels?

What would be the average price over the next twelve months if the sales volume were the same as current levels?

What would be the average price over the next twelve months if the sales volume were 10 percent above current levels?

As an example, the marketing manager in Region V would be required to fill in the following table with his price assessments for 10 percent changes in sales volume from current levels.

PRODUCT	REGION V CURRENT ANNUAL SALES VOLUME	REGION V AVERAGE UNIT SALES PRICE FOR NEXT YEAR'S SALES VOLUME IN RELATION TO CURRENT SALES VOLUME		
		10% LOWER	SAME	10% HIGHER
A	50,000			
B	30,000			
C	100,000			
D	40,000			

The marketing manager in Region V would be providing three price assessments for three volume figures. He should be sensitive to the effect on price with changing volume of sales through quantity discount policies by his granting permission for discounting above certain prescribed limits, and through direct contacts with major customers. A marketing manager should be able to assess what would happen to price if the volume of sales increased or decreased by 10 percent from current levels.

There is probably a non-linear relationship between price and volume. The price would probably not change much as one started to move away from the current level of sales in either direction. As one moved closer to either extreme—

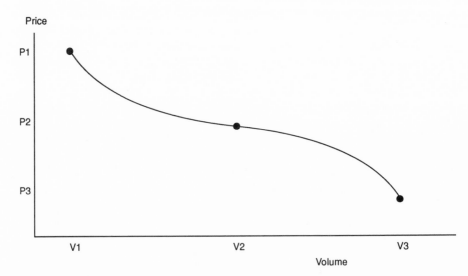

Exhibit 6.4.
Price/Volume Relationship

here defined as 10 percent more or less from current sales—there would be a greater price change per unit change in volume. If this were true, the resulting relationship between price and volume would be non-linear as illustrated in Exhibit 6.4.

P2 and V2 are the price/volume relationship for next year's sales being the same as current sales. P1 and V1 are the price/volume relationship for next year's sales being 10 percent lower than the current sales. P3 and V3 are the corresponding figures if next year's sales are 10 percent higher than current sales. These three sets of numbers can be translated into a price/volume simulator.

Suppose that the marketing manager in Region V responded with the following price sensitivities with regard to the various sales volume projections.

PRODUCT	REGION V CURRENT SALES VOLUME	REGION V AVERAGE UNIT SALES PRICE FOR NEXT YEAR'S SALES VOLUME IN RELATION TO CURRENT SALES VOLUME		
		10% LOWER	SAME	10% HIGHER
A	50,000	$35	$35	$35
B	30,000	20	20	17
C	100,000	18	17	15
D	40,000	25	20	10

Product A may be in the growth stage in the product life cycle. The market would not be affected, in terms of price, by changes in production. Cutting production, or increasing production, simply means a change in market share. In the case of Product D, where the market for the product is in the declining stage of the product life cycle, increasing the volume of sales would have disastrous repercussions on the pricing structure. One can see from the price figures that the pricing structure can be maintained only by cutting production. Products B and C are in the maturity stage of the product life cycle where changes in production have relatively modest repercussions on pricing. The assessments for price sensitivities for Products B and C are influenced more by the perceived state of the business cycle over the forecast period than by any other factor. The assessments for price sensitivities for Products A and D are influenced more by the perceived state of their respective positions in the product life cycle. These are assessments over the next twelve months. If the assessments were being made over the next month, or next quarter, then the seasonality aspects product sales would have to be taken into consideration.

A program to create a price/volume simulator is contained in the appendix to this chapter. This simulator derives the relationship between price and volume for one hundred increments between the low and high volume figures using a non-linear S-shaped curve as previously illustrated. Then each of these one hundred increments is assigned a corresponding random number between 1 and 100. The following table shows the simulator's assignment of price and volume for each of the products resulting from drawing the indicated random numbers. A complete table would contain all one hundred random numbers.

ASSIGNMENT OF PRICE AND VOLUME FOR INDICATED RANDOM NUMBERS

RANDOM NUMBER	PRODUCT A PRICE	VOLUME	PRODUCT B PRICE	VOLUME	PRODUCT C PRICE	VOLUME	PRODUCT D PRICE	VOLUME
1	$35.00	45000	$20.00	27000	$17.97	90000	$24.85	36000
5	35.00	45400	20.00	27240	17.85	90800	24.10	36400
10	35.00	45900	20.00	27540	17.70	91800	23.50	36720
15	35.00	46400	20.00	27840	17.55	92800	22.75	37120
20	35.00	46900	20.00	28140	17.40	93800	22.00	37520
25	35.00	47400	20.00	28440	17.30	94800	21.50	37920
30	35.00	47900	20.00	28740	17.20	95800	21.00	38320
35	35.00	48400	20.00	29040	17.13	96800	20.65	38720
40	35.00	48900	20.00	29340	17.05	97800	20.25	39120
45	35.00	49400	20.00	29640	17.03	98800	20.13	39520
50	35.00	49900	20.00	29940	17.00	99800	20.00	39920
55	35.00	50400	19.93	30240	16.95	100800	19.75	40320
60	35.00	50900	19.85	30540	16.90	101800	19.50	40720
65	35.00	51400	19.63	30840	16.75	102800	18.75	41120
70	35.00	51900	19.40	31140	16.60	103800	18.00	41520
75	35.00	52400	19.10	31440	16.40	104800	17.00	41920
80	35.00	52900	18.80	31740	16.20	105800	16.00	42320
85	35.00	53400	18.35	32040	15.90	106800	14.50	42720
90	35.00	53900	17.90	32340	15.60	107800	13.00	43120
95	35.00	54400	17.45	32640	15.30	108800	11.50	43520
100	35.00	59900	17.00	32940	15.00	109800	10.00	43920

As can be seen from this table, the volume increments evenly divide the difference between plus and minus 10 percent of the sales volume. Price changes near the annual sales figure change slowly as one moves away in either direction. However, price changes become more pronounced as one approaches either extremity of the volume range.

To maximize profitability in a sales region, one has to know the variable cost and the standard hours of effort to manufacture each of the four products. Suppose that the company has three plants which can manufacture all four products—some more efficiently than others. The actual scheduling of production to minimize shipping, inventory carrying, and production costs can be accomplished using linear programming techniques once the sales forecast for each of the four products in each of the five sales regions has been determined. The problem at this point is to obtain the sales forecast for all of the products in a given sales region.

Suppose that the average standard hours, and average variable costs, to manufacture each of the four products in the three plants are as follows.

PRODUCT	AVERAGE STANDARD HOURS	AVERAGE VARIABLE COST
A	2.8	$20
B	3.4	15
C	3.8	15
D	2.4	20

Standard hours of effort reflect the labor input, in terms of time, for the manufacture of the products for the given machine configuration. Variable costs include the average cost of labor and the average cost of material consumed in the manufacture of the product. Neglecting shipping costs between the manufacturing plants and the regional warehouses at this point, the gross margin in a sales region is the volume sold multiplied by the difference between the sales price and the variable cost. Standard hours consumed is the volume of a product sold in a sales region multiplied by the standard hours to manufacture one unit of the product.

The total standard hours of the system are fixed by the size of the work force, which can be varied within narrow limits, and the capacity of the machinery and equipment to produce the various products. The most profitable product may not be the product with the highest gross margin. This measure does not take into account the constraint of finite resources of machine capacity and the size of the work force. It could well be that the most profitable item is the one with the lowest unit gross margin because the work force and machine configuration are capable of producing so many more of these than any other product.

It is not known how many standard hours of effort can be consumed in any one sales region that would optimize the profitability of the company as a whole. To bracket the problem, it is first necessary to determine the gross margin and the total standard hours consumed if the minimum and maximum volumes for each product were sold in the sales region.

STANDARDS HOURS AND GROSS MARGIN FOR MINIMUM SALES VOLUME

	PRODUCT A	PRODUCT B	PRODUCT C	PRODUCT D
VOLUME	45,000	27,000	90,000	36,000
STD HOURS PER UNIT	2.8	3.4	3.8	2.4
TOTAL STD HOURS	126,000	91,800	342,000	86,400
PRICE PER UNIT	$35	$20	$18	$25

STANDARDS HOURS AND GROSS MARGIN FOR MINIMUM SALES VOLUME

	PRODUCT A	PRODUCT B	PRODUCT C	PRODUCT D
VAR COST PER UNIT	$20	$15	$15	$20
MARGIN PER UNIT	$15	$5	$3	$5
MARGIN	$675,000	$135,000	$270,000	$180,000

TOTAL STANDARD HOURS: 646,200

TOTAL GROSS MARGIN: $1,260,000

The simulator in the appendix generates slightly lower price figures than those previously indicated resulting in a slightly smaller gross margin. Redoing the table on the basis of maximum volume estimates results in a higher number of standard hours consumed and a different gross margin.

STANDARDS HOURS AND GROSS MARGIN FOR MAXIMUM SALES VOLUME

	PRODUCT A	PRODUCT B	PRODUCT C	PRODUCT D
VOLUME	55,000	33,000	110,000	44,000
STD HOURS PER UNIT	2.8	3.4	3.8	2.4
TOTAL STD HOURS	154,000	112,200	418,000	105,600
PRICE PER UNIT	$35	$17	$15	$10
VAR COST PER UNIT	$20	$15	$15	$20
MARGIN PER UNIT	$15	$2	$0	-$10
MARGIN	$825,000	$66,000	$0	-$440,000

TOTAL STANDARD HOURS: 789,800

TOTAL GROSS MARGIN: $451,000

Maximizing sales has an adverse effect on profitability because of the resulting price declines of Product D. One may argue that no sales manager would be permitted nor would permit sales to be pushed to the point where the price declines below the variable cost of production. The purpose in examining the two extremes is not to make a decision, but to take another step in the procedure for determining the optimal product mix that maximizes the profitability of the firm. The optimal product mix that maximizes the profitability of a company could be attained at the minimum sales volume, or at the maximum sales volume, or somewhere in between.

The bracketing which is of interest in examining the minimum and maximum sales volume is not the gross margin, but the standard hours of effort. Various values of standard hours can be assumed between the minimum and maximum extremes, and a simulation can be run to obtain the optimal mix of products which maximizes the total gross margin for that selected value of standard hours. The simulation program contained in the appendix was run for nominal intermediate values of 675,000, 700,000, 725,000, and 750,000 standard hours. This set of values is bracketed on the lower end by 646,200 standard hours associated with the minimum volume and, on the upper end, by 789,800 standard hours associated with the maximum volume of sales. The optimal product mix which maximized the gross margin in Region V for each of the intermediate values of standard hours follows.

OPTIMAL PRODUCT MIX FOR NOMINAL 675,000 STANDARD HOURS OF EFFORT

	PRODUCT A	PRODUCT B	PRODUCT C	PRODUCT D
VOLUME	53,000	28,020	90,800	36,240
STD HOURS PER UNIT	2.8	3.4	3.8	2.4
TOTAL STD HOURS	148,400	95,268	345,040	86,976
PRICE PER UNIT	$35.00	$20.00	$17.85	$24.40
VAR COST PER UNIT	$20	$15	$15	$20
MARGIN PER UNIT	$15.00	$5.00	$2.85	$4.40
MARGIN	$795,000	$140,100	$258,780	$159,460

TOTAL STANDARD HOURS: 675,684
TOTAL GROSS MARGIN: $1,353,340

OPTIMAL PRODUCT MIX FOR NOMINAL 700,000 STANDARD HOURS OF EFFORT

	PRODUCT A	PRODUCT B	PRODUCT C	PRODUCT D
VOLUME	53,800	28,740	96,200	36,000
STD HOURS PER UNIT	2.8	3.4	3.8	2.4
TOTAL STD HOURS	150,640	97,716	365,560	86,400

	PRODUCT A	PRODUCT B	PRODUCT C	PRODUCT D
PRICE PER UNIT	$35.00	$20.00	$17.17	$24.85
VAR COST PER UNIT	$20.00	$15.00	$15.00	$20.00
MARGIN PER UNIT	$15.00	$5.00	$2.17	$4.85
MARGIN	$807,000	$143,700	$208,750	$174,600

TOTAL STANDARD HOURS: 700,316

TOTAL PRODUCT MIX: $1,334,050

OPTIMAL PRODUCT MIX FOR NOMINAL 725,000 STANDARD HOURS OF EFFORT

	PRODUCT A	PRODUCT B	PRODUCT C	PRODUCT D
VOLUME	54,200	29,820	101,200	36,400
STD HOURS PER UNIT	2.8	3.4	3.8	2.4
TOTAL STD HOURS	151,760	101,388	384,560	87,360
PRICE PER UNIT	$35.00	$20.00	$16.93	$24.10
VAR COST PER UNIT	$20.00	$15.00	$15.00	$20.00
MARGIN PER UNIT	$15.00	$5.00	$1.93	$4.10
MARGIN	$813,000	$149,100	$195,320	$149,240

TOTAL STANDARD HOURS: 725,068

TOTAL GROSS MARGIN: $1,306,640

OPTIMAL PRODUCT MIX FOR NOMINAL 750,000 STANDARD HOURS OF EFFORT

	PRODUCT A	PRODUCT B	PRODUCT C	PRODUCT D
VOLUME	54,900	32,520	104,800	36,640
STD HOURS PER UNIT	2.8	3.4	3.8	2.4
TOTAL STD HOURS	153,720	110,568	398,240	87,936
PRICE PER UNIT	$35.00	$17.63	$16.40	$23.65
VAR COST PER UNIT	$20.00	$15.00	$15.00	$20.00

	PRODUCT A	PRODUCT B	PRODUCT C	PRODUCT D
MARGIN PER UNIT	$15.00	$2.63	$1.40	$3.65
MARGIN	$823,500	$85,530	$146,720	$133,740

TOTAL STANDARD HOURS: 750,464

TOTAL GROSS MARGIN: $1,189,490

The optimal product mix was selected on the basis of the highest gross margin for the approximately 1,000 random selections of different product mixes for the given number of standard hours. Running more simulations may have achieved even greater gross margins. However, one can observe the case of diminishing returns in the running of the simulation program for very long periods of time. The longer the program runs, the less frequent are changes to the product mix which create a higher gross margin and the smaller the degree of magnitude in the improvement of the gross margin.

The optimal product mix maximizes the gross margin. The maximum gross margins for the various intermediate values of standard hours are listed along with the gross margin associated with the minimum and maximum number of standard hours.

NUMBER OF STANDARD HOURS	GROSS MARGIN
646,200	$1,260,000
675,684	1,353,340
700,316	1,334,050
725,068	1,306,640
750,464	1,189,490
789,800	451,000

Of these, the highest gross margin is achieved by expending 675,684 standard hours of a company's total resources in Region V. The optimal product mix for this situation has already been derived.

PRODUCT	VOLUME SALES	UNIT PRICE
A	53,000	$35.00
B	28,020	20.00
C	90,800	17.85
D	36,240	24.40
Standard Hours:	675,684	
Gross Margin:	$1,353,340	

The optimal product mix maximizes the gross margin in a sales region. The derivation of the maximum gross margin is based on the impact on the sales price of plus and minus 10 percent incremental changes in the previous twelve months' sales volume. The marketing manager, in assessing the price sensitivities for incremental changes in volume, is examining what he should know best: the relationship between price and volume of the region for which he is responsible. The price/volume simulator for each product in a region is unique. Put another way, each region has its own set of price/volume simulators for its product line.

The optimal product mix which maximizes the profitability, or gross margin, has been assessed for Region V. By rerunning the simulation in the other four regions, a corporate planner will possess sufficient data to complete the following arbitrarily constructed matrix showing the optimal product mix which maximizes the gross margin for each of the five sales regions of the company.

OPTIMAL PRODUCT MIX TO MAXIMIZE GROSS MARGIN

REGION	PRODUCT A	PRODUCT B	PRODUCT C	PRODUCT D	MAXIMUM GROSS MARGIN
I	82,500	44,370	100,200	46,820	$2,124,540
II	75,600	40,320	115,700	40,600	1,967,810
III	179,830	92,670	273,400	104,300	3,980,730
IV	152,400	75,320	224,600	48,320	1,657,800
V	53,000	28,020	90,800	36,240	1,353,340
TOTAL GROSS MARGIN					$11,084,220
TOTAL PRODUCT VOLUME	543,330	280,700	804,700	276,280	
STD HRS PER UNIT	2.8	3.4	3.8	2.4	
TOTAL STD HRS	1,521,324	954,380	3,057,860	663,072	6,196,636

There is a maximum capacity of production of each product in each of the three manufacturing plants. This is primarily a function of plant layout and machine configuration. Moreover, there is a maximum permissible number of standard hours for each of the three manufacturing plans. This condition corresponds to all assembly lines and workshops being manned at a level which utilizes the full capacity of the system. Adding one more employee would not increase the physical output of products. There would be corresponding figures with, and without, overtime. There may also be a desired minimum level of production for each product in each plant for any number of reasons such as ensuring utilization of certain equipment or honoring employment obligations.

The aggregate 6.2 million standard hours of employment may, or may not, be within the existing manning level of the company. During the forecast period, some adjustment may have to be made through voluntary attrition or layoffs, on the one hand, and hiring more personnel, on the other, to balance the forecast for demand of labor with those presently employed. The aggregate number of the various products to be produced may necessitate closing down a plant, on one hand, or adding capacity or subcontracting production, on the other hand, to balance the forecast for demand of products with current machinery and equipment capacity.

Suppose that there is a sufficient number of employees and sufficient machine capacity to manufacture the products in the aggregate as indicated by the optimal product mix forecast, or that necessary steps have been taken to ensure that the aggregate demand can be satisfied in some fashion. The anticipated schedule of demand on an annual basis can be broken down on a monthly or, possibly, a quarterly basis. This brings into the picture the seasonal aspects of demand in preparation for generating the master production schedule. A linear programming model can be constructed incorporating labor and machine constraints and production costs for each product at each factory. The model can also include transportation costs of the various products from the three manufacturing plants to the five sales regions' principal warehouses and inventory carrying costs for the number of products in inventory at the end of each planning cycle. Solving the linear equations yields the assignment of the production of the four products to the three plants on a monthly, or quarterly, basis which minimizes total production, shipping, and inventory carrying costs. The master production schedule is tentative at this point. It becomes the input to a materials and capacity requirements planning model. If the system as a whole can deliver the requisite component parts either from outside vendors or from the company's workshops, then the tentative master production schedule can be finalized. If not, the tentative master production schedule has to be revised.

SUMMARY AND IMPLEMENTATION

This method of obtaining a volume forecast by considering price sensitivities to incremental changes to the present volume of sales backs into a volume forecast rather than obtaining a sales forecast directly. Pricing implications caused by incremental changes in the volume of sales are considered from the point of view of maximizing profitability. The forecast on the volume of sales is a result of this exercise, not an objective. Marketing would probably provide unbiased price sensitivities to incremental changes in volume without the B, P, and H factors because they would have no easy means to translate these assessments into a volume forecast upon which they could be judged. This method may encourage marketing managers to turn away from volume maximization as a means to maximize profits to integrating price and volume to achieve the same end.

This system should first be experimented with rather than adopted. As a planning tool, it could be evaluated along with the existing forecasting methods. It might be difficult to explain how the system worked to managers who are accustomed to forecasting volume on the basis of volume, not by using price sensitivities to incremental volume changes. Moreover, quantitative forecasting methodologies have a heavy reliance on historic data, whereas this technique has little connection with the past. Forecasting volume on the basis of first obtaining the optimal product mix is more closely associated with the forward orientation of marketing managers than with the autogeneration techniques associated with production planners.

A potential repercussion of this system may be its psychological impact on setting sales goals by marketing managers. This system is not conducive to assigning volume goals for each product in each sales region on the basis of exceeding last quarter's or last year's figures. Volume goals become entwined with maintaining a pricing structure as delineated by the optimal product mix. Focusing on the optimal product mix to maximize total profitability of a company may actually result in cutbacks in the sales of a product in a particular region so that the resources of the company can be dedicated to enhancing sales of another product in a different region where there is greater profit potential. Obviously, incentive programs based on borrowing from future sales with steep pricing discounts to enhance present sales will not fit into such a system. The thought process of marketing managers considering price sensitivities on incremental volume changes may have an impact on their attitude toward their function in a company. If this is the case, then the process of determining the optimal product mix has much deeper implications than just deriving a sales volume forecast.

Appendix to Chapter 6

OPTIMAL PRODUCT MIX SIMULATION PROGRAM

This is the program for obtaining the optimal product mix as discussed in this chapter. Statements 20–30, in conjunction with the subroutine starting at statement 800, generates the non-linear price/volume simulator. The CUMDIST program could not be used because the resulting slope of the simulator curve is positive, whereas a negative slope is desired to reflect a decreasing price as volume increases. It may have been possible to use the CUMDIST program and, by some programming sleight of hand, reverse the slope of the resulting curve. Nevertheless, statements 20–30 and statements 800–940 show another way to create a simulator.

Statements 50–65 enter the price sensitivities associated with 10 percent changes in the current annual sales volume. These statements would have to become operator input statements for more general application of the program. Statements 70–97 permit the viewing of the price/volume simulator for each product. The standard hours to produce one unit of a product, and its variable cost, are entered in statements 100 and 105. These, too, would have to be more general in format to handle other situations. Reformatting would also be necessary to incorporate something other than four products into the simulation.

The gross margin and standard hours consumed at minimum level of sales are calculated and printed in statements 110–190, while the corresponding figures for the maximum level of sales are calculated and printed in statements 200–310. The number of simulations to be run for a given standard hours is entered in statement 320. A random product mix is derived in statements 350–380. If the standard hours is above the desired level, the product mix is discarded, so to speak, and a new one created. If the standard hours is below the desired level, then, in statements 410–435, one of the products has its volume increased by one increment. The new standard hours for the mix of products is calculated in statements 440–470 and the process repeated until the standard hours first exceeds the desired standard hours. Then the gross margin associated with the product mix is calculated in statements 500–530 and compared with the previous largest gross margin. If a new record has been established, the result is printed in statements 560–595, and its gross margin becomes the new record to be beaten; otherwise, the results are discarded. Then a new product mix is generated and the process repeated for the desired number of simulations.

```
10 REM NAME OF PROGRAM IS PRODMIX
15 DIM B(10,100)
20 FOR I=1 TO 10:READ S(I)
25 DATA .3,.6,.8,.95,1,.05,.2,.4,.7,1
30 NEXT
```

```
50  V=50000!:P1=35:P2=35:P3=35:I=1:GOSUB 800
55  V=30000:P1=20:P2=20:P3=17:I=3:GOSUB 800
60  V=100000!:P1=18:P2=17:P3=15:I=5:GOSUB 800
65  V=40000!:P1=25:P2=20:P3=10:I=7:GOSUB 800
70  INPUT "SEE PRICE/VOLUME RELATIONSHIP  YES-1  NO-2: ";Z
75  IF Z=1 THEN 80 ELSE 100
80  PRINT:PRINT "PRODUCT CODE  A IS 1; B IS 3; C IS 5; D IS 7":PRINT
85  INPUT "PRODUCT CODE: ";I:PRINT
90  FOR K=1 TO 100:PRINT K,B(I,K),B(I+1,K):INPUT Z$:NEXT
95  PRINT:INPUT "ANOTHER?  YES:-1  NO-2: ";Z
97  IF Z=1 THEN 80
100 E(1)=2.8:E(3)=3.4:E(5)=3.8:E(7)=2.4
105 V(1)=20:V(3)=15:V(5)=15:V(7)=20:PRINT
110 PRINT "REVENUE IN $MM AND MM STANDARD HOURS CONSUMED"
115 PRINT
120 PRINT "AT MINIMUM LEVEL OF PRODUCTION"
130 A=0:B=0:M=1E+06
140 FOR I=1 TO 7 STEP 2
150 A=A+B(I,1)*(B(I+1,1)-V(I))
160 B=B+B(I,1)*E(I)
165 NEXT:C1=B/M
170 PRINT "TOTAL GROSS MARGIN FOR DISTRICT: ";A/M
180 PRINT "TOTAL STANDARD HOURS CONSUMED:    ";C1
190 PRINT:PRINT:PRINT
200 PRINT "AT MAXIMUM LEVEL OF PRODUCTION"
210 A=0:B=0
220 FOR I=1 TO 7 STEP 2
230 A=A+B(I,100)*(B(I+1,100)-V(I))
240 B=B+B(I,100)*E(I)
250 NEXT:C2=B/M
260 PRINT "TOTAL GROSS MARGIN FOR DISTRICT: ";A/M
270 PRINT "TOTAL STANDARD HOURS CONSUMED:    ";C2
280 PRINT:PRINT:PRINT
300 PRINT "BETWEEN ";C1;" AND ";C2;" MILLION STANDARD HOURS":PRINT
310 INPUT "MILLION STANDARD HOURS FOR OPTIMAL MIX SIMULATION: ";Z
320 PRINT:INPUT "NUMBER OF SIMULATIONS: ";S:PRINT
330 Z=Z*M:N=0
340 FOR L=1 TO S
345 B=0
350 FOR I=1 TO 7 STEP 2
360 X=INT(100*RND(X)+1)
365 N(I)=X
370 B=B+B(I,X)*E(I)
380 NEXT
390 IF B>Z THEN 345
400 IF B<Z THEN 410 ELSE 500
410 X=RND(X)
412 IF X>.75 THEN 422
414 IF X>.5 THEN 424
416 IF X>.25 THEN 426
418 GOTO 428
422 I=1:GOTO 430
424 I=3:GOTO 430
426 I=5:GOTO 430
428 I=7
430 IF N(I)=100 THEN 410
435 N(I)=N(I)+1
440 B=0
450 FOR I=1 TO 7 STEP 2
460 B=B+B(I,N(I))*E(I)
470 NEXT:GOTO 400
500 A=0:B=0
```

```
510 FOR I=1 TO 7 STEP 2
520 A=A+B(I,N(I))*(B(I+1,N(I))-V(I))
525 B=B+B(I,N(I))*E(I)
530 NEXT
540 IF A>N THEN 560 ELSE 600
560 PRINT "SIMULATION RUN: ";L
565 PRINT "GROSS MARGIN:    ";A:N=A
570 PRINT "VOLUME SALES AND UNIT PRICE PER PRODUCT"
575 PRINT "PRODUCT A: ";B(1,N(1)),B(2,N(1))
580 PRINT "PRODUCT B: ";B(3,N(3)),B(4,N(3))
585 PRINT "PRODUCT C: ";B(5,N(5)),B(6,N(5))
590 PRINT "PRODUCT D: ";B(7,N(7)),B(8,N(7))
595 PRINT "MILLIONS STANDARD HOURS: ";B/M:PRINT:PRINT
600 NEXT
610 INPUT "ANOTHER STANDARD HOURS CRITERIA  YES-1  NO-2: ";Z
620 PRINT:IF Z=1 THEN 300 ELSE 630
630 END
800 V1=(1.1*V-.9*V)/100
805 B(I,1)=.9*V
810 FOR K=2 TO 100:B(I,K)=B(I,K-1)+V1:NEXT
820 FOR K=1 TO 100:B(I,K)=INT(B(I,K)+.5):NEXT
825 B(I+1,0)=P1:B(I+1,1)=P1
830 FOR K=10 TO 50 STEP 10
835 B(I+1,K)=P1-(P1-P2)*S(K/10)
840 NEXT
850 FOR L=1 TO 5
855 D=(B(I+1,10*(L-1))-B(I+1,10*L))/10
860 FOR K=1 TO 9
865 B(I+1,10*(L-1)+K)=B(I+1,10*(L-1)+K-1)-D
870 NEXT:NEXT
900 FOR K=60 TO 100 STEP 10
905 B(I+1,K)=P2-(P2-P3)*S(K/10)
910 NEXT
920 FOR L=6 TO 10
925 D=(B(I+1,10*(L-1))-B(I+1,10*L))/10
930 FOR K=1 TO 9
935 B(I+1,10*(L-1)+K)=B(I+1,10*(L-1)+K-1)-D
940 NEXT:NEXT:RETURN
```

7

New Product Test Marketing

SYNOPSIS

Bringing out a new product is fraught with risks. The major risk is market acceptance. The fact of life is that few new products succeed. This is particularly true for consumer products such as toys, popular music, pop-cereals, games, hobbies, shoes, jeans, bathing suits, and other items whose sales depend on the fickleness of fad and fashion.

The question facing a marketing manager is whether or not to spend some money to test market the product before investing a larger amount of money to introduce the product to the national market. The test market acts as a gauge on the product's potential success when it is distributed nationally. As an alternative, a marketing manager may forgo the test market because of its expense, or its unreliability as an indicator of success, and introduce the new product to the national market to see what happens.

A test market provides useful information if there is some historical data upon which to assess the chances of success or failure. This chapter is not intended to judge the chances of success of a totally new product for which there is no precedent. It is intended to cover situations where there is historical data, which is the case with a record by a new musical group, a cereal under a new brand name, or a new type of toy.

The classic solution to this problem is decision tree analysis. This chapter translates the decision tree to a computer simulation. The decision tree is the forerunner to simulation in that it once was the only means of analyzing a situation based on subjective rather than objective information. The difference between decision tree analysis and simulation is that simulation provides the opportunity to create many more branches. Although there should not be any real differences in the expected value and the nature of the final decision, simulation does provide a richer harvest in creating a probability distribution of various outcomes.

The chapter sets up a hypothetical situation in the record industry to demonstrate the decision tree solution to the problem and then proceeds to obtain a solution by using simulation. The comparison of the two methods should provide a manager with the insights that both decision tree analysis and simulation can provide in helping him to arrive at a decision about test marketing a new product.

ACME Records is a recording company in the popular music market and specializes in introducing new groups. The company enters into contracts with a new group giving the company the right to issue one record, with an option to tie the musical group to the company if the single release is successful. If the record is a bust, ACME Records does not exercise its option, and there is no further contractual linkage between ACME and the disappointed hopefuls.

ACME Records lives and dies in a world where 95 percent of records by new musical groups flop. This is not to say that 95 percent of all new releases flop. Once a new musical group has a successful record, then the chances of success for follow-on records by the group are quite high. The historic return to a record company of a successful musical group, including follow-on records, net of all expenses including production and distribution costs and royalty fees to the musical group, has varied from breaking even to making $20 million. This explains why ACME Records is in business.

But success comes once in twenty new releases. Executive positions and advancement hinge on the outcomes of these new releases, which explains why most ACME executives have ulcers and suffer from stress-related psychological disorders. Turnover in the executive suites of ACME Records is very high, which explains why few executives actually die while employed at ACME Records, and why few of them are over forty years of age.

Remuneration at ACME Records is directly tied to the success of the new releases, which explains why there is a long list of applicants eager to obtain a position at ACME Records regardless of the psychological and physical costs. Young account managers can easily obtain high five-figure incomes if they can attract potentially successful musical groups who eventually have some degree of success in the market. Middle managers, appropriately called stable managers, can earn low six-figure incomes if they can attract young account managers who can, in turn, attract successful musical groups. Executives can earn high six-figure incomes if they can attract stable managers, who are capable of attracting young account managers, who are capable of attracting successful musical groups.

The principal shareholder of ACME Records is addressed as Top Dog. He is strictly a personnel man. Top Dog ensures that the executive suites are populated only with those who have not yet had a bad year. The executives, in turn, ensure that the stable manager ranks are populated with those who have not yet had a bad nine months. The stable managers ensure that their young account managers have each had at least one win, or near-win, in the past six months and have nurtured some promising contacts within three months of employment.

The entrance to ACME Records is under tight security control. Each month, the security guards are given a list of those who are permitted to enter ACME Records and severance envelopes for those who didn't make the list. ACME Records is not exactly a fun place to work. The high rate of pay is supposed to compensate for the fact that no one who works at ACME Records will depart with fond memories.

All new musical groups are test marketed, so to speak, by the sponsoring account manager. The odds of success may be low, but the sponsoring account manager must be a believer in the eventual success of the group. The first challenge a new musical group must face is to find an account manager who is willing to risk his longevity at ACME Records by sponsoring the group. The second challenge is for the account manager to persuade his stable manager to bear his share of the burden if his judgment proves wrong.

Once these two hurdles have been cleared, the stable manager overseeing the activities of the account manager is faced with the decision of whether to spend $100,000 to test market the group in a regional market before spending $1 million to take the group national. The decision can go either way. The same stable manager may insist on test marketing one group and, on another, take a fling and spend $1 million without the benefit of the results of a test market. With fairness to the stable managers, most new groups are test marketed before $1 million is spent to introduce them to the national market.

One might ponder why anyone would bypass the additional information gleaned by test marketing a product even if it does cost $100,000 before risking $1 million. The answer is easy—test market results are not infallible. A rousing success in the Cleveland test market does not necessarily mean that New York and Los Angeles will follow suit.

A young account manager does not make the final decision to enter into a contractual arrangement with a new musical group without obtaining prior permission from his stable manager. The stable manager does not make the decision on whether or not to test market a new musical group without reviewing the situation with his senior executive. And senior executives like to touch base with Top Dog. So, in actuality, Top Dog makes the final decision on whether or not to test market a new group by how he nods his head. Furthermore, his head nodding also provides the final say in spending $1 million to introduce the musical group to the national market. Nevertheless, it is the young account manager, and his stable manager, and his senior executive manager who pay the price if Top Dog's nodding proves wrong.

Top Dog is the one who is considering whether there should be a consistent policy toward test marketing new records. He ponders why it is that some musical groups are test marketed before being introduced to the national market while others, although relatively few in number, are introduced to the national market without the results of a test market. An analysis of this kind requires data.

As is common in most industries, there is a considerable swapping of data. Top Dog is willing to divulge, at least in general terms, the outcomes of certain records in return for learning what is happening with records released from competitive firms. As a matter of fact, the information is fairly precise. Figures rounded to the nearest $10,000 can be considered more than general in nature. With Top Dog's cooperation, along with the cooperation of Top Dog's competitors, the industry trade association has assembled the following data regarding the chances of winning or losing with a new musical group, and the amount of profits and losses associated with each.

Regardless of whether the record is test marketed, the results of releasing the first record of a new group to the national market are as follows.

CUMULATIVE PROBABILITY	RECORD IS A LOSER	RECORD IS A WINNER
0%	-$1,000,000	0
25	-900,000	$1,000,000
50	-700,000	5,000,000
75	-500,000	7,000,000
100	0	20,000,000

If a record is a loser, and most of them are, there are some sales to compensate for the million-dollar cost of distributing and promoting the record nationally. Relatively few records actually end up costing the company a full million dollars. If a record is a winner, half of the time aggregate profits for the record, including successive records by the group, will total less than $5 million. Relatively few of the successful records will have aggregate profits of eight digits.

The weighted average of losing and winning are $620,000 and $6,600,000 respectively, as calculated below.

WEIGHTING FACTOR		AMOUNT OF LOSS		
20%	X	$1,000,000	=	$200,000
20%	X	900,000	=	180,000
20%	X	700,000	=	140,000
20%	X	500,000	=	100,000
20%	X	0	=	0

WEIGHTED AVERAGE LOSS: $620,000

WEIGHTING FACTOR		AMOUNT OF PROFIT		
20%	X	$20,000,000	=	$4,000,000
20%	X	7,000,000	=	1,400,000
20%	X	5,000,000	=	1,000,000
20%	X	1,000,000	=	200,000
20%	X	0	=	0

WEIGHTED AVERAGE PROFIT: $6,600,000

The weighted average profit and loss are misleading numbers if the analysis were to end at this point. A cursory inspection might lead one to believe that the risk of loss of $620,000 is more than compensated by the reward of winning $6,600,000. And it does look good if the odds are kept out of the picture. Unfortunately for the players, there is only one chance in twenty that a new group will be accepted by the market. Bringing that fact into the picture changes the appearance of the illusion of large wins and relatively small losses.

The branch of the decision tree representing not using a test market and going straight for national introduction of the new music group is illustrated as follows.

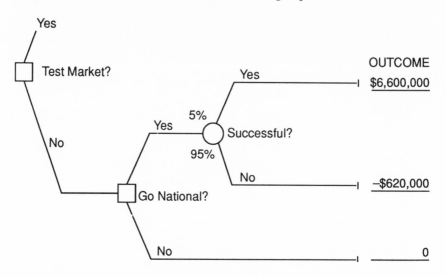

The expected outcome of a 95 percent chance of losing $620,000 and a 5 percent chance of winning $6,600,000 is 0.95 × −$620,000, or −$589,000, plus 0.05 × $6,600,000, or $396,000, for a total of −$193,000. Top Dog, and his competitors, are playing a losing game in going national without the benefit of a test market, assuming for the moment that there is a benefit in using the test market. They are better off not being in the game. This, of course, has nothing to do with playing the game. Each player feels that he can beat the odds on an individual basis, even if it is a negative-sum game for all the players. This is a crucial point that keeps Las Vegas, Atlantic City, and the New York State lottery alive.

In other words, Top Dog feels his organization can beat the others even if the whole group is losing money. The chance of backing a $20-million winner compensates for the risk of a maximum loss of $1 million regardless of the aggregate odds. What counts is the ability to pick the winner. One can still win, and win big, even playing against a stacked deck. Top Dog isn't the only one who feels this way—every player at the table shares his feelings.

However, even Top Dog has a penchant for test marketing a new group. Relatively few new musical groups go straight for the national market without a driving conviction on the part of management that the chances for a particular group to be successful are far above the average of 5 percent. Therefore, most new musical groups are test marketed prior to being introduced to the national market.

Although Top Dog is very conscious of his competition, and keeps tight security on the profits and losses of individual groups, he does not mind sharing his proprietary data with the industry trade association as long as his identity is not publicized. The reasons are not entirely altruistic. There is a desire on the part of Top Dog, and his competitors, to find out what is going on in the industry. And having the industry trade association fulfill this desire is the time-honored way of sharing the data base.

The trade association polled its members as to the number of times records were tested in the test market and their general results. The results of the survey were indexed to protect both the identities of the participants, and the nature of their results, from being revealed in the study. The publication of the results included nearly all the major firms belonging to the trade association.

An index of results was constructed on the basis of how much of the test market sales covered the cost of the test. An index value of zero meant that the company recovered essentially nothing in terms of sales in the test market. An index of 50 meant that 50 percent of the cost of the test market was recovered in sales. An index value of 100 meant that the sales were sufficient to recoup the entire cost of the test. From the point of view of the record companies, an index of 100 is a sellout indicating a strong chance of success if the record were marketed nationally. As one might expect, most new records fared poorly in the test market.

INDEX OF RESULTS IN TEST MARKET	DISCRETE PERCENTAGE OF RECORDS IN TEST MARKET	CUMULATIVE PROBABILITY
0	0	0
5	15	15
10	12	27
15	9	36
20	6	42
25	4	46
30	3	49
35	2	51
40	4	55
45	6	61
50	5	66
55	6	72
60	6	78

INDEX OF RESULTS IN TEST MARKET	DISCRETE PERCENTAGE OF RECORDS IN TEST MARKET	CUMULATIVE PROBABILITY
65	4	82
70	4	86
75	3	89
80	3	92
85	2	95
90	2	97
95	1	98
100	2	100

No company had taken a record national if it had scored less than an index of 30 in the test market. However, there were a few attempts to introduce a record nationally despite a poor showing in the test market. As can be seen in the next table, of those records that received a test market result of 30, and were introduced on a national scale, individual companies reported a success rate varying between 3 and 7 percent. For those whose test market results were indexed at 50, and that were also introduced on a national scale, individual companies reported a success rate varying between 6 and 12 percent. A test market result of 75 could be translated into a 20 to 30 percent chance of success if introduced to the national market. A runaway success in the test market with an index value of 100 meant only a 65 to 80 percent chance of success when the record was introduced nationally. As already noted, everyone in the industry realizes that a booming success in Cleveland could be a bust from New York to Los Angeles, except for Cleveland.

The trade association's complete compilation of ranges of success in the national market for various test market results, as reported by the individual companies, is as follows.

INDEX OF RESULTS IN TEST MARKET	PERCENTAGE OF SUCCESS IN NATIONAL MARKET
0	---
5	---
10	---
15	---
20	---
25	---
30	3 – 7

INDEX OF RESULTS IN TEST MARKET	PERCENTAGE OF SUCCESS IN NATIONAL MARKET
35	4 – 8
40	4 – 10
45	5 – 12
50	6 – 12
55	7 – 12
60	8 – 15
65	10 – 20
70	15 – 25
75	20 – 30
80	25 – 35
85	35 – 45
90	45 – 55
95	60 – 75
100	65 – 80

The range of success varies for each of the index numbers reflecting the results of individual record companies. For the index value of 100, at least one company reported that the probability of success of a record, which was a sellout in the test market, was 65 percent when the record was introduced to the national market. Another company had an 80 percent success rate for records which sold out in the test market. To some extent, the variance in the figures reflects the ability of management to pick winners. Other companies had results between these two figures. Top Dog was one of these. Next month's roster of those able to gain entrance to ACME Records' executive suites will reflect Top Dog's attempts to upgrade the success ratio.

The index numbers were ingeniously designed to indicate the fraction of the recovery of the test market costs by record sales in the test market. A sellout, which is an index of 100, means that all the costs of the test market were recovered by record sales. In other words, the net cost of the test market was zero. The ingenious aspect of the method of calculating the index numbers is the fact that test marketing a new record generally costs in the vicinity of $100,000 for all companies. The index tells everybody what they want to know while at the same time giving them a sense of illusion that there is still some remaining confidentiality in their proprietary data.

For the case of ACME Records, and basically for all other record companies, the index numbers provide a means for measuring the success of a test market for a new musical group and for calculating the net cost of the test market. An index of 30 can be translated to mean that the proceeds from the sale of the record covered 30 percent of the cost of the test market. Since test marketing usually costs $100,000, an index of 30 means that $30,000 is recovered in the sales of the record. The net cost was $70,000 to conduct a market acceptance test of a new musical group. Top Dog reviewed the results of the trade association survey. In his opinion, the results of the survey were reasonable assessments of the situation for ACME Records.

Top Dog has two questions to be answered. The first is this: Should he test market all new records, or should he forgo test marketing and go straight for the national market without the benefit of the information afforded by test marketing? There is another question nagging Top Dog. If he decides to test market all new records, what should he use as a prescribed cutoff point for making his decision to introduce the record in the national market? Should he introduce a new group to the national market only if it scores 95, or higher, in the test market? Or should another index value such as 90, or 80, or 70 be the demarcation point? In other words, what is the optimal decision point that best serves the interests of ACME Records and, therefore, Top Dog?

There is no doubt that conventional decision tree analysis can provide a solution. The branch of the decision tree taking care of the situation for not using the test market has already been illustrated. The branch of the decision tree for using the test market is shown here.

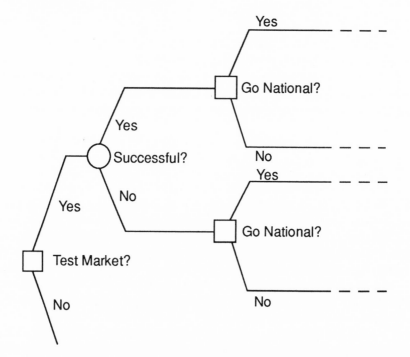

Classical decision tree analysis demands that all branches be evaluated. The branch that depicts bombing out in the test market and still introducing the record to the national market, and the branch depicting a rousing success in the test market yet deciding not to introduce the record to the national market have to be analyzed in terms of outcomes and probabilities. Both branches, in violation of conventional decision tree analysis, will be trimmed before the fact, so to speak, because they defy the whole purpose of the test market. There is no data available on the success or failure of records that bombed in the test market and were subsequently introduced to the national market. Nor is there any occurrence of a record not being introduced to the national market after having a rousing success in the test market.

The a priori, trimmed down decision tree is shown as follows.

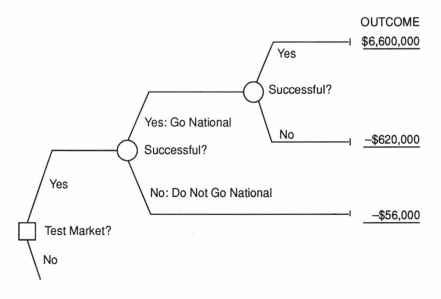

The cost of the test market is $100,000 less the weighted average of the index of test results (about 44) published by the trade association expressed in thousands of dollars. This implies that the weighted average cost of test marketing a new musical group is about $56,000 net of recoupment of actual record sales.

A minimum cutoff of the results of the test market has to be selected in order to assess the expected value of this branch of the decision tree. Only 3 percent of the records exposed to the test market obtain ratings of 95 or more. If a record obtains a rating of 95 or more, its chances of success are about 70 percent in the national market. The expected return on a record that was successful in the test market with an index score of 95 or more, where the chances of success are 70 percent and failure 30 percent, is calculated as $0.70 \times \$6,600,000 + 0.30 \times -\$620,000$, or $\$4,620,000 - \$186,000$, or $\$4,434,000$.

However, only 3 percent of the records exposed to the test market obtain ratings of 95 or more. Ninety-seven percent of the time there is a loss of $56,000.

Therefore, the entire branch representing utilizing the test market has an expected value of $78,700, calculated as 0.03 × $4,434,000 + .97 × −56,000, or $133,020 − $54,320, or $78,700.

The decision tree has been trimmed back to the main trunk, so to speak, and a decision can now be made as to whether or not to employ the test market.

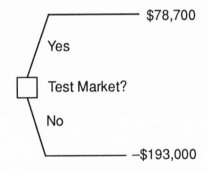

Decision tree analysis has indicated that there is no doubt that the test market should be used. Going national without the benefits of the insights provided by the test market, under the circumstances facing ACME Records, is foolish. However, this has little bearing on the actual decision to take a group national without the benefit of the test market because, in reality, this type of analysis is rarely performed. One can argue that this is caused by the fact that the underlying data is not available. One can counter this by observing that the underlying data usually is available, but no one bothers to go to the trouble to collect it. One can also argue that there is an irrational element in business decision making that would mitigate against the use of rational means of arriving at decisions. There is no counterargument for this one.

The first question raised by Top Dog about having a consistent policy toward test marketing has been addressed and resolved. He should test market all new releases. The second question now facing Top Dog, having decided to use the test market, is the selection of the optimal cutoff point.

Is an index value of 90 preferable to 95 as the optimal cutoff point? Using 95 as a point of demarcation, only about 3 percent of records survive the test market. However, their chances of success in the national market are about 70 percent. Using 90 as a point of demarcation, 5 percent of the records pass the test, but their chances of success in the national market are reduced to an average of about 60 percent. The previous calculations can be redone using these new assessments.

The expected return on a record that is successful in the test market with an index score of 90 or more, where the chance of success is 60 percent and the chance of failure is 40 percent, is calculated as 0.60 × $6,600,000 + 0.40 × −$620,000 or $3,960,000 − $248,000, or $3,712,000.

Suppose that the incremental cost of the test market for scores of 90 is $5,000;

$3,712,000 less $5,000 for the incremental cost of conducting the test is $3,707,000. Taking into consideration that 5 percent of the records exposed to the test market obtain ratings of 90 or more means that 95 percent of the time, one can expect a loss of slightly less than $56,000. Therefore, the entire branch representing utilizing the test market has an expected value of $132,150, calculated as $0.05 \times \$3,707,000 + .95 \times -\$56,000$ or $\$185,350 - \$53,200$ or $132,150.

Obviously, a cutoff at an index value of 90 on the test results is preferable to a cutoff point of 95 because the expected value has increased from $78,700 to $132,150. The cutoff point can be reduced again. If the expected value is higher than $132,150, then the exercise can be repeated with a lower cutoff point. When the expected value reaches its zenith, then that cutoff point becomes the optimal decision point that maximizes the expected return for ACME Records.

Decision tree analysis is the father of simulation. Before the advent of computers, decision tree analysis was employed as a means of evaluating the outcomes of decisions under conditions of uncertainty. Simulation provides the same results—that is, the conclusion reached by using simulation and that of decision tree analysis will be the same. This has to be because the simulation is modeled on the basis of the decision tree itself. The difference, as will be seen, is that simulation provides a more descriptive format including all possible outcomes, along with the expected outcome.

Using the branch of the decision tree depicting not using the test market, the probability of having a hit record was 5 percent, and the probability of having a record that can be best described as something less than successful was 95 percent. The outcome of a win was assessed at $6,600,000 which was the average of the possible outcomes being zero, $1 million, $5 million, $7 million, or $20 million. Or another way, the expected value of $6,600,000 was the weighted average of five individual branches each given the same probability weighting of 20 percent.

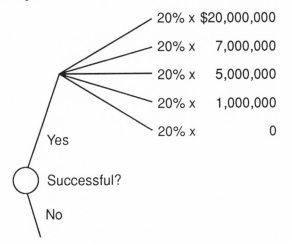

20% x $20,000,000
20% x 7,000,000
20% x 5,000,000
20% x 1,000,000
20% x 0

Yes

Successful?

No

SUCCESS IN NATIONAL MARKET

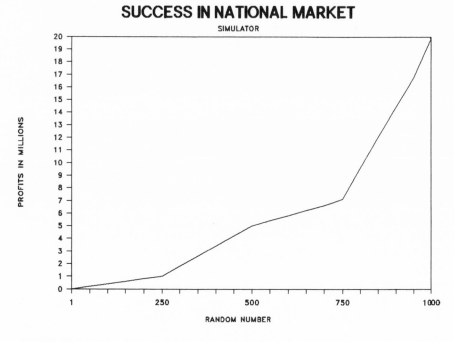

Exhibit 7.1.
Success in National Market (simulator)

In a simulation, there are 1,000 possible outcomes varying between zero and $20 million as depicted in Exhibit 7.1.

In a decision tree environment, six twigs, so to speak, represent the expected outcome of $6,600,000. In a simulation environment, there is a fan of twigs, 1,000 twigs as a matter of fact, modeling the totality of possible outcomes. Two hundred and fifty twigs have values between zero and $1 million. Another 250 twigs have values between $1 million and $5 million; another 250 with values between $5 million and $7 million; and another 250 with values between $7 million and $20 million. What is the expected outcome of simulating many successful records? It should be near $6,600,000 if the six twigs closely approximate the weighted average of a thousand.

The same holds true for the situation when record is a loser. In a decision tree as constructed herein, there are six outcomes fanning from a branch representing a losing situation. The weighted average of the six individual outcomes has been calculated to being equivalent to one branch having an outcome of −$620,000. The simulation represents a branch having a fan of 1,000 possible outcomes of

FAILURE IN NATIONAL MARKET

Exhibit 7.2.
Failure in National Market (simulator)

losing something between $1 million and breaking even. Two hundred and fifty possible outcomes have values between a loss of $1 million and $900,000. Another 250 outcomes represent losses between $900,000 and $700,000; another 250 for losses between $700,000 and $500,000, and the last 250 for losses between $500,000 and nothing. What is the expected outcome of simulating many losing records? Something around −$620,000 as long as the six outcomes of the decision tree closely approximate the 1,000 outcomes of the simulation. Exhibit 7.2 is the simulator for failure in the national market.

The appendix to this chapter contains a simulation program for using, and not using, the test market. In the case of not using the test market, a simulation was run on the basis of 10,000 new musical groups. There was a 5 percent chance of having a success and a 95 percent chance of having a failure. Win or lose, another random number between 1 and 1,000 was drawn from the bag, and the resulting profit or loss was stored. At the end of the exercise, the expected outcome was calculated to be −$334,000. This is a far cry from the −$193,000 previously calculated using the decision tree. There is something amiss.

The expected outcomes of losing were derived as follows from trade industry statistics.

```
WEIGHTING                 AMOUNT
FACTOR                    OF LOSS

  20%        X       $1,000,000   =   $200,000
  20%        X          900,000   =    180,000
  20%        X          700,000   =    140,000
  20%        X          500,000   =    100,000
  20%        X                0   =          0

WEIGHTED  AVERAGE  LOSS:             $620,000
```

Suppose a finer cut was made in arriving at the weighted average loss.

```
WEIGHTING                 AMOUNT
FACTOR                    OF LOSS

  11.1%      X       $1,000,000   =   $111,100
  11.1%      X          950,000   =    105,500
  11.1%      X          900,000   =     99,900
  11.1%      X          800,000   =     88,800
  11.1%      X          700,000   =     77,700
  11.1%      X          600,000            66,600
  11.1%      X          500,000            55,500
  11.1%      X          250,000            27,800
  11.1%      X                0                 0

WEIGHTED  AVERAGE  LOSS:             $632,900
```

On taking a finer cut to obtain the weighted average, the result is a somewhat different, and greater, weighted average loss. It is appropriate to redo the weighted average for the profit.

The original weighted average for the profit side of the equation was calculated as follows:

```
WEIGHTING                 AMOUNT
FACTOR                    OF PROFIT

  20%        X      $20,000,000   =   $4,000,000
  20%        X        7,000,000   =    1,400,000
```

WEIGHTING FACTOR		AMOUNT OF PROFIT		
20%	X	5,000,000	=	1,000,000
20%	X	1,000,000	=	200,000
20%	X	0	=	0

WEIGHTED AVERAGE PROFIT: $6,600,000

These calculations are also redone to obtain a better cut.

WEIGHTING FACTOR		AMOUNT OF PROFIT		
11.1%	X	$20,000,000	=	$2,220,000
11.1%	X	13,500,000	=	1,498,500
11.1%	X	7,000,000	=	777,000
11.1%	X	6,000,000	=	666,000
11.1%	X	5,000,000	=	555,000
11.1%	X	3,000,000		333,000
11.1%	X	1,000,000		111,000
11.1%	X	500,000		55,500
11.1%	X	0		0

WEIGHTED AVERAGE PROFIT: $6,216,000

The recalculated outcome using a better approximation of expected profit and loss is calculated as 0.05 × $6,216,000 plus 0.95 × −$632,900 or $310,800 − $601,300, or −$290,500.

The original −$193,000 was calculated on a fan of five branches representing the winning and losing situations. The −$290,500 was calculated on a fan of nine branches representing the winning and losing situations. The latter calculation is much closer to the simulated result of −$334,000 which represents a fan of 1,000 branches. This might lead one to conclude that one benefit of simulation over decision tree analysis is that simulation provides a more accurate expected outcome for a given probability distribution of possible outcomes. This is not an inherent advantage of simulation over decision tree analysis. All one has to do is provide sufficient branches on the decision tree, and the results of the simulation and the decision tree will be identical. It is the rapidity of the computer's ability to perform arithmetic calculations that causes one to abandon a limb of a decision tree with five or nine branches and substitute one with 1,000 branches.

The measurement of the efficacy of utilizing the test market contains an additional step. For each of the 10,000 new musical group records, each is first exposed to the test market. The resulting test market index is determined by a simulator built on the following cumulative probability table taken from the trade association study.

CUMULATIVE PROBABILITY	TEST MARKET INDEX RESULTS
0%	0
25	9
50	34
75	57
100	100

The test market index simulator (Exhibit 7.3) is created from this cumulative probability distribution.

After the test market index has been randomly selected, it is compared with a minimum cutoff point for determining whether or not to introduce the record nationally. For instance, if the cutoff point under consideration is a minimum index value of 60, and if the simulated test market index is 59, then the record is not introduced to the national market. The loss is the cost of the test which is

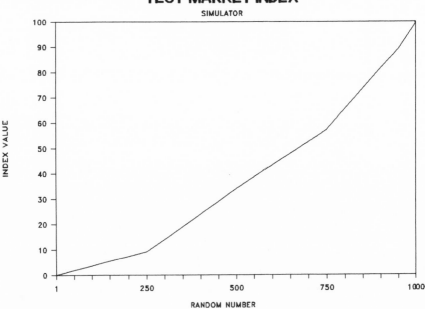

Exhibit 7.3.
Test Market Index (simulator)

$100,000 − $59,000, or $41,000 as previously discussed. Alternatively, if the simulated test market index is 61, the record is introduced to the national market. Its chances of success can vary between 8 and 15 percent. A random probability between 8 and 15 percent is selected and the dice are rolled again. If the number is less than the preselected probability for success, a number is drawn from the profit simulator. If not, a number is drawn from the loss simulator. The score, so to speak, is maintained for all 10,000 simulations.

This verbal description of the program contained in the appendix can also be set up as a flow diagram.

No Test Market Situation

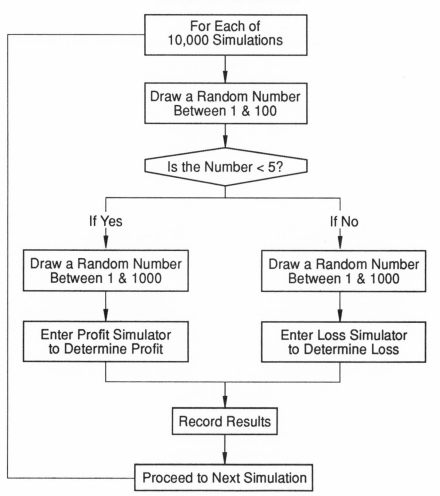

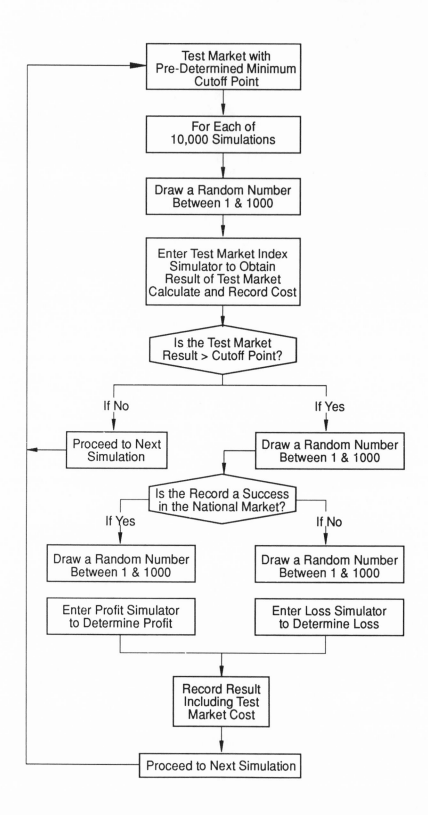

Test Market with
Pre-Determined Minimum
Cutoff Point

For Each of
10,000 Simulations

Draw a Random Number
Between 1 & 1000

Enter Test Market Index
Simulator to Obtain
Result of Test Market
Calculate and Record Cost

Is the Test Market
Result > Cutoff Point?

If No

Proceed to Next
Simulation

If Yes

Draw a Random Number
Between 1 & 1000

Is the Record a Success
in the National Market?

If Yes

Draw a Random Number
Between 1 & 1000

Enter Profit Simulator
to Determine Profit

If No

Draw a Random Number
Between 1 & 1000

Enter Loss Simulator
to Determine Loss

Record Result
Including Test
Market Cost

Proceed to Next Simulation

The simulation in the appendix is built on either the verbal description or the flow diagram. The outcomes for the various cutoff points on the index results of the test market are as follows.

SITUATION	EXPECTED OUTCOME
NO TEST MARKET	-$334,000
TEST MARKET WITH CUTOFF OF TEST RESULT INDEX OF:	
90%	$ 67,000
80	163,000
70	207,000
60	211,000
50	236,000
45	240,000
40	239,000
35	190,000
30	126,000

The expected outcome can be maximized by introducing every record which scores more than 45 on the test market index to the national market. If the record scores less than 45, which occurs more than half of the time, then the musical group, who, up to this point, has been wooed and dined, should be unceremoniously dumped.

The simulation permits a comparison to be made between using, and not using, the test market. This is done by comparing individual outcomes of using a test index of 45 as a decision point for determining whether or not to introduce the record to the national market with the individual outcomes of not using the test market. The first comparison is the chance of success of using, or not using, the test market.

	PERCENTAGE OF RECORDS INTRODUCED TO NATIONAL MARKET	
	SUCCESSFUL	NOT SUCCESSFUL
NO TEST MARKET	4.8%	95.2%
TEST MARKETED WITH CUTOFF AT INDEX OF 45	8.5	91.5

Although the test market did not set the world on fire in being able to dras-
tically improve the chances of success, it, nevertheless, materially improved the
expected outcome from a losing $334,000 to a profitable $240,000. This was
done mainly by reducing the number of records which would have created losses
of $500,000 or more, had they been introduced to the national market without the
benefit of the test market. This culling of the unpromising can be seen in the
following table.

PERCENTAGE FREQUENCY

AMOUNT OF LOSS	NO MARKET TEST	MARKET TEST CUTOFF > 45
$1,000,000	11.5%	6.5%
900,000	18.0	4.2
800,000	12.4	4.0
700,000	12.1	3.8
600,000	11.7	3.8
500,000	8.2	2.0
400,000	5.1	1.6
300,000	4.9	1.6
200,000	5.4	1.7
100,000	4.7	62.0
0	1.2	0.3

TOTAL PROBABILITY		
OF LOSING	95.2	91.5
OF WINNING	4.8	8.5

The 62 percent of the records generating losses of about $100,000 represents
approximately 60 percent of the records that did not receive a test market index
score above the minimum cutoff of 45. A high percentage of these records, if
introduced to the national market without the benefit of the test market, would
have generated losses considerably greater than $100,000.

The comparison of the different nature of losing with and without the test
market is illustrated in Exhibit 7.4.

The following table illustrates the differing nature of success with and without
the benefit of the test market.

PERCENTAGE FREQUENCY

AMOUNT OF PROFIT	NO MARKET TEST	MARKET TEST CUTOFF > 45
UP TO $5 MILLION	2.4%	4.4
$ 5 - 10 MILLION	1.5	2.4

	PERCENTAGE FREQUENCY	
AMOUNT OF PROFIT	NO MARKET TEST	MARKET TEST CUTOFF > 45
$10 - 15 MILLION	0.5	0.8
$15 - 20 MILLION	0.4	0.9
TOTAL	4.8%	8.5%

The same information is depicted in Exhibit 7.5.

An interesting aspect of the result of the simulation is the relatively low value of the optimal cutoff point. One might have been prone to select a higher value had such an opinion been asked prior to the running of the simulation.

An a posteriori explanation of this can be obtained by examining the underlying data. There is a sharp reduction in the chances of success as the test market index falls below 70. One would tend to conclude that the optimal point might be relatively high. The consequence of selecting a high cutoff point is that very few records would be introduced to the national market. While their chances of

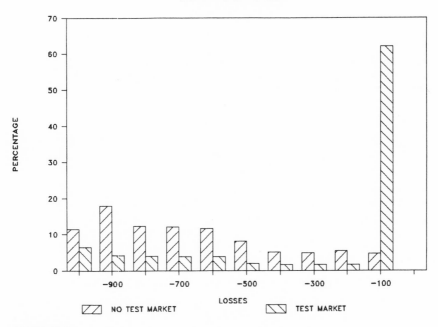

LOSS PROFILE

Exhibit 7.4.
Loss Profile

PROFIT PROFILE

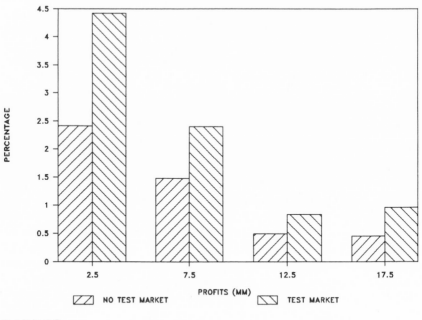

Exhibit 7.5.
Profit Profile

success are fairly high, the overall profitability of ACME Records would be hindered by the small volume of releases and, consequently, the small number of successful records.

Reducing the cutoff point has two repercussions—lowering the overall chances of success for the records being released to the national market, but permitting a higher number of releases where the incremental profits more than compensate for the incremental losses. This interplay raises the expected outcome until the cutoff point is around 40 to 45. Below this point, the interplay between declining chances of success and a greater number of releases becomes dysfunctional in that the expected outcome begins to decline. The greater number of releases has many more losers overpowering the relatively few winners as one approaches the proverbial bottom of the barrel. The situation continues to degenerate until the negative expected value of releasing all records regardless of the results of the test market is reached. This is equivalent, of course, to releasing all records without using the test market. It's worse, in fact, because the costs of conducting the test add to the negative expected value.

In conclusion, one benefit of simulation over decision tree analysis may be that the rounding error in obtaining a weighted average of expected outcomes is less in simulation than in decision tree analysis. However, it must be admitted that if better care had been taken in obtaining the weighted average, as was shown in this chapter, the net results of both simulation and decision tree analysis would have been essentially identical. This, of course, must be because simulation is modeled after decision tree analysis. Both methodologies would yield the same expected outcome for each branch, which, when pruned back to the trunk, would provide the same conclusion.

Therefore, the chief benefit of simulation over decision tree analysis is that there is a richer harvest. The spread of the individual outcomes can be examined in detail, whereas decision tree analysis leaves one solely with the conclusion. Both provide the same conclusion, but simulation permits the examination of the whole range of outcomes which enhances the appreciation of the nature of the conclusion.

Appendix to Chapter 7

NEW PRODUCT DECISION TREE SIMULATION

The cumulative probability distributions in this chapter were used as inputs to create the simulators using the CUMDIST program and were stored in the data files CUM1, CUM2, and CUM3. The graphical representations of the simulators presented earlier were derived from these data files.

  With reference to the program at the end of this appendix, the data files are called into the program in statements 30–170 and viewed in statements 280–330. Viewing of the data files is precautionary to ensure that subsequent cumulative distributions had not been generated and stored in these data files. Viewing also ensures that the simulators have not been confused with one another, which might lead to interesting, and thoroughly misleading, conclusions. Viewing is one way to reduce the chances of error. Another way is to have some idea what the nature of the results should be. In this example, for instance, the decision tree was worked out manually to assess the expected outcome. But the result of the simulation was not in agreement with the manual solution. The usual assumption is that there is a bug in the program. Having confirmed that the program was doing what was expected of it, it was discovered that the culprit turned out to be the manual solution. The simulation was simply doing a better job calculating the expected outcome, as was discussed in the chapter.

  Statements 180–270 create the internal data bases for the high and low estimates for success for given levels of the test market index. Statements 360–470 and statements 490–710 simulate winning and losing without, and with, the test market, respectively.

  Statement 450 and statements 690 and 700 store the results of the simulation for the two situations. Both perform the same function. The loss cannot exceed $2 million. The maximum win is $20 million. In the simulation, this is represented by −2000 and 20000 respectively. 3000 is added to the results to ensure that the result is a positive number. The possible outcomes can now range from about 1000 to 23000. The outcome is then divided by 100, transformed to an integer, and stored in the array S(I).

  Before doing this transformation, the number of possible outcomes was any value between −2000 and 20000. Including decimals, running 10,000 simulations would result in about 10,000 unique results. Storage would have to be in an external data file which, for 10,000 simulations, would consist of 10,000 results. This would have taken up a fair amount of space on the disk. After this transformation, the number of possible outcomes range in integer values between 10 and 230. Ten thousand unique results have been reduced to 220. One hundred thousand simulations, or millions of simulations, would be summarized in these same 220 integer values. This can be easily stored in an array S(I) consisting of 300 "mailboxes." This permits the results to be maintained internally within the program and printed out at the end of the program, or filed for later analysis in a much smaller data file.

The output statements starting at statement 720 reverses the process by subtracting 30 from the "mailbox" value in the array S(I) before multiplying it by 100. Statements 860–900 calculate and print out the expected outcome. No external files are required to store the results, although they could be added to the program, if desired.

```
10 REM NAME OF PROGRAM IS NEWPROD
20 DIM R(1000):DIM L(1000):DIM P(1000):DIM B(2,21):DIM S(300)
30 OPEN "I",#1,"CUM1"
40 FOR I=1 TO 1000
50 INPUT#1,K
60 R(I)=K
70 NEXT:CLOSE #1
80 OPEN "I",#1,"CUM2"
90 FOR I=1 TO 1000
100 INPUT #1,K
110 L(I)=K
120 NEXT:CLOSE #1
130 OPEN "I",#1,"CUM3"
140 FOR I=1 TO 1000
150 INPUT #1,K
160 P(I)=K
170 NEXT:CLOSE #1
180 FOR I=1 TO 21
190 READ B(1,I)
200 DATA 0,0,0,0,0,0,3,4,4,5,6,7,8
210 DATA 10,15,20,25,35,45,60,65
220 NEXT
230 FOR I=1 TO 21
240 READ B(2,I)
250 DATA 0,0,0,0,0,0,7,8,10,12,12,12
260 DATA 15,20,25,30,35,45,55,75,80
270 NEXT
280 PRINT "RANDOM","TEST","COST OF","PROFITS FROM"
290 PRINT "NUMBER","RESULTS","LOSING","WINNING"
300 PRINT 1,R(1),L(1),P(1)
310 FOR I=50 TO 1000 STEP 50
320 PRINT I,R(I),L(I),P(I)
330 NEXT:INPUT "PRESS RETURN TO CONTINUE";Z$
340 PRINT:INPUT "TEST MARKET   YES-1   NO-2: ";Z
350 ON Z GOTO 490,360
360 PRINT:INPUT "NUMBER OF SIMULATIONS: ";S
370 FOR K=1 TO S
380 X=RND(X)
390 I=INT(1000*X+.5)
400 IF I=0 THEN 380
410 X=RND(X)
420 IF X<.05 THEN 430 ELSE 440
```

```
430 T=P(I):GOTO 450
440 T=L(I)
450 T=T+3000:T=T/100:T=INT(T+.5)
460 S(T)=S(T)+1
470 NEXT
480 PRINT:PRINT "NO TEST MARKET":GOTO 740
490 PRINT:INPUT "% MINIMUM THRESHOLD (>30 & <95): ";B
500 IF B<30 THEN 490
510 IF B>95 THEN 490
520 PRINT:INPUT "NUMBER OF SIMULATIONS: ";S
530 FOR K=1 TO S
540 X=RND(X)
550 I=INT(1000*X+.5)
560 IF I=0 THEN 540
570 X=R(I)
580 T=-(100-X)
590 Y=RND(Y)
600 I=INT(1000*Y+.5)
610 IF I=0 THEN 590
620 IF X>=B THEN 630 ELSE 690
630 J=INT(X/5)+1
640 Y=RND(Y)
650 X=100*RND(X)
660 IF X<(B(1,J)+Y*(B(2,J)-B(1,J))) THEN 670 ELSE 680
670 T=T+P(I):GOTO 690
680 T=T+L(I)
690 T=T+3000:T=T/100:T=INT(T+.5)
700 S(T)=S(T)+1
710 NEXT
720 PRINT:PRINT "TEST MARKET WITH MINIMUM CUTOFF ";
730 PRINT "ON TEST RESULT INDEX OF";B
740 PRINT
750 PRINT "LOWER RANGE","UPPER RANGE","% FREQUENCY"
760 FOR I=1 TO 300 STEP 10
770 I1=I:I2=I+9
780 A=0:FOR J=I1 TO I2:A=A+S(J)*100/S:NEXT
790 PRINT 100*(I1-30),100*(I2-30),A:INPUT Z$:NEXT
800 PRINT:INPUT "SEE INDIVIDUAL VALUES?   YES-1   NO-2: ";Z
810 IF Z=1 THEN 820 ELSE 860
820 FOR I=1 TO 300
830 IF S(I)=0 THEN 850
840 PRINT 100*(I-30),S(I)*100/S:INPUT Z$
850 NEXT
860 A=0
870 FOR I=1 TO 300
880 A=A+100*(I-30)*S(I)/S
890 NEXT
900 PRINT:PRINT "EXPECTED OUTCOME: ";A
910 PRINT:INPUT "RERUN-1   END-2: ";Z
920 IF Z=1 THEN 930 ELSE 940
930 FOR I=1 TO 300:S(I)=0:NEXT:GOTO 340
940 END
```

8

Personnel Recruitment Planning

SYNOPSIS

Most large organizations have a training program for new employees. It may not be a formal training program in the sense of classroom lectures, although this may be part of the program. Often it takes the form of assigning new personnel as assistants to executives, to managers, to administrators, to engineers, to technicians, or to any person with a certain professional or technical background. This is often referred to as on-the-job training, which is one way to transfer the acquired expertise of a person with a professional or technical skill to a novice or a recruit. The word *recruit* in this chapter simply stands for a new hire, or employee, to an organization. A steady supply of recruits is required to replenish, or expand, the body of professionals. Without this supply of new blood, the body of professionals would wither away through attrition.

On-the-job training is usually associated with the transfer of proficiency in a profession, trade, or specialty. However, on-the-job training goes far beyond the transfer of expertise. Every occupation requires some sort of indoctrination. The process of indoctrination includes encouraging the recruit to adopt the company value system, of learning the social dos and don'ts, of molding his or her expectations of reward and punishment. Indoctrination means developing appropriate behavior patterns for dealing with co-workers, superiors, and lower-level staff, and for dealing with clients and customers. This process may take two years before a raw recruit is converted to a fully contributing member of an organization. This is not to say that the novice is a total financial drain on the organization during this period of time. It is to say that he is probably not covering his costs to the organization in a commercial sense for corporations or a functional sense for non-commercial entities. The payback on the organization's investment in a new hire is recouped, and then some, when he does become a fully contributing member of the organization.

This chapter focuses on recruitment objectives that support a contingent of fully contributing members of an organization. A change in the long-term goal to expand, maintain, or shrink a group of professionally trained personnel has an immediate impact on recruiting because of the time lag between recruitment and a recruit becoming a member of the professional staff.

Not to alarm the sensibilities of the reader, but with a change in the interpretation of the phasing-out probabilities, the same system for planning the recruitment of personnel can be adapted to the replacement of equipment. The difference is in the nature of the phasing out—with people, phasing out may be beneficial in that an individual may be advancing himself in the organization in such a way that others have to be recruited to replace him. Or it may be that an individual has garnered a better position with another firm. Death is not the driving force behind attrition in personnel planning. In equipment replacement, death is the driving force. After some years of service, the equipment is worn out, or has become technologically obsolete, and must be replaced. Although the nature of the exit is different between humans and machines, the same methodology can be applied to both personnel recruitment planning and equipment replacement planning.

Where do bank officers come from? Do people graduate from colleges or business schools fully qualified to become bank officers with, perhaps, BANK OFFICER stamped on their diplomas? Far from it. A bank recruits graduates from various institutions today to supply tomorrow's needs for professional bankers. A bank cannot function without experienced lending officers, experienced administrators of loan documents, experienced operations managers, and experienced people in a dozen other disciplines. The key word here is *experienced*. Experience comes partly by training, partly by imitation, and always requires time—time on the part of the recruit to learn the new trade; time on the part of a professional staff member to teach, and to indoctrinate, the recruit. The feudal journey from apprentice to master still exists for those who desire to take their place as a blue-collar, white-collar, or military professional.

The evaluation of a person during the training phase of his employment is quite different from evaluation during the professional stage of his employment. The former is on his prospects of becoming a productive professional member, and the latter is on his actual performance as a professional member of the organization. This change in the mode of evaluation may be a convenient way of differentiating between being a recruit and being a professional member of a staff.

How long does it take a recruit to gain experience in credit analysis, loan administration and documentation, clearing of checks, transfer of funds, data processing, and other aspects of bank operations? One might conclude that there must be at least a two-year period of time before a new recruit can gain the experience necessary to be considered a fully contributing member of the bank.

This is not to say that a new employee at a bank is a total drain on the bank's operation during this two-year period. The new hire probably is in his first hours of employment as he searches for the restroom. On the other hand, the new recruit may well be a fully contributing member of an organization at the end of the two years. But during this two-year period, he does not contribute to the organization to the degree that someone with five or ten years' experience (it is hoped) does.

The question that needs to be answered is this: If it takes one, two, three, or whatever years for a person to gain the experience to be counted as a contributing member of the professional staff of an organization, regardless of the function being considered, how many people should be recruited into the organization to maintain the size of the professional staff? How many people should be recruited over the next five years to satisfy management's ten-year goal to expand the level of services, or products, to be offered to the public?

Personnel recruitment planning is a critical consideration in strategic planning because building a new factory requires, to some degree, skilled workers to operate certain pieces of equipment who cannot be hired from a pool of untrained laborers. An insurance company, which desires to increase its market share by 50 percent in five years, may have to expand its professional staff by a commensurate degree. The manager in charge of personnel recruitment plays a vital role in fulfilling management's objectives to maintain or expand its level of business. The key phrase is *to maintain* or *to expand* the staff of professionals. If an organization is shrinking its staff of professionals, recruitment of new personnel is hardly a serious consideration. However, it may be of interest to be able to quantify the natural attrition of the professional staff before an organization resorts to termination as a means to shrink the staff.

The general methodology of forecasting recruitment objectives to satisfy the future manpower needs of the professional staff is similar to other applications of simulation to business problems. The structure should be simple and understandable. There is no law which states that simulations must have a simple structure, but simulations related to practical business applications should not be inherently more complicated than doing a hand calculation of the situation. All the applications of simulation have been nothing more than endless repetitions of a simple, or relatively simple, hand calculation. Simulations also require input in the form of data or a businessman's assessments of the key variables. For the application of simulation to personnel planning, the required data exists within the organization's personnel files, although there may be some effort expended to collect and summarize the data. The application of simulation to personnel planning can best be shown through an illustration.

Suppose that an organization has the following profile of natural attrition: high attrition during the first few years after initial recruitment, followed by a period of high retention, then another period of relatively high attrition followed by a lull culminating in a phasing-out period. This would be a fairly typical profile for professionals.

During the first two or three years of experience in an organization, there is a high attrition rate among the new recruits. This is the time when the new recruit decides that he may not be cut out to be a banker, a data processor, an artillery officer, or a welder of titanium steel. One might consider the indoctrination to be a failure as these recruits flock to the door. This is hardly the case. One may view the indoctrination program as a success in that the loss of investment in a recruit is being minimized by an early decision to cut and run. Banking, data processing, military service, welding, and a thousand and one other occupations aren't for everyone. And if a person finds out that he made a mistake joining a bank, a data processing firm, the artillery corps, or a specialized metal-working firm, the earlier the discovery of this fact, the better it is for the individual and for the organization.

True, recruits might be flocking out the door not because they don't want to be part of a particular profession, but because they just don't want to be part of that particular organization. Again, this can't be blamed solely on the indoctrination program. In fact, it may show that the indoctrination program is very effective in attempting to mold professional behavioral characteristics to the organization's ideal. In fact, the program may be too effective. The recruits take one look at the iron maiden of acceptable organizational conformity and bolt for the door. Whatever the cause, the point is that there is a relatively high probability of a recruit leaving during his first two or three years with the organization.

After this initial period of time, there is a sharp drop-off in those leaving. This holds up to the time of the seven-year itch. Between the seventh and twelfth years of employment, there is a greater chance of people leaving. These are the years of search for greener pastures. However, once a person has twelve years of service, his chances of remaining with the organization for the rest of his professional career are quite high. However, there is still attrition, be it sickness or death, promotion within to high-level executive positions that cannot be considered part of the professional staff in an operational sense, or promotion without to other organizations or businesses.

In addition to voluntary attrition on the part of an individual, there may be involuntary attrition which can be described as culling. Perhaps the organization has found that those leaving during the seven-year-itch years are the superior performers who are obtaining better positions in other organizations at a quicker pace than waiting for death and retirement to open the positions to which they aspire within the organization. The quality of the professional staff would then diminish if action were not taken to weed out, or cull, the poorer performers from the staff.

Culling can be done with great deliberation where the individual is given fair warning of what is in store for him when the carpet is removed from his office, which was the customary way of communicating such intentions in the 1960s. Or it could be the less gentile, but more efficient, "ten minutes to pack up and get out" practice of the 1980s. Nonetheless, the very act of culling obviously has an impact on voluntary attrition. Some will find positions elsewhere and be counted with those who suffered from the seven-year itch rather than wait around and be counted with those who were axed. In other words, those voluntarily leaving a firm, and those culled from the ranks, are not mutually exclusive. These two categories, voluntary and involuntary attrition, need not be separated. For the sake of illustration, they are treated separately in this chapter to provide an organization the means to examine recruitment goals for various policies concerning culling of the professional staff. The caveat here being that an organization eager to ax its professional staff cannot depend on the loyalty of those who escaped being axed when better opportunities came their way.

The central question is how many people should be recruited in a given year to either shrink, maintain, or expand the professional core of personnel. The answer to that question is how big does the organization want to be in the future in terms of the size of its professional staff. And that depends on the goals of top management. If the goal of the organization is to double in size in five years, recruitment has to be aggressive. If the goal of the company is to maintain its market share and the size of its professional staff, recruitment will be normal. If the goal of the bank is to cut overhead, with or without sacrificing market share, recruitment is curtailed. For this latter case, the methodology described here will provide an organization with the natural attrition curve of the professional staff, which, for most companies embarking on this road to enhanced efficiency, is usually much too slow.

It is true that one does not have to speed recruitment if there is a need for a larger professional staff. Recruiting can simply take the form of hiring away professional staff from competitive organizations. For purposes of illustration, it is assumed that the practice of the organization under consideration is to groom its own professional staff by recruiting inexperienced individuals. Outside hiring is limited to those occasions when there are insufficient numbers of new recruits entering the mainstream of the professional staff to satisfy the needs of the organization. In other words, there is a preference to hire from within the organization through promotion rather than hire from without through remuneration.

Suppose that the organization under consideration has the following time of service profile.

Years of Service	Number Professionals in Years of Service Group
1	525
2	490
3	437
4	452
5	398
6	372
7	401
8	379
9	323
10	297
11	257
12	223
13	198
14	172
15	153
16	96
17	72
18	25

Years of Service	Number Professionals in Years of Service Group
19	23
20	18
21	15
22	11
23	9
24	7
25	12
26	15
27	4
28	3
29	7
30	5

After thirty years' service, an individual either retires or achieves a very high ranking within the company that takes him outside of what is considered the professional staff in an operational sense.

In any given year, people leave the firm. Those culled can be identified by the nature of the paperwork in their personnel files. Those not culled are considered to be part of natural attrition. A review of the records shows the longevity of service of those who left in any given year. The data, in this format, is not what is desired. What is desired is the historic record of those remaining who belonged to a particular years of service group.

As shown in the following table for 1982, 43 of the 372 with two years' service left the company voluntarily. This is equivalent to 11.6 percent attrition by voluntary means for the two-year service group. In 1983, 40 of the 298 with two years' service left the firm voluntarily. This is equivalent to 13.4 percent attrition for the two years of service group. Note that this is an entirely different group of people from those counted with two years' service in 1982. The 1982 two years of service group is the 1983 three years of service group. The following table can be constructed using this procedure.

	NUMBER WITH TWO YEARS' SERVICE	NUMBER LEAVING VOLUNTARILY	PERCENTAGE LEAVING VOLUNTARILY
1982	372	43	11.6%
1983	298	40	13.4
1984	355	60	16.9
1985	332	42	12.7
1986	363	36	9.9
etcetera			

The range of the percentage of those leaving voluntarily, at least for the indicated years, varies between 10 and 17 percent. The same survey could be done for those who involuntarily left the organization. As previously cited, it is not necessary that there be a separation in the survey between voluntary and involuntary parting of company. The separation does not permit an analysis of recruiting needs if there were a change in the company policy with regard to the magnitude of involuntary dismissals. As already mentioned, such changes with regard to culling would have an impact on those voluntarily leaving the company as these two categories of separation cannot be considered independent of one another.

A table can be constructed for voluntary and involuntary departures from an organization for each years of service group. The range of those leaving, in percentage terms, can be determined for each service year group. The following table, showing the minimum percentage of a particular years of service group who had left over the time span of the survey, and the maximum percentage of those who had left, can be compiled from data contained in the personnel files of a company.

PERCENTAGE RANGE OF THOSE LEAVING:

YEARS OF SERVICE	VOLUNTARILY MINIMUM	VOLUNTARILY MAXIMUM	INVOLUNTARILY MINIMUM	INVOLUNTARILY MAXIMUM
1	8	15	0	0
2	10	17	0	0
3	6	9	0	0
4	2	5	0	0
5	1	3	2	4
6	1	3	3	7
7	2	4	4	8
8	6	9	5	10
9	5	7	6	12
10	4	7	0	0
11	3	6	0	0
12	2	4	0	0
13	1	3	0	0
14	1	3	0	0
15	1	3	0	0
16	1	3	0	0
17	1	3	0	0
18	1	3	0	0
19	1	3	0	0
20	1	3	0	0
21	2	4	0	0
22	5	7	0	0
23	6	8	0	0
24	8	10	0	0
25	10	12	0	0
26	10	15	0	0
27	15	20	0	0
28	20	25	0	0
29	25	50	0	0
30	100	100	0	0

There is a high degree of voluntary departures during the first two or three years of service as the recruits decide that this profession, or organization, is not their cup of tea. Departures drop until the seven-year-itch years which run from about the seventh through twelfth years. Most of these departures may be individuals from the upper end of the performance scale heading for greener pastures. Thereafter, voluntary resignations from the organization become quite small until the silver anniversary of service. This is the phase-out period for members of the professional staff. Much of the attrition is promotions within the organization to high levels of responsibility where the individual can no longer be counted as part of the professional staff in an operational sense. For example, an experienced lending officer in a bank may now be in charge of marketing, planning, Washington relations, and so forth. Although he is still with the organization, he is no longer fulfilling the function of an experienced lending officer. He has to be replaced. Other reasons may be retirements or assuming high-level positions in other firms. The 100 percent probability ensures that there is nobody left in the operational staff with more than thirty years of service. This may come about by surveying the professional staff and noting that there are none, or essentially none, with more than thirty years' experience. It is not essential to cut off the simulation at any particular years of service other than simplifying the modeling of the situation.

Realizing that its best people may well be the ones departing during the seven-year-itch years, the organization has a procedure for culling the lower end of the performance scale. No culling takes place during the first four years in order to permit sufficient passage of time for an individual to pass through the indoctrination period and establish some sort of a performance record to be judged. If a marginal performer can survive to his twelfth year without being culled, then his position is fairly secure for the rest of his career. After all, there is a role to be played by middling performers. Someone has to establish a measure against which the overachievers can overachieve. The existence of mediocrity is essential for measuring achievement.

Before a forecast can be performed, the professional staff has to be defined. Its definition will be all professional personnel with three or more years of experience with the organization. Those with one or two years' service act as a manpower reservoir to replenish the ranks of professionals who are being depleted from attrition, voluntary or otherwise. The rules for forecasting the size of the professional staff are simple and straightforward: the hallmarks of hand calculations of business problems.

1. Determine the recruitment levels to be examined over some period of time.

2. Total up all those with three or more years of service. This is the year 0, or present size of the professional staff. In this example, there are 4,384 professional staff members with three or more years of experience.

3. Determine the number of forecasts to be run and analyzed. This is the number of simulations.

4. For each year of a single forecast:

   A. For each of the thirty years of service groups (year groups 1, 2, 3, etc.), select a percentage between the allowable minimum and maximum values for both voluntary and involuntary departures. For instance, for the three-year group, this would be some random selection between 6 and 9 percent as there are only voluntary leavings. For the nine-year group, the number leaving would be the total of some random selection between 5 and 7 percent plus another random selection between 6 and 12 percent to include both forms of exit from the company.

B. Reduce each year group by the applicable percentage.

C. Age the entire professional staff by one year. In other words, that which was in the fifth year of service group is now in the sixth. Total up the new size of the professional staff, which is the total of those with three or more years' experience.

D. As the first-year group is now the second-year group, and is lacking a value, assign the applicable year's recruitment objective as the new first year of service group.

5. At the end of each forecast, compare the results with all previous forecasts. Keep track of the largest and smallest size of the professional staff for each year of the forecast along with the average size of the professional staff.

6. At the end of the total number of simulations, print out the results. These would be the smallest and largest size of the professional staff forecasted by the simulations along with the average size of the professional staff for each year of the forecast period.

These are straightforward, repetitive rules that do not exceed the computer's ability to perform simple arithmetic calculations and logic functions. These rules are incorporated in the program contained in the chapter's appendix that has been set up to perform a ten-year forecast of the size of the professional staff.

Suppose that all recruitment ceases. There are still two years of personnel supply, so to speak, in the pipeline—that is, those already in the system. The number of personnel increases in years one and two as those surviving two years of apprenticeship join the journeymen of the company. Thereafter, the size of the professional staff declines as there are no longer any replacements, at least from within the company, for those leaving. This can be seen in Exhibit 8.1, which can be interpreted to be the natural attrition curve of the company. If a company were cutting back its operations, this is the natural decay of the professional staff. Termination would have to be used to increase the rate of natural decay.

The minimum and maximum levels were based on 10,000 simulations. In a statistical sense, the minimum and maximum curves represent three or four standard deviations from the average. In a layman's sense, it would be highly unusual to find oneself close to the minimum and maximum lines. The most likely variation about the average size of the professional core would be about half of that shown in the exhibit.

What would the average size of the professional staff be like for various constant rates of recruitment? The three curves in Exhibit 8.2 are the average sizes of the professional staff for three different, and constant, recruitment rates of 300, 325, and 350 new recruits per year. The average size of the professional staff is not affected by differences in recruitment rates during the first two years of the forecast because the first year's recruitment, no matter what the level of recruitment, can only affect the size of the professional staff in the third year.

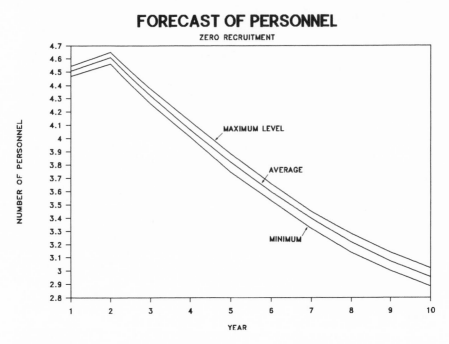

Exhibit 8.1.
Forecast of Personnel (zero recruitment)

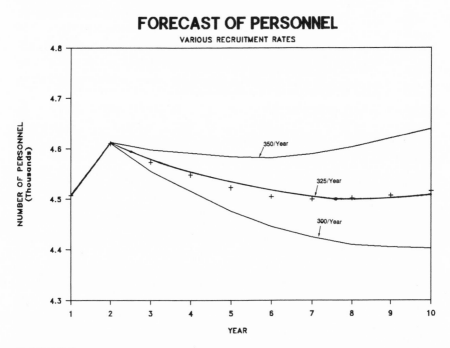

Exhibit 8.2.
Forecast of Personnel (various recruitment rates)

In this illustration, recruitment level inputs into the simulation are not needed for years nine and ten because these would affect the size of the professional staff in years eleven and twelve, which are beyond the forecast period. It is interesting to note that none of the selected recruitment programs would satisfy a corporate objective of maintaining the core of professional personnel at a constant level. The best, 350 people per year, barely holds the line for a few years before the professional core starts to increase at a slow pace. One would have to experiment with different recruitment levels to achieve the combination that holds the core of professional personnel at a constant level.

Rather than find a recruitment level that keeps the professional staff at the present level, suppose that management has a goal of expanding its professional staff from the present number of just under 4,400 to 5,000 in six years. A little trial and error is needed, but it doesn't take too long to come up with a recruitment objective of 500 new recruits for the first four years followed by 375 new recruits per year thereafter. As one can see in Exhibit 8.3, it does achieve management's goal fairly closely.

Again, in reviewing the spread between the minimum and maximum size of the professional core, it should be kept in mind that there is one chance in 10,000 of finding oneself at either extremity. The width of the band could probably be

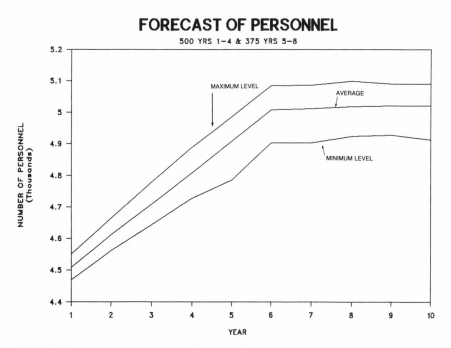

Exhibit 8.3.
Forecast of Personnel (500 yrs 1–4 & 375 yrs 5–8)

cut in half if one were interested in the most likely variation from the indicated average size of the professional group over the forecast period.

The simulation does provide a means to forecast the size of the professional staff using a data base which should be part of the personnel records of any large organization. This approach to personnel planning with regard to the number of new recruits to be brought into an organization should have results that are better than ad hoc decisions as to the proper size of a group of new recruits to an organization. One, however, cannot dismiss the efficacy of ad hoc decision making since it does lie at the core of much of what transpires for planning in many organizations. And these organizations have survived quite well picking numbers out of the air.

EQUIPMENT REPLACEMENT PLANNING

The conversion of personnel replacement planning to equipment or machine replacement planning is easy, and perhaps, uncomfortably easy. The point is that there is no conversion other than labeling. The supply of equipment is not all pieces of equipment with more than two years of service, but all equipment that has been installed. The attrition of equipment is not through voluntary and involuntary departures, but from failure of components of the unit, or the failure of the unit itself.

Suppose that an electric utility has thousands of a particular type of electrical transfer device. Material records would show when the device fails, or when its performance deteriorates to a point where the device must be replaced. Thus one can obtain a minimum and maximum percentage failure rate for each year of service using exactly the same procedure as in personnel planning. Different types of failures can be handled in the same way as different forms of personnel attrition. Multiple types of failure may require the services of a statistician to derive the applicable probabilities and to examine whether or not the probabilities are mutually exclusive, or independent, of one another. The simulator builder would have to incorporate the statistician's model of how to handle the probabilities for different ways of failure into the simulation.

The failure rate could have the same general shape as cited for personnel attrition. The relatively high failure rate in the early years reflects individual units which may have had a manufacturing defect, or lower quality standard, than other units. After the initial sorting out of the poorer quality transfer devices, the failure rate remains quite low until one approaches the end of life of a key element. Simulation could provide the framework of analysis for the following considerations.

1. Should the key element, which had failed, be replaced, which would extend the life of the transfer device for a certain period of time until other elements begin to fail, or should the whole unit be replaced at the time when the key element failed?

2. Should the annual maintenance effort be cut back, which will result in a higher rate of

failure of individual units, or should the annual maintenance effort be expanded, which will result in a lower rate of failure?

3. Should a more expensive unit be used that has a lower failure rate, or should a less expensive unit be used that has a higher failure rate?

These questions can be addressed once the economic factors associated with the various issues are quantified. This is not a tall order for those involved with the analysis of equipment policies. But the same economic analysis, which pertains to equipment decision making, can be brought to bear on personnel planning.

Here the economic assessments may be more subjective than with equipment planning. Nevertheless, an economic component can be added to personnel planning simulation to deal with the following considerations.

1. Should money be expended for upgrading the proficiency of workers or professional people, bearing in mind the limited number of remaining years of service, or should they be terminated and replaced with new personnel who will be, or already are, trained in the new areas of expertise?

2. Should annual pay be below industry standards which will lead to a higher rate of departures, or should annual pay be increased which will enhance retention rates?

3. Should more proficient people, who can garner higher earnings, be replaced by less proficient people who are willing to work for less pay?

From a simulation point of view, there is no real difference between the three sets of questions except in the area of the hardness of data. One might surmise that data for equipment and machinery on failure rates for different levels of maintenance would be more reliable than retention rates for individuals when the base pay is below, at, or above industry standards. This may or may not be true. It doesn't matter if it is true or not. The hardness of data, or its greater reliability, affects the range, or probability distribution, of the results of a simulation. The harder, or more reliable, the data, the less spread there will be in the results of the simulation. The greater the reliance on assessments rather than data, the more spread there will be in the results. Either way, simulation can be brought to bear on personnel and equipment replacement with equal ease.

Appendix to Chapter 8

PERSONNEL RECRUITMENT PLANNING SIMULATION

The simulation program discussed in the chapter is listed at the end of this appendix. Statements 30–280 are the data base for the present size of each years of service group and the upper and lower range limits on the voluntary and involuntary attrition rates. The verbal rules for writing the simulation are reproduced here, along with the applicable statement numbers.

1. Determine the recruitment levels to be examined over some period of time (statements 290–450).

2. Total up all those with three or more years of service. This is the year 0, or present size of the professional staff. In this example, there are 4,384 professional staff members with three or more years of experience (statements 460–470).

3. Determine the number of forecasts to be run and analyzed. This is the number of simulations (statement 480).

4. For each year of a single forecast:

   A. For each of the thirty years of service groups (year groups 1, 2, 3, etc.), select a percentage between the allowable minimum and maximum values for both voluntary and involuntary departures. For instance, for the three-year group, this would be some random selection between 6 and 9 percent as there are only voluntary leavings. For the nine-year group, the number leaving would be the total of some random selection between 5 and 7 percent plus another random selection between 6 and 12 percent to include both forms of exit from the company (statements 520–550).

   B. Reduce each year group by the applicable percentage (statement 560).

   C. Age the entire professional staff by one year. In other words, that which was in the fifth year of service group now is in the sixth. Total up the new size of the professional staff which are all those with three or more years' experience (statements 580–590).

   D. As the first-year group is now the second-year group, and is lacking a value, assign the applicable year's recruitment objective as the new first year of service group (last part of statement 580).

5. At the end of each forecast, compare the results with all previous forecasts. Keep track of the largest and smallest size of the professional staff for each year of the forecast along with the average size of the professional staff (statements 600–650).

6. At the end of the total number of simulations, print out the results. These are the smallest and largest size of the professional staff forecasted by the simulations along with the average size of the professional staff for each year of the forecast period (statements 660–690).

The program is simply the translation of instructions given in a human language to a language understood by a computer. Some people mistakenly feel that this translation is universal—that is, the translation of human thought to a form that is understood by a computer covers all aspects of thinking. The translation only applies to that rather limited form of thought that lends itself to numerical expression. Those who feel that "artificial intelligence" is a form of intelligence, in and of itself, have been sadly misled by those who introduced that terminology. At best, all one can say is that the computer output can be presented in such a way that it appears that the computer has intelligence, when, in fact, it has none.

```
10 REM NAME OF PROGRAM IS PERSON
20 DIM P(30):DIM V(30):DIM B(2,30):DIM C(2,30):DIM M(3,10)
30 FOR I=1 TO 30
40 READ P(I)
50 DATA 525,490,437,452,398,372,401,379,323,297
60 DATA 257,223,198,172,153,96,72,25,23,18
70 DATA 15,11,9,7,12,15,4,3,7,5
80 NEXT
90 FOR I=1 TO 30
100 READ B(1,I)
110 DATA 8,10,6,2,1,1,2,6,5,4,3,2,1,1,1
120 DATA 1,1,1,1,1,2,5,6,8,10,10,15,20,25,100
130 NEXT
140 FOR I=1 TO 30
150 READ B(2,I)
160 DATA 15,17,9,5,3,3,4,9,7,7,6,4,3,3,3
170 DATA 3,3,3,3,3,4,7,8,10,12,15,20,25,50,100
180 NEXT
190 FOR I=1 TO 30
200 READ C(1,I)
210 DATA 0,0,0,0,2,3,4,5,6,0,0,0,0,0,0
220 DATA 0,0,0,0,0,0,0,0,0,0,0,0,0,0,0
230 NEXT
240 FOR I=1 TO 30
250 READ C(2,I)
260 DATA 0,0,0,0,4,7,8,10,12,0,0,0,0,0,0
270 DATA 0,0,0,0,0,0,0,0,0,0,0,0,0,0,0
280 NEXT
290 PRINT:PRINT "RECRUITMENT OBJECTIVES OVER NEXT EIGHT YEARS"
300 PRINT:INPUT "ENTER INDIVIDUALLY-1   INCREMENTALLY-2: ";Z
310 IF Z=1 THEN 320 ELSE 340
320 PRINT:PRINT "FOR INDICATED YEAR, ENTER RECRUITMENT LEVEL":PRINT
330 FOR I=1 TO 8:PRINT I:INPUT R(I):PRINT:NEXT:GOTO 440
340 PRINT:INPUT "NEXT YEAR'S RECRUITMENT LEVEL: ";R(1):PRINT
350 INPUT "ENTER STEPPING INCREMENT TO APPLY THEREAFTER: ";Z
360 INPUT "UNTIL YEAR: ";Y
370 FOR I=2 TO Y:R(I)=R(I-1)+Z:NEXT
380 IF Y=8 THEN 400
390 FOR I=Y+1 TO 8:R(I)=R(I-1):NEXT
400 FOR I=1 TO 8
```

```
410 IF R(I)<0 THEN 420 ELSE 430
420 R(I)=0
430 NEXT
440 PRINT:PRINT "YEAR","RECRUITMENT":PRINT
450 FOR I=1 TO 8:PRINT I,R(I):NEXT:PRINT
460 A=0:FOR I=3 TO 30:A=A+P(I):NEXT
470 PRINT:PRINT "PRESENT CADRE OF PERSONNEL IS";A
480 PRINT:INPUT "NUMBER OF SIMULATIONS: ";S:PRINT
490 FOR I=1 TO 10:M(1,I)=100000!:M(2,I)=0:M(3,I)=0:NEXT
500 FOR K=1 TO S
510 FOR I=1 TO 30:V(I)=P(I):NEXT
520 FOR I=1 TO 10
530 FOR J=1 TO 30
540 X=RND(X):Y=RND(Y)
550 D=B(1,J)+X*(B(2,J)-B(1,J))+C(1,J)+Y*(C(2,J)-C(1,J))
560 V(J)=INT(V(J)*(1-D/100)+.5)
570 NEXT
580 FOR J=30 TO 2 STEP -1:V(J)=V(J-1):NEXT:V(1)=R(I)
590 A=0:FOR J=3 TO 30:A=A+V(J):NEXT:N(I)=A:NEXT
600 FOR I=1 TO 10
610 IF N(I)<M(1,I) THEN 620 ELSE 630
620 M(1,I)=N(I)
630 IF N(I)>M(3,I) THEN 640 ELSE 650
640 M(3,I)=N(I)
650 M(2,I)=M(2,I)+N(I):NEXT:NEXT
660 FOR I=1 TO 10:M(2,I)=INT(M(2,I)/S+.5):NEXT
670 PRINT "TEN YEAR FORECAST ON CADRE OF PERSONNEL":PRINT
680 PRINT "YEAR","RECRUITMENT","MINIMUM","AVERAGE","MAXIMUM"
690 PRINT:FOR I=1 TO 10:PRINT I,R(I),M(1,I),M(2,I),M(3,I):NEXT
700 PRINT:INPUT "RERUN-1   END-2: ";Z
710 IF Z=1 THEN 290
720 END
```

9

Assessing an Unknown Market

SYNOPSIS

Sometimes a new market emerges for products and services. A recent example is the computer virus. Ingenious programmers are tampering with software disks. This practice can have predictable results from the point of view of the programmers, but unsettling implications for the users of these disks. The most harmless form of the virus is simply a message appearing on the screen on a certain day proclaiming universal peace day or a reminder about Mother's Day. A more imaginative message may be an advertisement for a firm whose business is to sanitize computers of the virus.

A much more virulent form of the computer virus can, after a suitable waiting period, contaminate data bases. Variations of these themes can include simply eating up portions of data bases or programs much to the dismay of the operator.

The virus is spread when disks are copied. A contaminated disk will infect the computer itself with the virus program. The virus program then attaches itself to every disk that is inserted into the computer. The virus spreads through copying of disks, and the interchange of disks among users.

How does one measure the potential market for a service to treat the computer virus? In other words, is the potential damage of the computer virus sufficient to invest in the development of an anti-virus treatment? The scope of the market is unknown because of the delay between the time a computer is infected and the start of the destructive process. Moreover, the extent of copying and the exchange of disks among users is not known.

The same technique used to assess the size of the market for the computer virus can be used to judge the potential market for human disorders. A company in the health care business, for example, would want to estimate the potential size of the market before dedicating a major portion of its research and development funds to trying to discover a treatment for a particular disease. This is not to say that companies are heartless in deciding not to risk millions of dollars trying to find a cure, or a treatment, for a disease that has infected a total of ten people. This is the natural consequence to a situation where no one is willing to share the risk of a company not being able to find a cure.

Suppose that the world is being plagued by a new virus that affects a certain segment of the population. The hard data is that the virus, dubbed Virus, seemingly infects only those who practice the Lifestyle. But not all who are part of the

Lifestyle are afflicted by the disease. Suppose that those who practice the Lifestyle are usually associated with a Group. A Group, which can vary in size from two to any number of individuals, is usually a closed set of individuals who practice the Lifestyle among themselves. If the integrity of a Group is maintained, the Group will not become infected with the Virus. The Virus can only be transmitted through a Liaison, which is the practice of the Lifestyle with someone outside the Group. If a member of the Lifestyle group has a Liaison with someone who is infected with the Virus, and if the Virus is transmitted through the act of the Liaison, then the infected member will eventually infect his entire Group.

These are the general descriptive facts associated with the transmission of the Virus. The hard data is in the form of hospital admissions of new patients for treatment of the Virus. Trend lines can be drawn which give some indication of what the case load might be like over the next month or so. However, an ever-ascending trend line cannot be extrapolated too far into the future because this will infer that the whole world will eventually have to be treated. The problem is that the nature of the hard data, the historic record of admissions to hospitals, is not amenable to assessing the eventual size of the market.

This chapter shows that simulation can analyze the opinions of experts who have made assessments of the situation and translate these assessments into a forecast of what might be the size of an unknown market. This may not be the answer—that is, the correct answer. No one knows the correct answer because no one knows all the facts. Simulation permits qualitative assessments based on analysis of available data to be translated to a quantitative portrayal of the potential demand for a service or a product.

The Virus, of course, is fictitious. The figures and assessments are created to demonstrate a possible methodology to evaluate a situation where the hard data is indicative of a potential market, but not necessarily amenable to answering a question concerning the size of the market.

The discussion on assessing the size of an unknown market can best be handled by setting up a situation. This provides the background for focusing on the various points concerning the use of simulation in forecasting demand in an unknown market. To do this, a scenario of events has to be established, and terms pertaining to this scenario defined. These terms include the Alpha Incursion, the incubation period, and the incidence period.

THE ALPHA INCURSION

The existence of the Virus was not even known until the first victims showed up at the hospital door. As most of the victims were members of the Lifestyle, and in observing the characteristics of the Virus, and in extensive interviews with the victims, it took some time to name the Virus, identify its distinguishing features, and isolate its chief means of transmittal.

The transmission of the Virus can only be accomplished through a Liaison. The only way for a Group to be infected is for an individual of the Group to have a Liaison with an infected carrier. A Liaison is the practice of the Lifestyle with someone outside the Group. More particularly, Liaison is a kind of relationship where neither participant knows the name of the other before, during, or after the Liaison. There is, in Liaison, what amounts to a random selection of partners.

Among the first victims was an individual who came to be known as the Alpha Incursion. He was a particularly flamboyant practitioner of the Liaison who prided himself on sheer numerical accomplishments. It is not known how the Alpha Incursion became infected. What is known is that the overwhelming preponderance of the first wave of victims of the Virus had a Liaison with the Alpha Incursion. And for those who did not have a direct Liaison with the Alpha Incursion, an overwhelming percentage of these were members of the Groups of those who did have a direct Liaison with the Alpha Incursion. Among the first wave of victims, all roads lead to the Alpha Incursion.

THE INCUBATION PERIOD

The incubation period is the time from the transmittal of the Virus to the individual until the individual reacts positively to a Virus identification test. This lapse of time between transmittal of the Virus and the Virus entering a stage where it reacts positively to the test can last several years. During this time, the Virus appears to be in a dormant stage within the body. Nevertheless, the infected person is now a carrier of the Virus and is capable of infecting others within, or without, his Group. What is unusual about the incubation period with the Virus is its length. Most diseases make their presence known in a much shorter period of time than does the Virus. Thus actions that may reduce the spread of the disease can be taken sooner to contain the extent of the outbreak of the disease. One of the worst aspects of the Virus was the long period of time between the Alpha Incursion and the recognition of the fact that the Alpha Incursion had occurred.

THE INCIDENCE PERIOD

At the end of the incubation period, the Virus advances to a state where it reacts positively to a test. All this means is that the individual now knows that he has the Virus. The Virus, however, is not afflicting the individual in any way other than making its presence in the body known. In a physical sense, an individual can continue to live a seemingly normal life. In a psychological sense, the individual may be living in fear of when the Virus will enter its active state. The end of the incidence period is marked by the Virus entering its active phase. This is the point where the potential market for a product or service becomes real.

THE NATURE OF THE UNKNOWNS

The nature of the problem in addressing the magnitude of the potential market is that three unknown quantities have to be assessed. One is the size of the total population that might be harboring the Virus. The second is the incubation period, which, as will be seen, has a large impact on the size of the potentially infected population. The third unknown is the incidence period. All three unknowns have to be dealt with in order to be able to quantitatively assess the ultimate size of the market.

The total Lifestyle population is not at risk. Those members of the Lifestyle population whose liaisons, spelled with a small "l," are restricted to members of the Group are not at risk as long as no member of the Group entered into a Liaison, spelled with a capital "L," with a carrier. Sociologists, or experts in the behavioral aspects of the Lifestyle community, might be able to assess the two principal segments of the population.

One segment is the aggregate of Groups whose integrity has not been compromised by any individual of the Group entering into a Liaison. The Virus can only be transmitted by an individual having a Liaison with a carrier. A carrier is one who belongs to a Group whose integrity has been violated by a member of the Group having a Liaison with the Alpha Incursion, or with those who have had Liaisons with members of Groups that had been infected by the Alpha Incursion. These, naturally, form the other principal segment of the Lifestyle population. And it is this segment that is at risk.

Other than being unusually long, there are problems associated with quantifying the length of the incubation period. The first victims, showing up at the doorsteps of hospitals, had already passed through the incubation and incidence periods. Through interviews, some assessment could be made as to when the Virus entered the body. This marks the start of the incubation period, and the hospital admission marks the end of the incidence period.

Ideally, the incubation period could be assessed by establishing the timing of a Liaison with a known carrier that may have resulted in the transmittal of the Virus. Once this has been established, the individual could start taking a series of identification tests. When the results of the tests turn from negative to positive, then one would have an idea of the incubation period. If this could be done with a sufficient number of individuals, then the more defined estimates of the actual incubation period could be transformed to a probability distribution to be applied against the at-risk population.

All of this sounds logical, but the nature of those who enter into Liaisons is not amenable to testing, even if they knew that they were placing themselves at risk. Furthermore, there is a great reluctance among the Lifestyle population to be tested. Ignorance is bliss in that a negative reading does not mean that the Virus is not in the body. A negative test means either that the Virus is not present, or is present, but is in its dormant stage. Not much solace there. And a positive reading from the test merely transforms life from uncertainty to the stark realization that better days are not ahead. The most negative aspect of testing is the feeling that the timing of its availability may already be too late. Perhaps, under these circumstances, ignorance is bliss.

Thus one could argue that the incubation and incidence periods really ought to be combined. And, perhaps, they should be. However, they will be treated separately for discussion purposes here.

THE FIRST UNKNOWN—THE DEGREE OF PREVALENCE

The first expert who has to be called to the witness stand will have to be a sociologist, or someone knowledgeable about the size and behavior patterns of the Lifestyle population. One assessment is required. What is the population of the at-risk segment of the Lifestyle population? This can be arrived at by a direct question, or indirectly, by estimating the total Lifestyle population and the segment of the Lifestyle population which has maintained its integrity. The integrity of a Group can be protected by members of the Group maintaining their activities within their respective Groups. The difference between these two assessments is the critical assessment. This process may require a number of experts who are sufficiently knowledgeable about these matters to make such assessments for different localities.

The at-risk population are the members of the Lifestyle population. They belong to Groups whose membership includes individuals who practice Liaison. It is in practicing Liaison that the Virus can be transmitted from an infected Group to a non-infected Group. And there are those who do practice Liaison; otherwise, the Alpha Incursion could not have taken place. The most damage the Alpha Incursion could have done was to infect his own Group. But this was, unfortunately, not his style. And even more unfortunate was the time span between the Alpha Incursion planting the seeds of the Virus and the reaping of the harvest. The time span from the start of Alpha Incursion's career to the publication of warnings upon which individuals could take protective actions was about five years.

Suppose that the experts cannot agree on the size of the population that may be at risk. An alternative course of action is to make up a certain set of assumptions, simulate the spread of the disease with these assumptions, and view the results. Knowing the results of the simulation, one can then return to the experts for an opinion on the nature of the assumptions. One might conclude at this point that there is too much "flying in the dark" to proceed further. One always has the time-honored alternative of doing nothing and, therefore, having no idea of what the potential market may be. A planner has a right to make that choice.

If the latter choice is not acceptable, the planner has to start somewhere to begin the market assessment process. One beginning step would be to assume that there is a total population of 10,000 at-risk Groups. The next step would be to assume that the Alpha Incursion infected one Group per week. The planner could ponder the question as to what total percentage of the population would be infected at the end of five years. This would be one data point in addressing the issue as to how prevalent the disease might be among the at-risk Lifestyle population.

At the rate of infecting one Group per week, the Alpha Incursion is responsible for infecting fifty-two Groups in one year's time, or 0.5 percent of the total population. In five years, 2.5 percent of the total population would be infected— an eminently controllable situation.

Or is it?

This estimate assumes that no Group infected with the Virus would spread it to other Groups. This means that all Liaisons were restricted to involvement with the Alpha Incursion. Although the Alpha Incursion wouldn't mind such a distinction, such was not the case. After all, many people believed what a great modern-day philosopher said about the conduct of consenting adults behind closed doors. Everything, and anything, is fine as long as the adults consent to what is going on behind the closed door. And consent they did.

One might feel much more comfortable if the results of a poll of sociologists as to their feelings on the frequency of Liaisons among the at-risk Groups were available. It is not necessary that they be polled. One might experiment with various assumptions to see what might be the magnitude of the problem before polling the experts. If the information gleaned from a poll falls within a certain range of the parameters covered by the experiments, then one has a fair idea of the situation without further ado.

Liaison, with a capital "L," has been defined as a liaison between total strangers. This fits a model of a purely random relationship between two at-risk Groups. Again, for purposes of illustration, suppose that in a given week, there is a 98 percent chance that no member of an at-risk Group enters into a Liaison. That means that there is a 2 percent chance that a Liaison would take place in any given week of each of the presumed 10,000 at-risk Groups. That is equivalent to one Liaison in fifty weeks, or about one Liaison per year by one member of an at-risk Group. If the Liaison is between members of non-infected Groups, then, naturally, there would be no spread of the Virus. If the Liaison involves two individuals of whom one is a carrier, the risk of transmission is assumed to be 50 percent. Thus one has a 50 percent chance of walking away from a Liaison with a carrier in a pure state of health. Once an individual of a Group becomes a carrier, he will infect every member of his Group either directly, or indirectly by infecting those who, in turn, infect others in the Group. In other words, liaisons within any Group occur with sufficient frequency to assure the transmittal of the disease to every member of the Group.

Offhand, these parameters do seem reasonably modest from the point of view of examining the preponderance of the Virus five years after the Alpha Incursion made his debut. There are 10,000 Groups each involved, on average, with one Liaison with another Group per year. If the Liaison does involve a carrier of the Virus, the non-infected individual has a 50 percent chance of walking away from the encounter unscathed. On average, there is a time span of the order of two years for an infected Group to infect another Group. Viewed on this basis, it would appear that the number of infected Groups might not be appreciably higher than the fifty-two infected Groups per year who were the direct victims of the Alpha Incursion.

There is another way to view this same situation. Each week there will be 200 Liaisons (2 percent of 10,000). These Liaisons will be randomly assigned between two Groups from the total population. There are two ways to spread the disease. A member of an infected group may end up having a Liaison with a member of a non-infected group with a 50 percent chance of there being an actual transmission of the disease. If one notes that there are only 52 infected Groups at the end of the first year caused by the Alpha Incursion, and that the chances are only 2 percent that any of these Groups will have entered into a Liaison, then there will be one potentially infectious Liaison. Potential meaning that there is still a 50 percent chance that the transmission may not occur at all. Therefore, one might expect fifty-two known cases of the Virus from the Alpha Incursion plus possibly a few other cases stemming from Liaisons between infected and non-infected Groups. Here, again, the number of cases is controllable from a superficial examination of the circumstances.

And that is the fault with this examination. It is superficial. What is being considered is the chance of an individual from an infected Group having a Liaison with an individual from a non-infected Group. What is being neglected is the chance of an individual from a non-infected Group having a Liaison with an individual from an infected group. One tends to think of the spread of the Virus being accomplished by individuals of an infected Group entering into a Liaison with an individual of a non-infected Group. That is one side of the coin. The other side of the coin is non-infected individuals arranging a Liaison with infected individuals.

At the end of the first year where there are presumably fifty-two infected Groups, there are still 200 Liaisons being arranged of which nearly all of them represent the 9,948 non-infected Groups. All are casting dice, or more precisely, drawing a random number from a bag of 10,000 numbers. If the number they draw happens to be an infected Group, then there is a 50 percent chance that that Group might become carriers. The spread of the Virus is caused not by the one infected person out of the 200 Liaisons being arranged by reaching into the bag and drawing a number of a non-infected individual. The spread of the Virus is caused by the 199 non-infected individuals reaching into the bag and drawing the number of an infected individual.

The simulation in the appendix to this chapter is based on the points contained in this discussion. The program simulates the spread of the Virus on a weekly basis. For the circumstances assumed in the discussion, the number of infected Groups at the end of the first quarter (thirteen weeks) after the Alpha Incursion makes his debut is sixteen. Thirteen of these are the responsibility of the Alpha Incursion, but three are not. And the additional three cases are not so much the infected thirteen having a Liaison with an innocent party, but an innocent party having the rotten luck of having a Liaison with an infected individual. Although the odds are small for one non-infected Group selecting an infected Group, the cumulative effect of 200 randomly selected Liaisons per week, or 2,600 randomly selected Liaisons over the course of the thirteen-week quarter, adds three more infected Groups to the roster generated by the Alpha Incursion.

During the second quarter, there is a total of thirty-four infected Groups. Twenty-six of these can point to the Alpha Incursion as the culprit as he is spreading the disease to one member of a different Group for each week of his life. The remaining eight cases are primarily individuals from non-infected Groups choosing the wrong partner. Thus at the end of the first year, there is a total of ninety-two cases of which fifty-two can be blamed on the Alpha Incursion, and the remaining forty are the bad luck of the draw. The bad luck is primarily of non-infected individuals selecting infected individuals as Liaison partners, and not vice versa.

An interaction rate of 2 percent means that there is a 98 percent chance that a particular Group will not have a Liaison in any given week. This is equivalent to one Liaison per year per Group. The number of Liaisons averages about 200 per week in a total population of 10,000 Groups. The following table relates the interaction rate to the number of Liaisons per Group per year and to the total weekly number of Liaisons.

INTERACTION RATE	APPROXIMATE NUMBER OF LIAISONS PER GROUP PER YEAR	APPROXIMATE NUMBER LIAISONS PER WEEK FOR TOTAL POPULATION OF 10,000 GROUPS
2%	1.0	200
3	1.5	300
4	2.0	400

The following table summarizes the number of infected Groups for the three interaction rates on a quarterly (thirteen-week) basis. The simulation incorporates the point that there is a 50 percent chance of the Virus not being transmitted from an infected individual to a non-infected individual.

	PERCENTAGE INTERACTION RATE PER WEEK		
	2%	3%	4%
Year 1			
Qtr			
1	16	18	18
2	34	45	42
3	64	79	92
4	92	137	160

Year 2

Qtr			
1	140	224	296
2	192	344	494
3	263	492	850
4	369	748	1380

Year 3

Qtr			
1	491	1080	2108
2	620	1563	3154
3	791	2112	4341
4	1021	2817	5586

Year 4

Qtr			
1	1306	3663	6856
2	1664	4610	7837
3	2089	5584	8621
4	2551	6530	9109

Year 5

Qtr			
1	3111	7359	9458
2	3684	8059	9676
3	4367	8573	9799
4	5012	8985	9875

Year 6

Qtr			
1	5722	9298	9921
2	6316	9490	9952
3	6851	9648	9973
4	7381	9759	

Year 7

Qtr		
1	7796	9830
2	8168	9885
3	8528	9911
4	8809	9931

Year 8

Qtr		
1	9030	9956
2	9231	9970
3	9383	
4	9499	

Year 9

Qtr	
1	9594
2	9683
3	9742
4	9788

Year 10
  Qtr
    1   9825
    2   9861
    3   9896
    4   9916

The data in the table show that the Alpha Incursion's work is over the first year. The system feeds on itself after that. Moreover, the critical mass from which a chain reaction sets in, greatly magnifying the scope of the problem, is the 10 percent infection level. Once 10 percent of the population is infected, the annual progression from that level is approximately the same regardless of the interaction rates. The annual progression is about 10, 25, 50, 75, and 90 percent rate of infection of the at-risk Groups regardless of the interaction rates. If this model has any validity in reality, the sociologists need not be asked for an assessment of the interaction rates. What is important from these specialists is the overall size of the at-risk Lifestyle population. Then public health experts can be queried as to their opinion when there was a 10 percent infection rate among the at-risk population. If a few years had passed since that time, then the appropriate answer to the query as to the prevalence of the Virus among the at-risk Lifestyle population should include the word *significant*.

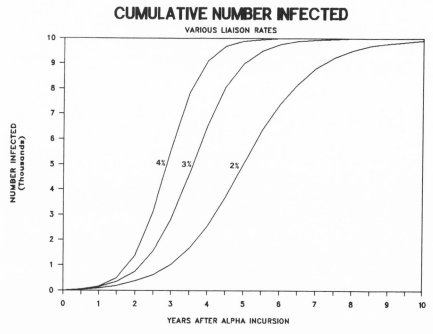

Exhibit 9.1.
Cumulative Number Infected (various liaison rates)

This point is shown in Exhibit 9.1 of the cumulative number of those infected out of a total population of 10,000 for the three interaction rates under consideration.

THE SECOND UNKNOWN—THE INCUBATION PERIOD

The incubation period starts at the time of infection. For a non-infected Group, an individual having a Liaison with a carrier, and not walking away unscathed by the encounter, starts a series of liaisons within a Group that eventually infect the entire Group. The Virus is dormant during this period and does not respond positively to identification tests. Yet the person infected with the Virus is a carrier. The incubation period ends when the Virus reacts positively to an identification test. This marks the point when the Virus is one step away from its active stage where medical attention, or hospitalization, is required. The period of time from the point that the Virus reacts positively to a test until it enters its active stage is the incidence period. In reality, it may not be possible to separate the incubation and incidence periods. Here, they are treated separately.

Suppose a knowledgeable observer of the Virus makes a public statement: In his opinion, there is a small chance that the incubation could be as short as three years and as long as seven. A simulation model builder might interview the person in order to obtain a more definitive opinion as to the incubation period. After all, the opinion is rather qualitative, and the simulation requires a more precise cumulative probability distribution. The conversation between the model builder and the expert might run like this:

"Mr. Expert, you mentioned that there is a small chance that the incubation period may be as short as three years."

"Yes, I did."

"How small is small?"

"What do you mean?"

"Well, do you mean 1 percent chance of the incubation period being as short as three years, or 5 percent, or 10 percent, or what?"

"I don't know."

"Well, does 1 percent sound too small?"

"I don't know. I don't have too much data to go on. I'm dealing with people who have tested positively. I don't know how long they have been in this state. It's a guess. And I don't know when they picked up the Virus. That, too, is a guess because they can't pin down the who, when, and where of the circumstances. All I can say is that, based on scores, if not hundreds of interviews, there appears to me to be a small chance of the incubation period being as short as three years. I feel that the incubation period seems to be about four to six years, with a small chance of being over six years."

"Well, does 5 percent sound too small?"

"Didn't I just explain to you the fuzziness of this whole situation?"

"I know, but I need to put a probability value on three years."

"Why is that my problem?"

"How about 10 percent? Does that sound about right?"

"You are desperate for a number, aren't you?"

"No, I wouldn't say that I'm desperate. But for me to model the situation, I do need a probability distribution of the length of time of the incubation period. Therefore, I need from you an assessment of the probability of the incubation period being as short as three years, and as long as seven years. Then we can look at the intervening years."

"But I have little in the way of data. I have arrived at certain conclusions based on medical records and personal interviews."

"And all I'm asking you is to take these feelings, if you will, and translate them into a probability. For instance, does 10 percent sound about right for the number of people you have interviewed whom you feel may have had an incubation period as short as three years?"

"Yes, it does have a sonorous ring about it."

"You agree with this assessment?"

"Sounds fine to me."

And so the expert, in the interest of ending the conversation as soon as possible, because he cannot be as definitive as to the discrete probabilities for each year of the incubation period as he is being asked to be, agrees to anything that sounds fine to the interrogator. Suppose that the two agree to the following table.

YEAR	DISCRETE PROBABILITY DISTRIBUTION
3	10%
4	20
5	30
6	30
7	10

The simulation model builder then translates this to a cumulative probability distribution table.

YEAR	CUMULATIVE PROBABILITY DISTRIBUTION
3	10%
4	30
5	60
6	90
7	100

Once it has been established when the individual became infected, then a simulation can be run to determine the incubation period for the individual. This can be done by directing someone, figuratively, to reach into a bag of one hundred numbered ping-pong balls. If the number on the ball is under ten, then the incubation period is three years. If the number on the ball is between ten and thirty, the incubation period is four years; if the number on the ball is between thirty and sixty, then the incubation period is five years. Ping-pong balls numbered between sixty and ninety assign six years to the incubation period, whereas those numbered above ninety establish a seven-year incubation period.

All of this is well and good except for two points. The first point is that the discrete probability table was created by cajoling and intimidating the expert. The expert had almost nothing to do with the creation of the discrete probability distribution. The expert simply acquiesced to the probability values put forth by the simulation builder. What sounded good to the expert, sounded good to the model builder, and what sounded good to the model builder, sounded good to the expert. This is a singing duet, not an assessment on the discrete probability distribution.

The second point is that the whole conversation is a waste of time for both individuals. All the model builder has to do is run the CUMDIST program using three years as the lower value, five years as the median, seven years as the upper value, and a scaling factor of 0.3. This would not generate the exact same cumulative distribution as in the previous table, but it certainly would be just as valid with no cajoling.

THE THIRD UNKNOWN—THE INCIDENCE PERIOD

The incidence period starts from the time the Virus leaves the dormant stage, which is marked by positive test results, until the time the Virus enters the active stage and the individual requires medical attention. Suppose that there is a 1 percent chance that the Virus will activate during any particular month. A person who has tested positively would interpret this to mean that, on any given month, he reaches into a bag of one hundred ping-pong balls, all of which are colored white except for one black ball. (Alternatively, all the ping-pong balls could be colored black except for one white ball.) Nevertheless, a person who has tested positive might feel confident that he can last forever because the survival rate is 99 percent. And the survival rate is 99 percent each month, but the survival rate is not 99 percent after reaching into the bag twelve times over the course of a year, or 120 times over the course of a decade. The probability of survival after reaching into a bag 120 times, where the odds are 99 percent in one's favor on each individual draw, is about one chance in three.

Suppose that there are 10,000 individuals who have passed from the incubation period to the incidence period at the same point in time. Suppose that the incidence rate is 0.5, 1, and 1.5 percent per month. What would be the expected number of individuals afflicted with the Virus entering its active state? This is the point where the potential demand for health care services and products becomes real, as illustrated here.

YEARS INCIDENCE PERIOD	DEMAND FOR SERVICES AND PRODUCTS PER TEN THOUSAND TOTAL POPULATION FOR VARIOUS INCIDENCE RATES/MONTH		
	0.5%	1.0%	1.5%
1	649	1166	1686
2	559	1049	1402
3	522	894	1158
4	467	777	974
5	486	747	760
6	432	641	703
7	397	568	587
8	395	478	460
9	353	393	416
10	328	353	325

The previous table was derived by a simulation program contained in the accompanying appendix. Classical probability theory could also have been used to derive this table. The question of interest is not the choice of methodology but the percentage of the total population that will require health care services, or products, during the first ten years of the incidence period. If the incidence rate is 0.5 percent per month, about 46 percent of the total population will be afflicted during the first ten years after the incubation period is over. If the incidence rate is 1 percent, about 71 percent will require hospital care. And if the incidence rate is 1.5 percent, then about 85 percent will be hospitalized during the first ten years of the incidence period.

An expert in these matters might expect most of those afflicted by the Virus to require hospitalization during the first fifteen years of the incidence period. This would imply an incidence rate between 1 and 1.5 percent.

Of course, there is no law that states that the incidence rate has to be constant year after year, or could not vary among individuals. But if it were constant, or nearly so, the rate of affliction for a given population is relatively high in the beginning and tapers off because of the declining portion of the population which has not yet been afflicted. Exhibit 9.2 illustrates the percentage of those stricken with the Virus entering its active stage at an incidence rate of 1 percent per month.

THE THREE UNKNOWNS IN TANDEM

One reason for separating the incubation and incidence periods was to show the sharp divergence in the characteristics of the probability curves that describe the

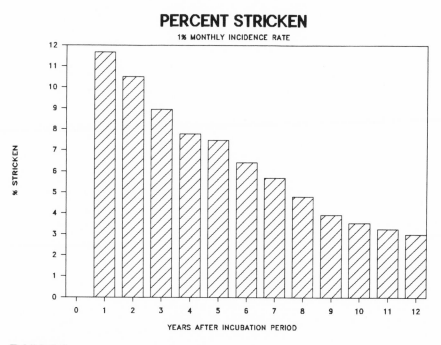

Exhibit 9.2.
Percent Stricken (1% monthly incidence rate)

three periods of time which separate a healthy individual from the hospital bed. At the beginning of the Alpha Incursion, the probability distribution for contracting the Virus for the at-risk population is very small. Indeed, up to the point where about 10 percent of the population was infected, the chances of contracting the Virus were modest. After that, the chances of contracting the Virus mushroomed, not unlike other chain reactions. Once the Virus is in the body, the incubation period marking the dormant stage of the infection was the typical "normal" type of probability distribution where the highest probabilities centered around the middle point with probabilities tailing off quickly as one moved away from the center. Once the incubation period is over, the incidence period begins. Here, the probability distribution is shaped just the opposite as the first one describing the contracting of the Virus. Where before, the chance of contracting the Virus is small in the early years and increases thereafter, the chance of developing the disease is relatively large in the early years, tapering off thereafter.

For purposes of illustration, suppose that there are 10,000 infected individuals. Suppose that the experts feel that the timing of the contraction, the incubation, and incidence periods of the Virus have the following probability distributions.

PROBABILITY DISTRIBUTION FOR TIMING OF INFECTION

YEARS AFTER START OF ALPHA INCURSION	DISCRETE PROBABILITY	CUMULATIVE PROBABILITY
1	1%	1%
2	3	4
3	6	10
4	15	25
5	25	50
6	25	75
7	15	90
8	5	95
9	3	98
10	2	100

PROBABILITY DISTRIBUTION FOR LENGTH OF INCUBATION PERIOD

YEARS AFTER INFECTION BY VIRUS	DISCRETE PROBABILITY	CUMULATIVE PROBABILITY
3	10%	10%
4	20	30
5	30	60
6	30	90
7	10	100

PROBABILITY DISTRIBUTION FOR LENGTH OF INCIDENCE PERIOD

YEARS AFTER INCUBATION PERIOD	DISCRETE PROBABILITY	CUMULATIVE PROBABILITY
1	11%	11%
2	10	21
3	9	30
4	8	38
5	7	45
6	6	51
7	5	56
8	4	60
9	4	64
10	4	68
11	3	71
12	3	74

YEARS AFTER INCUBATION PERIOD	DISCRETE PROBABILITY	CUMULATIVE PROBABILITY
13	3	77
14	2	79
15	2	81
16	2	83
17	2	85
18	1	86
19	1	87
20	1	88
21	1	89
22	1	90
23	1	91
24	1	92
25	1	93
26	1	94
27	1	95
28	1	96
29	1	97
30	1	98
31	1	99
32	1	100

These probability distributions form a scenario for predicting the demand for health care services and products. The assessment of the size of the market can be first related to the demand for services for a population of 10,000 infected individuals. The heart of a simulation for forecasting the market demand for health care services and products for a population of 10,000 infected individuals is described as follows.

FOR EACH OF THE 10,000 INDIVIDUALS

DRAW A RANDOM NUMBER BETWEEN ONE AND ONE HUNDRED
DETERMINE TIMING OF INFECTION FROM START OF ALPHA INCURSION

DRAW A RANDOM NUMBER BETWEEN ONE AND ONE HUNDRED
DETERMINE LENGTH OF INCUBATION PERIOD

DRAW A RANDOM NUMBER BETWEEN ONE AND ONE HUNDRED
DETERMINE LENGTH OF INCIDENCE PERIOD

ADD UP THE THREE TIME PERIODS

KEEP TRACK OF THE RESULTS

This is the essence of the program contained in the appendix. In addition, the entire process was repeated one hundred times. The following table shows the minimum, maximum, and average demand for health care services, or products, from these one hundred simulations for a twenty-year period after the Alpha Incursion made his debut.

YEAR AFTER START OF ALPHA INCURSION	FORECAST OF DEMAND FOR HOSPITAL BEDS		
	MINIMUM	AVERAGE	MAXIMUM
1		0	
2		0	
3		0	
4		0	
5	0	1	4
6	1	7	12
7	12	22	34
8	39	63	90
9	123	151	191
10	254	287	323
11	428	473	515
12	585	641	695
13	675	753	810
14	716	772	830
15	683	730	810
16	597	654	718
17	531	578	640
18	452	504	571
19	401	447	495
20	351	398	435

Exhibit 9.3 illustrates the forecast for the demand for beds for a presumed infected population of 10,000.

Exhibit 9.3 can be normalized—that is, the figure holds for 10,000 infected individuals or any multiple of 10,000. The general shape of the figure would not differ for 100,000 or 1 million infected individuals. At the peak year, roughly 6 to 8 percent of the total infected population will require hospitalization. If, hypothetically, this were a valid model for the Virus, and if this were the tenth year after the Alpha Incursion, then the current annual demand for hospital beds represents about 3 percent of the total case load and the demand for hospital beds will more than double over the next three or four years.

Unfortunately, how does one know if this is a valid model? The experts disagree on everything. Suppose, for the sake of discussion there is general agreement on the structure of the model. That is, there are three distinct time elements—the timing of the spread of the Virus, the incubation period, and the incidence period. However, there are three opinions on the probability distribution associated with the spread of the disease, four opinions on the probability distribution of the incubation period, and five opinions on the probability distribution of the incidence period. This would generate sixty individual forecasts.

Now the problem becomes selecting the right forecast out of sixty. This may not be quite as impossible as it might appear. First, those forecasts containing longer incubation periods and shorter incidence periods may be very similar to forecasts of shorter incubation periods and longer incidence periods. In other words, there may be combinations of assessments by the experts that end up with a very similar forecast. Thus the sixty individual forecasts may be represented by

NUMBER BEDS VERSUS TIME

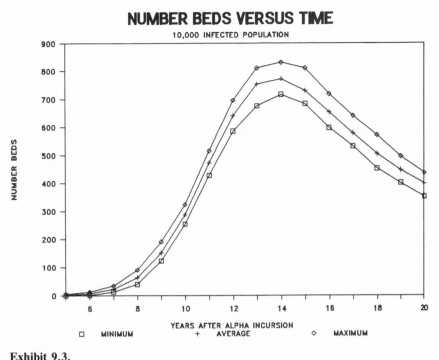

Exhibit 9.3.
Number Beds Versus Time (10,000 infected population)

as few as six aggregate or "families" of forecasts. Each family of forecasts has approximately the same profile as to the future demand for hospital beds, but are made up of different combinations of assessments by the various experts.

Which of these is best? Or is the task of predicting the number of hospital beds essentially impossible? Where there is breath, there is hope. Now the hard data of the historic demand for beds can be put to work. Of the six or so families of forecasts, there may be one or two that cannot be made to fit the actual case history of bed demand. There is no assumed size of an infected population that would generate a forecast of demand for hospital beds that would fit the actual history of demand. The forecast of demand is either leading or lagging actual demand for any reasonable estimate on the total infected population. Therefore, it appears reasonable to eliminate these particular families of forecasts.

However, more information can be gleaned from this culling of forecasts. The family of forecasts is made up of combinations of individual forecasts, which, more or less, ended up with the same general forecast. Could it be that certain experts have individual forecasts that make up the family of forecasts which are about to be discarded? It is not the family of forecasts that should be culled, but the experts who seem to be heavily represented in these forecasts.

Thus there begins a reiterative process where time adds hard data which may or may not confirm the assessments of particular experts. The culling of experts, whose assessments of the situation lead to forecasts that cannot be confirmed with actual data, reduces the number of combinations of opinions which have to be considered. And, hopefully, with the passing of time, the opinions of the experts hone in on the actual factors that describe the situation. The desired end result is when all the eligible families of forecasts can be boxed into one neat little package where one can say that the peak load will be in A to B years, at a level which represents L to M multiple of the current number of patients, and that the total case load over the next ten years is expected to be between X and Y number of patients. And, equally as hopeful, the values of A and B, L and M, X and Y are reasonable estimates of what will actually transpire.

Appendix to Chapter 9

ASSESSING AN UNKNOWN MARKET SIMULATION

Three simulation programs are mentioned in this chapter. The first concerns the spread of the Virus among a population of 10,000 at-risk Groups and is entitled SPREAD. The second involves the determination of those requiring medical attention once the incidence period starts. This program is entitled AFFLICT. The third simulation program is the forecast for the demand for hospital beds and is entitled BEDFORC.

SPREAD Program

An array of 100 by 100 represents each individual Group for a total of 10,000 Groups. A value of 0 means that the Group is not infected, whereas a value of 1 means that the group is infected. Statement 30 ensures that the simulation starts with a non-infected population. Over a 400-week period (statement 50), the Alpha Incursion infects one Group randomly (statements 60–140). Statement 60 permits any number of Groups to be infected by the Alpha Incursion on a weekly basis, but this was hardly necessary. One a week was damaging enough. Statements 150–340 give each of the 10,000 Groups a 2 percent chance (statement 180) to enter into a Liaison. If one of the parties associated with a Liaison is infected (statements 280 and 290), then there is a 50 percent chance that the infection will not be transmitted (statement 300). If it is, both parties walk away from the encounter infected (statement 320). The N value in statement 190 permits more than one Liaison—again, hardly necessary in view of the speed which the Virus can spread with a Liaison restricted to one Group at a time.

The program entitled PSPREAD listed at the end of SPREAD printed out the results in thirteen-week intervals.

```
10 REM NAME OF PROGRAM IS SPREAD
20 DIM A(100,100)
30 FOR I=1 TO 100:FOR J=1 TO 100:A(I,J)=0:NEXT:NEXT
40 OPEN "O",#1,"SPREADF"
50 FOR W=1 TO 400
60 FOR K=1 TO 1
70 X=RND(X)
80 I=INT(100*X+.5)
90 IF I=0 THEN 70
100 X=RND(X)
110 J=INT(100*X+.5)
```

```
120 IF J=0 THEN 100
130 A(I,J)=1
140 NEXT
150 FOR I=1 TO 100
160 FOR J=1 TO 100
170 X=RND(X)
180 IF X<.02 THEN 190 ELSE 200
190 N=1:GOTO 210
200 N=0
210 IF N=0 THEN 340
220 X=RND(X)
230 I1=INT(100*X+.5)
240 IF I1=0 THEN 220
250 X=RND(X)
260 J1=INT(100*X+.5)
270 IF J1=0 THEN 250
280 IF A(I,J)=1 THEN 300
290 IF A(I1,J1)=1 THEN 300 ELSE 330
300 X=RND(X)
310 IF X<.5 THEN 320 ELSE 330
320 A(I,J)=1:A(I1,J1)=1
330 N=N-1:GOTO 210
340 NEXT:NEXT
350 A=0
360 FOR I=1 TO 100
370 FOR J=1 TO 100
380 A=A+A(I,J)
390 NEXT:NEXT
400 PRINT W,A
410 WRITE #1,W,A
420 NEXT
430 CLOSE #1:END


10 REM NAME OF PROGRAM IS PSPREAD
20 DIM B(900)
25 FOR I=1 TO 900:B(I)=0:NEXT
30 OPEN "I",#1,"SPREADF"
40 INPUT #1,W,A
45 B(W)=A
50 IF EOF(1) THEN 60 ELSE 40
60 CLOSE #1
100 FOR I=13 TO 897 STEP 13
105 IF B(I)=0 THEN 120
110 PRINT I,B(I):INPUT Z$
120 NEXT
130 END
```

AFFLICT Program

Over a 480-month period (statement 50), the unafflicted population represented by the variable P is exposed to a monthly lottery (statement 90) as to whether the Virus enters its active stage when medical treatment is required. Statements 70–110 perform this lottery over the 480-month period and keep track of the results. Statements 120–190 print out a summary of those afflicted annually.

```
10 REM NAME OF PROGRAM IS AFFLICT
20 DIM A(480):DIM F(40)
30 INPUT "MONTHLY AFFLICTION RATE AS %: ";M
40 P=10000:A=0
50 FOR I=1 TO 480
60 A=0
70 FOR J=1 TO P
80 X=100*RND(X)
90 IF X<=M THEN 100 ELSE 110
100 A=A+1
110 NEXT:A(I)=A:P=P-A:A=0:NEXT
120 A=0:FOR I=1 TO 240:A=A+A(I):NEXT
130 PRINT "TOTAL AFFLICTED: ";A
140 FOR Y=1 TO 40
150 A=0
160 FOR I=12*(Y-1)+1 TO 12*Y
170 A=A+A(I)
180 NEXT:F(Y)=A:NEXT
190 FOR I=1 TO 40:PRINT I,F(I):INPUT Z$:NEXT:END
```

BEDFORC Program

The number of repetitions to obtain the minimum and maximum values of the forecast for the demand for hospital beds is assigned in statement 40. The summary description of this program provided in the chapter is repeated here with the appropriate statement numbers appended.

FOR EACH OF THE 10,000 INDIVIDUALS
(Statement 80)

DRAW A RANDOM NUMBER BETWEEN ONE AND ONE HUNDRED
DETERMINE TIMING OF INFECTION FROM START OF ALPHA INCURSION
(Statements 90–290)

DRAW A RANDOM NUMBER BETWEEN ONE AND ONE HUNDRED
DETERMINE DURATION OF INCUBATION PERIOD
(Statements 300–400)

DRAW A RANDOM NUMBER BETWEEN ONE AND ONE HUNDRED
DETERMINE DURATION OF INCIDENCE PERIOD
(Statements 410–1050)

ADD UP THE THREE TIME PERIODS
(Statement 1060)

KEEP TRACK OF THE RESULTS
(Statements 1070–1150)

The results of the simulation are printed in statements 1170–1210.

```
10 REM NAME OF PROGRAM IS BEDFORC
20 DIM B(100):DIM D(3,100)
30 FOR J=1 TO 100:D(1,J)=100000!:D(2,J)=0:D(3,J)=0:NEXT
40 PRINT:INPUT "ENTER NUMBER OF SIMULATIONS: ";S
50 FOR J=1 TO S
60 FOR I=1 TO 100:B(I)=0:NEXT
70 PRINT J
80 FOR I=1 TO 10000
90 X=100*RND(X)
100 IF X<1 THEN 200
110 IF X<4 THEN 210
120 IF X<10 THEN 220
130 IF X<25 THEN 230
140 IF X<50 THEN 240
150 IF X<75 THEN 250
160 IF X<90 THEN 260
170 IF X<95 THEN 270
180 IF X<98 THEN 280
190 GOTO 290
200 Y1=1:GOTO 300
210 Y1=2:GOTO 300
220 Y1=3:GOTO 300
230 Y1=4:GOTO 300
240 Y1=5:GOTO 300
250 Y1=6:GOTO 300
260 Y1=7:GOTO 300
270 Y1=8:GOTO 300
280 Y1=9:GOTO 300
290 Y1=10:GOTO 300
300 X=100*RND(X)
310 IF X<10 THEN 360
320 IF X<30 THEN 370
330 IF X<60 THEN 380
340 IF X<90 THEN 390
350 GOTO 400
360 Y2=3:GOTO 410
370 Y2=4:GOTO 410
380 Y2=5:GOTO 410
390 Y2=6:GOTO 410
```

```
400  Y2=7:GOTO 410
410  X=100*RND(X)
420  IF X<11 THEN 740
430  IF X<21 THEN 750
440  IF X<30 THEN 760
450  IF X<38 THEN 770
460  IF X<45 THEN 780
470  IF X<51 THEN 790
480  IF X<56 THEN 800
490  IF X<60 THEN 810
500  IF X<64 THEN 820
510  IF X<68 THEN 830
520  IF X<71 THEN 840
530  IF X<74 THEN 850
540  IF X<77 THEN 860
550  IF X<79 THEN 870
560  IF X<81 THEN 880
570  IF X<83 THEN 890
580  IF X<85 THEN 900
590  IF X<86 THEN 910
600  IF X<87 THEN 920
610  IF X<88 THEN 930
620  IF X<89 THEN 940
630  IF X<90 THEN 950
640  IF X<91 THEN 960
650  IF X<92 THEN 970
660  IF X<93 THEN 980
670  IF X<94 THEN 990
680  IF X<95 THEN 1000
690  IF X<96 THEN 1010
700  IF X<97 THEN 1020
710  IF X<98 THEN 1030
720  IF X<99 THEN 1040
730  GOTO 1050
740  Y3=1:GOTO 1060
750  Y3=2:GOTO 1060
760  Y3=3:GOTO 1060
770  Y3=4:GOTO 1060
780  Y3=5:GOTO 1060
790  Y3=6:GOTO 1060
800  Y3=7:GOTO 1060
810  Y3=8:GOTO 1060
820  Y3=9:GOTO 1060
830  Y3=10:GOTO 1060
840  Y3=11:GOTO 1060
850  Y3=12:GOTO 1060
```

```
860  Y3=13:GOTO 1060
870  Y3=14:GOTO 1060
880  Y3=15:GOTO 1060
890  Y3=16:GOTO 1060
900  Y3=17:GOTO 1060
910  Y3=18:GOTO 1060
920  Y3=19:GOTO 1060
930  Y3=20:GOTO 1060
940  Y3=21:GOTO 1060
950  Y3=22:GOTO 1060
960  Y3=23:GOTO 1060
970  Y3=24:GOTO 1060
980  Y3=25:GOTO 1060
990  Y3=26:GOTO 1060
1000 Y3=27:GOTO 1060
1010 Y3=28:GOTO 1060
1020 Y3=29:GOTO 1060
1030 Y3=30:GOTO 1060
1040 Y3=31:GOTO 1060
1050 Y3=32
1060 Y=Y1+Y2+Y3
1070 B(Y)=B(Y)+1
1080 NEXT
1090 FOR I=1 TO 100
1100 IF B(I)<D(1,I) THEN 1110 ELSE 1120
1110 D(1,I)=B(I)
1120 IF B(I)>D(3,I) THEN 1130 ELSE 1140
1130 D(3,I)=B(I)
1140 D(2,I)=D(2,I)+B(I)
1150 NEXT
1160 NEXT
1170 FOR I=1 TO 100:D(2,I)=D(2,I)/S:NEXT
1180 FOR I=1 TO 100
1190 IF D(2,I)=0 THEN 1210
1200 PRINT I,D(1,I),D(2,I),D(3,I):INPUT Z$
1210 NEXT:END
```

10

Establishing an Economic Benefit

SYNOPSIS

Those who are responsible for dispersing funds, private or public, possess the inherent right to establish the rules by which requests and proposals are submitted and judged. If requests or proposals are not submitted in the proper format with all the required supporting documentation, they are returned to the originator with a curt note either to comply with the rules or withdraw the request. Once a request or proposal is in compliance with the applicable rules and regulations, then it is placed in the hopper for further consideration.

Until recently, the administrators responsible for selecting environmental improvement projects for funding did not require an analysis of the economic benefit of the project. The analysis was not part of the request for consideration for funding. Arguments in favor of a particular project—for example, a project that would result in a cleaner ocean environment—were supported by qualitative assertions on the benefits of having clean ocean waters. This was all that was needed for the justification for the expenditure of public funds.

The consequence of this form of justification was that an environmental improvement project for cleaner ocean waters found itself in the same domain with other desirable projects such as medical care for the elderly and the war against drugs. All these projects are desirable. All should be accomplished if desirability were the sole criterion. However, the availability of public funds cannot support all desirable projects. Some have to be eliminated.

Suppose that the government agency responsible for administrating applications for funding of environmental improvement projects changes the rules by which requests are evaluated. Now the agency requires that proposals for spending public funds on environmental improvement projects, such as cleaner ocean waters, be accompanied with documentation supporting the economic justification of the project.

The motive for changing the rules is not to prevent environmental improvement projects for cleaner ocean waters from being funded. Rather, the purpose is to transform an expense item on an operating budget into a capital investment whose economic benefits self-liquidate the cost of the project. The transformation of an expenditure into a capital investment also transforms the funding of the project. Before the transformation, the funding of an environmentally attractive project to clean up the ocean waters contributed to the government's operating deficit. After the transformation, the project can be financed by the issuance of bonds where the economic benefit of the project, in the form of enhanced tax revenues, can meet the interest and amortization payments of the bonds issued to fund the project.

The administrators of public funds for environmental improvement projects are asking for something they had not asked for before: the economic justification of the project itself. As understandable as that request might be from the point of view of those funding the project, a company in the business of constructing large-scale waste treatment plants finds itself in a position of trying to economically justify something that has never been economically justified before.

The company had no difficulty dealing with the qualitative desirability of having clean ocean waters. No one challenged the points that the tourist and fishing industries had been adversely affected by polluted offshore waters. There is no question that these industries would benefit from cleaner waters. However, there is a question on how one would quantitatively measure a qualitatively desirable course of action.

The essential nature of the problem is that the data, which is available to describe the problem, is not in a form that makes it amenable to addressing the nature of the question being posed. The question being posed is how would the expenditure of funds for an improvement of the ocean environment be justified as a return on investment before the fact—that is, as a precondition for approving the project. The data supports the obvious in that the ocean has been degradated through pollution. The data, at least in the present format, does not directly address the issue of how the tourist and fishing industries would benefit from actions taken to clean up the environment in quantitative terms.

This chapter proposes a framework of analysis that a company could take in response to this requirement. The requirement to economically justify environmental improvement projects is understandable. However, there is no existing basis for analyzing the economic benefits of a cleaner ocean because there has never been a requirement to do so. How would a company go about estimating the economic benefit of a cleaner ocean environment? Simulation can be part of a general framework of analysis to accomplish this objective.

The framework of analysis discussed in this chapter is not simply another example of the use of simulation in the planning process for making decisions. The framework of analysis is a response that could be taken by a company in the waste treatment business to the challenge posed by government administrators to economically justify an environmental improvement project for cleaner ocean waters.

THE GENERAL NATURE OF THE FRAMEWORK OF ANALYSIS

The general nature of the proposed framework of analysis is to utilize a combination of statistics, assessments by marine biology and pollution control experts on the impact of a particular project on the ocean environment, and computer simulation. A conventional statistical methodology is used to link economic indices such as number of tourists and the quantity of fish caught in offshore waters to various indices of environmental degradation. Assessments by marine biology experts as to how a proposed project will affect the ocean environment is incorporated into a simulation. The simulation model combines the assessments made by marine biologists with the statistical relationship linking the economic factors with indices of environmental degradation. Its output will be in the form of a probability distribution describing the range of likely results to the tourist industry, and to the fishing industry, of a particular environmental improvement project.

The impact of the proposed environmental improvement project on the enhanced number of tourists and on the enhanced fish catches is then analyzed as to its implication to the economy of the shore communities. Enhanced levels of business have a direct bearing of incremental tax receipts for the government. The incremental tax receipts can then be compared to the cost of the project. The comparison of the cost of the project with the incremental tax receipts stemming from the restoration of the tourist trade and the revival of the fishing industry form the basis of assessing the capacity of a project to self-liquidate. If the economic benefits are sufficient to justify the self-liquidation of the proposed project, then the project can be funded as a capital investment whose return can support the interest and amortization payments of the underlying debt.

The framework of analysis consists of four elements. The first is the construction of a statistical relationship between economic and environmental indices. The second is an assessment by marine biologists and environmental engineers as to the impact of a particular project on the environmental indices of pollution. The third is the translation of this assessment to an economic benefit through a simulation program that links the statistical model of economic and environmental indices to the assessment by knowledgeable experts as to the project's ability to reduce offshore pollution. The fourth, and final step, is the linking of the economic benefit to the cost of the project to measure its capacity to self-liquidate.

THE STATISTICAL LINKING OF THE ECONOMY AND THE ENVIRONMENT

The statistical relationship linking indicators of economic activity of the shore to indicators of pollution of the offshore waters is known as regression analysis. As regression analysis plays an important role in the methodology being proposed, perhaps an explanation would be appropriate.

Suppose that an indicator of economic activity is the number of tourists visiting the shore. Actually what would be more desirable is the number of tourist-days, as the length of stay is just as important as the number of tourists. This could be expressed as the actual number of tourist-days, or as an index to a base year. As an example, suppose that the base year index was 12 million tourist-days, and the current year has an estimate of 8 million tourist-days. The data can be expressed either in absolute terms as millions of tourist-days or in relative terms as an index value to the base year.

YEAR	MILLIONS TOURIST–DAYS	INDEX OF TOURIST–DAYS
BASE	12.0	100
•	•	•
•	•	•
•	•	•
CURRENT	8.0	67

An index value is obtained by taking the current figure of tourist-days and comparing it with the base year figure. The current figure of 8 million tourist-days is compared to the base year of 12 million tourist-days to obtain the current index value of 67 (8 million is 67 percent of the base of 12 million). Once the index value for any year is determined, it can be referred to the base year to obtain the absolute figure. Sixty-seven percent of 12 million tourist-days yields the current 8 million tourist-days. Index values will be used here as a substitute for the real data. Obviously, the potential success of the proposed framework of analysis does rely on the existence of a data bank of information concerning both economic activity of the shore community and the degradation of the ocean environment.

There are a number of indicators of environmental degradation. These include bacteria count in the water, turbidity or degree of clarity of the water (or lack thereof), flotsam or floating debris, and rainbow tides, which are uncontrollable outbreaks of various algae. For the sake of illustration, suppose that one type of bacteria count is selected as an indicator of environmental degradation, and further suppose that the following indices of economic well-being and environmental degradation are applicable over a ten-year period of time.

YEAR	INDEX OF TOURIST–DAYS	INDEX OF BACTERIA COUNT
1	88	127
2	86	130
3	86	128
4	87	132
5	84	134
6	82	130
7	80	135
8	81	137
9	83	140
10	80	138

A cursory examination of the two columns of data shows that the economic index (tourist-days) is decreasing while the environmental degradation index (bacteria count) is increasing. Regression analysis is a statistical method to measure the correlation between tourist-days and bacteria count without reference to time. Time does link two data points of tourist-days and bacteria count, but the end result is an assessment of the relationship between tourist-days and bacteria count. Correlation is the measure of the fit between tourist-days and bacteria count in terms of a linear relationship: Tourist-Days=a + b (Bacteria Count) where a is a constant and b is the slope of a straight line.

Exhibit 10.1 is the scatter diagram of the data of tourist-days versus bacteria count and the ''best fitting'' straight line passing through the data points. The best fitting straight line will eventually be used as the basis for obtaining predictions of the index value for tourist-days for a given index value of bacteria count.

A perfect correlation is defined as all the data points falling on the best fitting straight line. Under these conditions, the coefficient of correlation is defined to have a value of 100 percent. Obviously, from Exhibit 10.1, the data points do not fall on the straight line. The best fitting line, which is called the regression equation, passes through the data points in such a way that the vertical distances between the observed points, and the points on the line, are minimized. Regres-

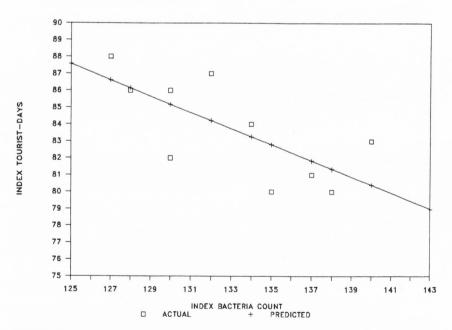

Exhibit 10.1.
Tourist-Days versus Bacteria Count

sion analysis calculates the constant, or y-intercept, and the slope of the best fitting line. The resulting regression equation can be used to predict the index of tourist-days for a given index level of the bacteria count depending on the degree of correlation: Index Tourist-Days=147.3962 − 0.47855 (Index Bacteria Count).

The degree of correlation (technically, the coefficient of determination) between the data points and the best fitting straight line is 51.2873 percent. Fifty percent is usually considered the minimum value for utilizing the regression equation for prediction purposes.

Multiple regression is an attempt to create a better model by adding more variables. Suppose that the previous data base can be examined by including an index for flotsam.

YEAR	INDEX OF TOURIST-DAYS	INDEX OF BACTERIA COUNT	INDEX OF FLOTSAM
1	88	127	156
2	86	130	153
3	86	128	157
4	87	132	161
5	84	134	163
6	82	130	165
7	80	135	167
8	81	137	170
9	83	140	168
10	80	138	172

Regression analysis can calculate the best fitting line through the data points, bearing in mind that the line is now a plane in three-dimensional space. The resulting regression equation is this: Index Tourist-Days=181.267 − 0.04127 (Index Bacteria Count) − 0.57332 (Index Flotsam).

The coefficient of determination, or degree of correlation, is 80.1811 percent, a marked increase from the earlier model. Generally, the degree of correlation improves as the number of variables and the volume of data increase. The Standard Error of the Estimate, the SEE, is 1.487. The SEE is used to obtain an estimate of the spread, or the range, of values around a specific prediction. This can be best demonstrated by an illustration.

Note that the latest year has a tourist-day index of 80 with a bacteria count index of 138 and a flotsam index of 172. Suppose that there is a project being considered which is anticipated to reduce the bacteria count to 130 and the flotsam index to 160. What would be the predicted tourist-day index for these values of the bacteria count and flotsam indices?

Index Tourist-Days=181.267 − 0.04127 (Index Bacteria Count) − 0.57332 (Index Flotsam)

Index Tourist-Days=181.267 − (0.04127)(130) − (0.57332)(160)

Index Tourist-Days=181.267 − 5.3651 − 91.7312 = 84.1707

The predicted impact of the project under consideration is to increase the tourist-days from a current reading of 80 to 84, or about a 5 percent increase in the level of business. This is a statistical prediction, not a law of nature. The prediction depends on the causal relationship between tourist-days, as the dependent variable, and the changes in the independent variables (indices of bacteria count and flotsam), remaining unchanged as the indices of pollution are reduced. This may, or may not, be reflected in reality. The nature of a statistical relationship is not the same as the physical relationship describing the distance an object will cover for a given speed and time. One can be 100 percent confident that if a person travels at a speed of 50 miles per hour for one hour, he will cover fifty miles regardless of the circumstances. This same degree of certainty does not hold for a statistical relationship such as a regression equation linking economic activity to the ocean environment.

However, if the causal relationship underlying the statistical equation does hold, then the predicted tourist index will be 84 plus and minus a certain range of values to take into consideration the inherent spread in the data that makes up the regression equation. The SEE provides the basis for the likelihood for the actual value to fall within prescribed ranges about the predicted value. Basically, one can be about 68 percent confident that the actual index of tourist-days will fall within the range of the predicted index of tourist-days plus or minus the SEE. One can be 95 percent confident that the actual index of tourist-days will fall within the range of the predicted index plus or minus twice the SEE.

The 68 percent confidence level is 84.1707 +/− 1.487, or a range in index of tourist-days from 82.6837 to 85.6577. The 95 percent confidence level is achieved in the range of 84.1707 +/− 2.974 (2 × SEE), or a range in the index of tourist-days between 81.1967 and 87.1447.

Regression analysis can be used to identify which variables have the greatest influence, in a statistical sense, on the index of tourist-days. In the previous example, which is a purely arbitrary set of data, a given reduction in the index of flotsam has a much greater impact on the increase in tourist-days than does an equivalent reduction in the index of bacteria count. Such a model might suggest that it might be a better investment to take actions to reduce open ocean dumping than to reduce the bacteria count. This can be appreciated by the fact that tourists see flotsam, whereas bacteria are not usually apparent to the naked eye.

The t-statistic is a mechanism to measure the effect a particular variable is having on the final model. Variables with low t-statistic values can be eliminated from the model because they are not contributing to the final regression equation. In other words, removing a variable with a low t-statistic from the final model may not change, or may even improve, the degree of correlation.

Measurements of collinearity between variables can be used to reduce the number of variables. For instance, there may be three different types of bacteria counts. Yet having the data on all three bacteria counts may not be necessary because all are rising and falling in unison. A high degree of collinearity means that the final model may be just as good with one, or two, rather than three types of bacteria counts.

The t-statistic associated with individual variables and measures of collinearity between variables are merely details for building a multiple regression model. The importance of this discussion is to point to the general methodology of creating separate models for the two chief components that measure the activity of the shoreside economy: the tourist and fishing industries. The two multiple regression models would be similar in many respects but would have some differences in structure. The following is an initial proposal for the construction of two multiple regression models to illustrate their basic structure.

	TOURIST INDUSTRY	FISHING INDUSTRY
DEPENDENT VARIABLE	Tourist-Days	Annual Catch

The dependent variable is the economic activity being measured and is the object of the prediction. Its value depends on what values are assigned to the independent variables. Tourist-days are the number of tourists multiplied by the days spent on the shore. It is a physical measurement and is not expressed in monetary terms. This eliminates inflation from the model. Once the number of tourist-days has been predicted, it can then be changed to a monetary measurement when multiplied by the average amount of money spent per tourist-day.

The same consideration holds for the measure of the economic activity of the fishing industry. It is preferable that its measurement be in physical, not monetary, terms as pollution affects the fish population in offshore waters. If the annual catch is expressed in monetary terms, the model is muddled with the changing price of fish, which is not germane to the intent of the analysis.

	TOURIST INDUSTRY	FISHING INDUSTRY
INDEPENDENT VARIABLES		
ENVIRONMENTAL	Bacteria Count Turbidity Flotsam Rainbow Tides	Bacteria Count Turbidity Flotsam Rainbow Tides
DEMOGRAPHIC	Population within Access of Shore Region	
ECONOMIC	Gross National Product Discretionary Spending	
DIETARY		Fish Consumption

This is an initial listing of a possible modeling of both the tourist and fishing industries. Some of the data may not be available, which might eliminate a variable. Perhaps other variables may be added. This is a function of the nature of the underlying data base. Nevertheless, the objective of this phase of the project would be to construct a multiple regression model linking these variables, or others, to a physical aspect of both the tourist and fishing industries. The two models act as links between the economy and the environment. The general format of the resulting regression equations based on the proposed initial listing of independent variables would be as follows.

$$\text{Tourist-Days} = a1 + b1(\text{Bacteria Count}) + b2(\text{Turbidity}) +$$
$$b3(\text{Flotsam}) + b4(\text{Rainbow Tides}) +$$
$$b5(\text{Population}) + b6(\text{Gross National}$$
$$\text{Product}) + b7(\text{Discretionary Spending})$$
$$\text{Annual Catch} = a2 + b8(\text{Bacteria Count}) + b9(\text{Turbidity}) +$$
$$b10(\text{Flotsam}) + b11(\text{Rainbow Tides}) +$$
$$b12(\text{Fish Consumption})$$

ASSESSMENTS BY EXPERTS

The opinions of experts are required in two areas. One is an opinion as to the reduction in the degree of pollutants entering the offshore waters for the project under consideration. The second opinion evolves around the impact on the indicators of pollution if the project were completed. The former opinion is an engineering opinion. A designer of a waste treatment plant can perform an input/output analysis of the proposed project to arrive at an opinion as to what degree of reduction of pollution will be achieved by the construction of the plant. This assessment would be quantitative in nature with a fairly high degree of confidence in that the variation around the assessment would be quite narrow.

The opinion as to the impact on the quality of offshore waters if the waste treatment plant were built probably would be more qualitative in nature requiring the combined efforts of a team of marine biologists, and possibly other specialists. This assessment will have to include a knowledge of the total amount of pollution entering the offshore waters, the reduction in pollution associated with the proposed project, and the impact of this reduction of pollution on the various indicators describing the ocean environment. The assessment will require the knowledge of specialists in tides, currents, wind, and other factors affecting the dispersal, and movements, of pollutants in the marine environment. Probably other disciplines associated with the study of the marine environment may have to be involved. Regardless of who has to be involved, these specialists must come up with assessments as to the environmental impact of a pollution control project on the indicators of pollution of the offshore waters incorporated in the model linking the economy with the environment.

Their assessments need not be discrete, or single value. The assessments would be in the following format for each of the indicators of pollution that are contained in the final model linking the number of tourist-days and the quantity of the fish catch to the measure of the degree of environmental degradation.

What is the minimum impact the project would have on the measure of pollution?
What is the most likely impact the project would have on the measure of pollution?
What is the maximum impact the project would have on the measure of pollution?

These three assessments would have to be asked about each of the measures of environmental degradation. Presumably the marine biologists and other specialists can make these assessments. Various techniques can be brought to bear to encourage the expeditious conclusion of this matter. Some degree of expeditiousness is necessary as the querying of expert opinions is not an invitation to start a decade-long study, but to bring to the table the experience of a lifetime in a particular discipline for the purposes of arriving at an assessment.

One such way of arriving at opinions with some degree of efficiency is the Delphi method. The Delphi method has certain variations built around a central theme. Basically, the Delphi method is a meeting of experts—hopefully, in not too comfortable circumstances or surroundings. The purpose of the meeting is for the experts to arrive at a consensus concerning the environmental consequences of a proposed project.

Prior to the meeting, the experts are supplied with the factual material pertaining to the project under consideration. Drawing on their respective areas of expertise, the experts make their private assessments as to the impact of the project on improving the marine environment. These assessments are written down and forwarded to the organizer of the meeting. The organizer collates the information and publishes a summary of the results of the survey. The summary does not reference the opinions of particular individuals. The summary of the survey is given to the participants before the meeting is scheduled, or at the initial meeting. Either way, the purpose of the meeting is for experts of diverging views to express their opinion backed up with whatever factual documentation of their past endeavors reinforces their own opinions or demolishes the opinions of others.

After due deliberation, the survey is repeated and another discussion follows. This process continues until there is general agreement as to what impact the project will have on the various measures of the environmental degradation of the offshore waters. Again, discrete values are not necessary. The consensus is in the form of a minimum, most likely, and maximum assessments as to the impact of a project on the ocean environment.

For purposes of illustration, suppose that the final model for predicting the tourist-day index is as follows: Tourist-Day Index $= 250 - 0.5$ (Pollution Measure 1) $- 0.4$ (Pollution Measure 2) $- 0.3$ (Pollution Measure 3) $+ 0.1$ (Population Index) $+ 0.2$ (Discretionary Spending Index).

The experts were called together concerning what impact a proposed project might have on the three measures of pollution. Prior to the meeting, the experts made their initial estimates. The findings were publicized without reference to the individuals making the estimates and were discussed at the initial meeting. Then the experts were again polled, and results of the survey were discussed again in an open forum. The procedure was repeated until consensus was reached as to the impact of the project on the three measures of ocean pollution. Suppose that the consensus of the experts is shown as follows.

		ASSESSMENT OF POLLUTION MEASURE IF PROJECT WERE COMPLETED		
POLLUTION MEASURE	PRESENT READING	MINIMUM READING	MOST LIKELY READING	MAXIMUM READING
1	210	170	180	200
2	150	120	135	140
3	175	150	165	170

The next step in the framework of analysis is to take these assessments and make a judgment as to their impact on the shore economy.

THE SIMULATION TO DERIVE THE ECONOMIC BENEFIT OF A PROJECT

The CUMDIST program can take the assessments of pollution measures and translate them into a simulator. The simulator is actually the cumulative distribution curve where the minimum reading represents the 0 percent cumulative probability point, the mostly likely reading represents the 50 percent cumulative probability point, and the maximum reading represents the 100 percent probability point. The scaling factor built into the computer program addresses the issue as to how unlikely are the minimum and maximum readings. If the assessment to the degree of unlikeliness is that it is quite unlikely that the project would actually experience the minimum or maximum readings, then a scaling factor of 0.3, or lower, would be appropriate. If the assessment on the degree of unlikeliness is couched in less emphatic terms, then a higher scaling factor is appropriate. A consensus on this matter would have to be reached at the Delphi meeting in addition to the previously provided assessments.

In terms of Pollution Measure 1, a scaling factor of 0.3 creates the following cumulative distribution.

POLLUTION MEASURE 1	CUMULATIVE PROBABILITY DISTRIBUTION
170	0
177	25
180	50
186	75
200	100

The following simulators for the three measures of pollution (illustrated in Exhibits 10.2, 10.3, and 10.4) are merely the cumulative probability distribution curves with the horizontal scale changed from 0 to 100 to a scale of 1 to 1,000. A scaling factor of 0.3 was used to generate the simulators.

As previously mentioned, the presumed model linking the economic activity of the shore community in terms of tourist-days with the quality of the ocean environment and with the population who may visit the shore region, and with the willingness to spend money on vacations, is presumed to be as follows: Tourist-Day Index=250 − 0.5 (Pollution Measure 1) − 0.4 (Pollution Measure 2) − 0.3 (Pollution Measure 3) + 0.1 (Population Index) + 0.2 (Discretionary Spending Index).

Suppose that the independent variables have the following values prior to the approval of the environmental improvement project under consideration.

INDEPENDENT VARIABLE	CURRENT VALUE
Pollution Measure 1	210
Pollution Measure 2	150
Pollution Measure 3	175
Population Index	145
Discretionary Spending Index	165

These values can be substituted into the regression equation to obtain a tourist-day index value if the project is not completed.

Tourist-Day Index=250 − 0.5 (Pollution Measure 1) −

0.4 (Pollution Measure 2) − 0.3 (Pollution Measure 3) +

0.1 (Population Index) + 0.2 (Discretionary Spending Index)

Tourist-Day Index=250 − 0.5(210) − 0.4(150) − 0.3(175) +

0.1(145) + 0.2(165)

Tourist-Day Index=250 − 105 − 60 − 52.5 + 14.5 + 33 = 80

The tourist-day index of 80 is the base from which economic benefit of the project under consideration can be measured. The measurement of the economic benefit of the project is done by running the simulation contained in the accompanying appendix to this chapter. The simulation consists of the following steps.

FOR EACH OF 100,000 SIMULATIONS

DRAW A RANDOM NUMBER BETWEEN 1 AND 1,000
ENTER THE SIMULATOR FOR POLLUTION MEASURE 1
SELECT AN INDEX VALUE FOR POLLUTION MEASURE 1

DRAW A RANDOM NUMBER BETWEEN 1 AND 1,000
ENTER THE SIMULATOR FOR POLLUTION MEASURE 2
SELECT AN INDEX VALUE FOR POLLUTION MEASURE 2

DRAW A RANDOM NUMBER BETWEEN 1 AND 1,000
ENTER THE SIMULATOR FOR POLLUTION MEASURE 3
SELECT AN INDEX VALUE FOR POLLUTION MEASURE 3

SUBSTITUTE THESE VALUES ALONG WITH THE CURRENT VALUES
FOR POPULATION AND DISCRETIONARY SPENDING
INTO THE REGRESSION EQUATION

RECORD RESULTS

AFTER 100,000 SIMULATIONS
CALCULATE PROBABILITY DISTRIBUTION
AND EXPECTED VALUE OF TOURIST-DAY INDEX

PRINT RESULTS

If the project is not completed, the tourist-day index has a value of 80. If the project is completed, and if this modeling technique is valid, the expected tourist-day index would be 104.3. The probability distribution of the tourist-day index resulting from running the simulation contained in the appendix is tabulated as follows.

PERCENTAGE PROBABILITY OF OUTCOMES
(ROUNDED TO NEAREST TENTH)

TOURIST-DAY INDEX	PERCENTAGE PROBABILITY	TOURIST-DAY INDEX	PERCENTAGE PROBABILITY
90	0	105	11.2
91	0	106	10.6
92	0	107	9.2
93	0.1	108	7.3
94	0.3	109	5.3
95	0.7	110	3.3
96	1.3	111	2.0
97	2.0	112	1.0
98	2.9	113	0.5
99	4.1	114	0.2
100	5.0	115	0.1
101	6.1	116	0
102	7.2	117	0
103	8.9	118	0
104	10.7	119	0

The percentage probability of outcomes is illustrated in Exhibit 10.5.

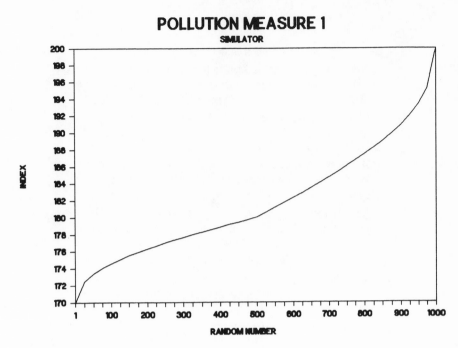

Exhibit 10.2.
Pollution Measure 1 (Simulator)

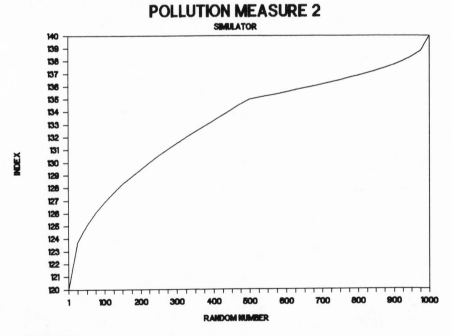

Exhibit 10.3.
Pollution Measure 2 (Simulator)

196

POLLUTION MEASURE 3

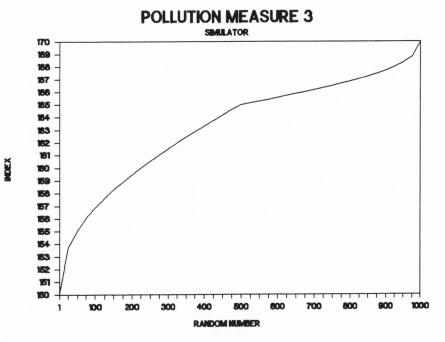

Exhibit 10.4.
Pollution Measure 3 (Simulator)

PROBABILITY DISTRIBUTION

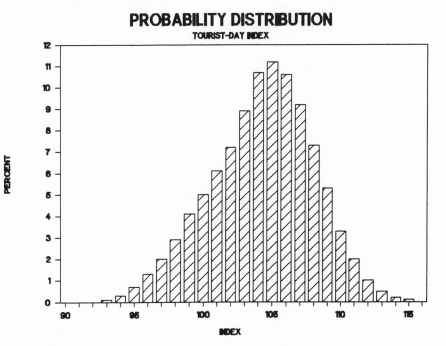

Exhibit 10.5.
Probability Distribution (tourist-day index)

THE MEASURE OF THE PROJECT'S SELF-LIQUIDATION POTENTIAL

This exercise would have to be repeated to measure the economic benefit of the environmental improvement project on the fishing industry. Presumably, the economic benefit of the project under scrutiny would accrue to both segments of the shore economy, but not necessarily to an equal degree.

Whether the model is constructed in relative terms with indices like those illustrated here, or whether the model is constructed in absolute terms, is immaterial. It is merely a matter of convenience for those involved in the project. The probability of outcomes for the tourist-day index can be translated into absolute terms as to the number of tourist-days one would expect if the project materializes. The difference between the expected number of tourist-days, and the base figure that corresponds to an index value of 80, provides both the incremental number of tourist-days, and the probability distribution about the expected incremental number of tourist-days. The probability distribution is the same as that of the simulation for the probability distribution for the tourist-day index. All that needs to be done is the relabeling of the vertical axis.

At this point, the number of incremental tourist-days must be converted to a monetary value. How much does a tourist spend per day while on the shore? This may have to be addressed in terms of a consumer survey. The survey may have a discrete value in that a tourist, on average, will spend a stipulated amount of money. The results could also be expressed in a minimum, most likely, and maximum format: A tourist is not likely to spend less than A dollars per day, nor more than C dollars, and is most likely to spend B dollars per day. With some statistical analysis, the appropriate scaling factor can be determined to build these assessments into a simulation model to create the expected amount of incremental revenue, and its probability distribution, for a given project.

This model would also put a dollar value on the incremental fish catch if the project under consideration were to materialize. Again, the price of fish can be either a discrete value, or a range of values, that can be incorporated into the simulation model. The remaining factor that has to be analyzed is the incremental tax receipts to the state and federal governments for each incremental dollar spent by tourists, or received by fisherman. A statistical examination of the returns by shore businesses, such as restaurants, retail shops, motels and hotels, and other businesses that depend on the tourist trade, would provide the necessary data. This process would have to be repeated for those businesses related to the fishing industry. A regression equation based on aggregate tax returns, both personal and corporate, for ZIP code numbers of shore communities would be another method of arriving at the relationship between tax receipts and gross revenues.

The calculated incremental tax receipts can be converted to incremental tax rates. The incremental tax rates can then be applied to the incremental revenue which is expected to be experienced by the tourist and fishing industries were the environmental improvement project approved, funded, and completed. The combined incremental tax revenues from both pillars of the shore community would yield the minimum, expected, and maximum incremental tax receipts to the state and federal governments, which could be set aside for the interest, and amortization, of the debt issued to finance the project.

Suppose that the minimum incremental tax revenue of a major environmental improvement project is $25 million. The expected incremental tax revenue is $40 million, and the maximum is $60 million. If the project can be funded with taxable thirty-year bonds with a coupon of 12 percent, the annual capital recovery factor necessary to pay the interest and retire the debt, on a semi-annual basis, is 12.375 percent. If the project can be funded with thirty-year tax free bonds with a coupon of 9 percent, the capital recovery factor is 9.7 percent to satisfy all obligations. The size of the project that can be funded with taxable, and tax free, bonds for the incremental tax revenue expected to be generated by having a cleaner ocean environment is shown in the following table.

MAXIMUM INVESTMENT FOR INDICATED TAX REVENUE AND FINANCING

	INCREMENTAL TAX REVENUE		
	$25 MM	$40 MM	$60 MM
30 YEAR BONDS AT 12%	$202 MM	$323 MM	$485 MM
30 YEAR BONDS AT 9%	$258 MM	$412 MM	$619 MM

A comparison can now be made between the cost of the project and the amount of an issue of bonds that can be supported by the incremental tax revenue. Risk in the project can be analyzed by the amount of potential shortfalls, and the probability distribution associated therewith, between incoming incremental tax revenue and outgoing interest and amortization payments. The security of a project can be analyzed with equal ease in terms of the degree of coverage provided by the incremental tax revenues with respect to the magnitude of the bond obligations. The analysis of the relative risk, or security, of several projects can be used to establish a priority listing from the point of view of the degree of self-liquidation inherent in each project.

CONCLUSION

One understandable conclusion is that all of this represents a great deal of effort. The response to this is that the proposed framework of analysis does represent a great deal of effort. However, the proposed analysis is basically a planning tool whose totality in cost and in effort is minuscule compared with the magnitude of the cost and effort that will be required to complete an environmental improvement project such as a large-scale waste treatment plant. This is apparent once one realizes that environmental improvement projects, capable of improving offshore waters, are capital investments whose costs are expressed in terms of eight-, nine-, or ten-digit numbers.

The proposed framework of analysis represents the minimum effort required to quantify the economic repercussions of an environmental improvement project. Its validity can be no better than the validity of the proposed model linking the shore economy with environmental factors and in the validity of the assessments provided by experts of a project's impact on the environment. There is no magic in the methodology—it incorporates available data with statistical analysis and simulation to assess the economic impact of an environmental improvement project. The proposed framework of analysis is designed to be cost-effective as a planning tool for evaluating the economic benefits of environmental improvement projects.

Appendix to Chapter Ten

ESTABLISHING AN ECONOMIC BENEFIT SIMULATION

Of the two programs used in the chapter, one was CUMDIST that created the cumulative distribution probability curves, which then became the simulators for Pollution Measures 1, 2, and 3.

The second is the simulation program to assess the impact of a project on the environment. Statements 30–90 feed in the data files created by CUMDIST for the three measures of pollution. Statements 120–130 print the data files for confirmation prior to running the simulation. The logic of the simulation is repeated here with the appropriate statements of the program appended.

FOR EACH OF 100,000 SIMULATIONS
(Statements 140, 150, 230)

DRAW A RANDOM NUMBER BETWEEN 1 AND 1,000
ENTER THE SIMULATOR FOR POLLUTION MEASURE 1
SELECT AN INDEX VALUE FOR POLLUTION MEASURE 1
(Statements 160–190)

DRAW A RANDOM NUMBER BETWEEN 1 AND 1,000
ENTER THE SIMULATOR FOR POLLUTION MEASURE 2
SELECT AN INDEX VALUE FOR POLLUTION MEASURE 2
(Statements 160–190)

DRAW A RANDOM NUMBER BETWEEN 1 AND 1,000
ENTER THE SIMULATOR FOR POLLUTION MEASURE 3
SELECT AN INDEX VALUE FOR POLLUTION MEASURE 3
(Statements 160–190)

SUBSTITUTE THESE VALUES ALONG WITH THE CURRENT VALUES
FOR POPULATION AND DISCRETIONARY SPENDING
INTO THE REGRESSION EQUATION
(Statement 200)

RECORD RESULTS
(Statements 210–220)

AFTER 100,000 SIMULATIONS
CALCULATE PROBABILITY DISTRIBUTION
AND EXPECTED VALUE OF TOURIST-DAY INDEX
PRINT RESULTS
(Statements 240–300)

```
10 REM NAME OF PROGRAM IN ENVIRON
20 DIM D(3,1000),R(200)
30 OPEN "I",#1,"CUM1"
40 FOR I=1 TO 1000:INPUT #1,D:D(1,I)=D:NEXT
50 CLOSE #1:OPEN "I",#1,"CUM2"
60 FOR I=1 TO 1000:INPUT #1,D:D(2,I)=D:NEXT
70 CLOSE #1:OPEN "I",#1,"CUM3"
80 FOR I=1 TO 1000:INPUT #1,D:D(3,I)=D:NEXT
90 CLOSE #1
100 PRINT " ","POLL MEAS 1","POLL MEAS 2","POLL MEAS 3"
110 PRINT "1",D(1,1),D(2,1),D(3,1)
120 FOR I=50 TO 1000 STEP 50
130 PRINT I,D(1,I),D(2,I),D(3,I):NEXT
140 PRINT:INPUT "NUMBER OF SIMULATIONS: ";S
150 FOR K=1 TO S
160 FOR J=1 TO 3
170 X=1+INT(1000*RND(X))
180 M(J)=D(J,X)
190 NEXT
200 M=250-.5*M(1)-.4*M(2)-.3*M(3)+.1*145+.2*165
210 M=INT(M+.5)
220 R(M)=R(M)+1
230 NEXT
240 PRINT "PROBABILITY DISTRIBUTION OF OUTCOMES":PRINT
250 FOR I=1 TO 200
260 IF R(I)=0 THEN 280
270 PRINT I,100*R(I)/S:INPUT Z$
280 NEXT
290 A=0:FOR I=1 TO 200:A=A+I*R(I):NEXT
300 PRINT "EXPECTED OUTCOME VALUE: ";A/S:END
```

11

Financial Strategic Planning

SYNOPSIS

"I can't believe it! The third motel mortgage this year to go down the drain!"

"The motel operators are having a tough time this year."

"And last year. And the year before that. And probably next year. And probably next week someone else will come in unable to make his mortgage payments."

"What will you do?"

"What can I do? Recast the mortgage in terms that the owner can meet or foreclose on the motel and operate it myself. Which would you recommend? And, by the way, do you want to join me in telling the president what has just happened?"

This is the conversation between a lending officer and his assistant. It is one that occurs at irregular intervals during troughs in the business cycle. This conversation took place during the trough in the motel business cycle.

There was an earlier conversation. This time it was between the president and the lending officer during the previous peak of the motel business cycle.

"Why did we lose the Featherweight motel deal?"

"We haven't lost it yet. But First Savings is offering Featherweight a better deal."

"How so?"

"Better terms. We offer 80 percent financing. They are offering 85 percent. Our interest rate is 11.75 percent, theirs is 11.65 percent. Our upfront fees are 2 percent of the deal, theirs is 1.75 percent."

"How do you know all that?"

"Featherweight told me. Said if we can do 90 percent financing, match their interest rate, and knock something off the upfront fees, he'll have enough equity money to build two motels, and we can finance both of them."

"Motel business sure is booming, isn't it?"

"Sure is. Featherweight has money for one motel if we finance at 80 percent. At 90 percent financing, he has the equity for two motels. Instead of booking $1 million in one motel mortgage, we can book $2 million for two with virtually no extra work."

"Double the mortgage doubles the amount of money we make on our spread between what we pay for funds and what we will receive from the mortgages."

"And no risk. Have you seen the figures on occupancy rates for the last two years? And the profits the motel owners are making?"

"Doesn't Featherweight own that motel on Ocean Avenue? I bet we could refinance that one, throw that baby into the collateral pot, and he'll have enough equity to build three motels, and we can book about $3 million or so in our motel mortgage portfolio including the refinancing of the one he owns. That'll leave old First Savings gasping for breath."

Expansion of capacity during boom times in an industry is the free market at work. It is the hallmark of laissez-faire economics. The problem is that everybody wants to expand capacity. The problem is compounded by bankers lining up outside the doors of prospering businessmen with deals that no one can turn down. Borrowers cannot resist the temptation to borrow and expand their businesses even more than their equity funds can support. Featherweight had the equity to build one motel, he asked for financing to build two motels, and was offered a deal to build three motels. Why should he resist? Business has never been so good.

Yet, in a few years time, the bankers are wondering how the loans are going to be repaid, and the borrowers are in real danger of losing everything they have. And if these conditions persist long enough, and they usually do, the banks foreclose on the borrowers leaving them with nothing much more than the shirts on their backs. The bankers are not left unscathed by foreclosing. The mortgages eventually have to be written down to the true value of the underlying asset. At some point in time, the banks can no longer maintain the fiction that a million-dollar mortgage in a motel that no one is willing to buy for even a small fraction of a million dollars is really worth a million dollars.

This chapter focuses on financial strategic planning from the point of view of establishing safe lending limits for a business whose revenue is volatile and unpredictable. The motel business merely serves as a prop in a scenario describing financial strategic planning in a business environment where revenue can best be described in terms of volatility and unpredictability. The same general procedure can be applied to any industry for purposes of determining not only safe lending limits, but also optimal levels of equity and debt in the capital structure of the company including the optimal payout of dividends in relation to earnings.

"Come here, my erstwhile assistant. I have a task for you."

"What do you want me to do?"

"I want you, first of all, to meet Mr. Featherweight."

"How do you do, Mr. Featherweight."

"Mr. Featherweight wants to recast his entire mortgage loan portfolio. But I am putting one more condition on this one. Mr. Featherweight has agreed to cooperate with us to create some sort of a model to tell us what is the safe lending limit on financing motels. It is perfectly clear to me that we have been lending to motel operators on far too generous terms. That is why all these loans are going bad as soon as the wind changes direction. You two get together and give me a tool—something that tells me what the safe level is for financing motels and something that tells me what risk of loss I face should I decide to lend beyond the safe level. Do you understand what I want?''

''I think so.''

''Good, now sit down with Mr. Featherweight and let's get on with it.''

''I think we'll be comfortable here in my office, Mr. Featherweight. Sit down and make yourself comfortable. I'm sorry to hear about your difficulties.''

''What difficulties?''

''Well, the whole situation with your mortgages.''

''Do you think recasting the mortgages for a larger amount to give me the cash needed to pay this year's mortgage payments is a difficulty for me? All I have to do is promise that, when things get better, any excess cash that I earn over my mortgage payments to you will be dedicated to reducing the amount of the mortgage. What difficulty are you talking about?''

''I don't understand.''

''You have a chance to take away my motels and you don't. You ensure my survival. Then, as punishment, your boss gives me this assignment to cooperate with you. Some punishment. I'm probably more interested in the results than you are. Talk about throwing B'rer Rabbit into the briar patch!''

''You could lose all your motels over this.''

''Yes, I could. But you'll take one helluva bath. My investment at this point is pretty small. What is yours? It's millions, now you tell me who is in hot water.''

''I think I would like to get off this subject. For me to analyze the motel business, I guess you better tell me something about it.''

''How can you make loans to motel operators and not understand the business to begin with?''

''Well, I'm only an assistant, I did not make the loan.''

''You might be only an assistant, but the person who gave you this assignment makes the loans. Do you think that he understands this business?''

''Well . . .''

''. . . he doesn't. Why do you have this assignment if he knew what he was doing? He doesn't know this business. I told him all these things. Maybe not exactly in the same words, but I've told him. I told him he made a big mistake letting me build all those motels with his money. At worse, I may lose four motels for which I have already got most of my money back. He can't throw me out because he can't operate a motel. He can't sell the motels because they wouldn't fetch a small fraction of what is needed to pay off the mortgages. He can't bring in a new operator because there really is no point for a new operator to come into this situation. I am the best operator. No one can operate those motels better than I can. And besides, it isn't the operation that needs improvement, but the number of motel customers that needs to be increased.''

''He could throw you out—from a legal standpoint.''

''Sure he could. My loans are in default, and he has the legal right to throw me out. But then he would have to write down the loans. Then the bank would have to post a loss. A real big loss. But as long as he recasts the mortgages to ensure my survival, then the loans are classified as good loans. As long as the loans are classified as good loans, his superiors have no reason to be upset with him. And the last thing his superiors want to report to the stockholders are extraordinary losses taken in their motel loan portfolio. So it is to everyone's advantage to paper over the situation for as long as possible.''

''Papering over has its limits. But I think we better get off this discussion and get on with the assignment.''

''Okay, here is the motel business in a nutshell. I don't have to tell you that it is seasonal. The Shore Motel Association keeps statistics for us. We send in information every month, and they compile it leaving out the individuals' names, of course. This way we all know what's going on without having to snoop around the neighborhood to find out.''

''Makes life convenient.''

''Sure does. But I don't need to look at the information. It is all in my head. You don't spend twenty years in this business and not know the facts. The facts are simple. Business stinks nine months of the year. Nearly all of our entire gross income is earned during the months of June, July, and August. In other words, my whole well-being depends entirely on the summer season.''

''That certainly is a nutshell description.''

''The total capacity of the existing motels in the Shore Area is 20,000 rooms. There are about 400 motels in the Shore Area which means that the average motel has fifty rooms. All the figures I'm going to be giving you come from the Shore Motel Association. I have the reports with me and I'll leave them with you. We can cut through much of what is in these reports by simply remembering this. The total revenue from nine months of the year covers all our direct operating costs for those nine months and that is all. That would include such things as real estate taxes, maintenance, utilities, repairs, refurbishing, cleaning people, and something for the operator to live on. Direct operating costs, which do not include mortgage payments, amount to about $20 per room per day filled or not filled. You got that?''

''Yes.''

''Now the daily rental rate is a function of how busy we are. The Shore Motel Association shows that, on average, we can get $85 per day if the occupancy rate for all motels in the shore area is 90 percent or above. Between 80 and 90 percent occupancy, the daily rental falls to $60. Between 70 and 80 percent, it is $50. And below 70 percent, we average $45 per night.''

''Yes, let me write it down.''

PERCENTAGE OCCUPANCY ALL MOTELS	AVERAGE DAILY ROOM RENTAL
90% OR MORE	$85
80–90%	60
70–80%	50
70% OR LESS	45

"See how profitable this business can be?"

"I guess so . . ."

"When people flock to the shore and the occupancy rate for all motels in the shore area rises above 90 percent, it becomes a sellers' market. We can raise rates up to about $85 per day and get away with it. I tell you that is heaven."

"Heaven . . ."

"Yes, heaven. Look, the average motel has fifty units, or rooms, and costs $1 million to build, right?"

"Right."

"Let's say we have 90 percent occupancy for three months at $85 per day, less $20 per day per room in operating costs, how much do we make?"

"Your gross revenue is 90 percent of fifty rooms times $85 per day for ninety days, or . . ."

"About $344,000. I've done the calculation a thousand times. Filled or empty, a motel room costs $20 per day in direct operating costs. The gross operating cost is 50 rooms times $20 per day for 90 days or $90,000. So our gross income, before financing charges, is $254,000. At full capacity, our gross income will be about $293,000. Now a motel of that size costs about $1 million. Why with that kind of income, you can pay off a motel in four years. And the banks will give you 80 or 90 percent financing over twenty years. Don't you see the simple arithmetic of being in the motel business?"

"You couldn't get 10 percent financing from us right now."

"That's because business stinks. When it's good, I came to you to finance one motel. First Savings might have let me do two, but you guys wrapped up my Ocean Avenue motel and let me build three."

"That's because you could demonstrate the ability to make sufficient profits to cover the mortgage payments."

"Only because you were looking at the current market at that time. We had a couple of extraordinarily good years back then, if you remember."

"Let's talk about why the good years don't last."

"Well, there are two reasons. During good times, we build motels, which, when they are completed, flood the market with capacity. Excess capacity, may I add."

"And the other?"

"The tourist trade at the shore jumps hither and yon from year to year with no apparent rhyme or reason. Some years it's way up, others it's way down, and sometimes there is little change."

"Do you have any figures?"

"Of course I've got figures. Why do we all support the Shore Motel Association? To have figures. Figures are the life blood of our business."

"Let's have some."

"Here they are. I was showing these to your boss when he got the idea of having you do this study. The Shore Motel Association did a summary of the chief features of our business. Look here. The data show that 55 percent of all years are up-years and 45 percent are down-years. Up-years are years when the demand for motel space, expressed in room-days, is up from the previous year. I guess I don't have to explain what a down-year is.''

''No.''

''Okay, here are some more figures. For the up-year, the highest increase was 15 percent from the previous year, and the lowest, well, essentially zero. They have figures for the average. Do you want to write them down?''

''I guess I better.''

PERCENTAGE CHANGE IN DEMAND FOR MOTEL-DAYS
FROM PREVIOUS YEAR

	UP YEARS	DOWN YEARS
MINIMUM	0	0
AVERAGE	7	−6
MAXIMUM	15	−12

''You can have as much as a 27 percent swing between a very good year and a very bad one.''

''Yes, but the key point from your point of view is that there is an upward trend. We have clean water down here. As pollution gets worse and worse up north, people are coming farther and farther south to swim in our clean waters. This is what is going to save you in the long term. Our clean water, our clean beaches.''

''You keep saying 'you.' You have a vested interest in all this.''

''Technically, no. Not the way you financed me. Actually, yes. I am interested in seeing this thing through. I'm going to end up with four motels. And you can't get a better operator than myself because I want those four motels. But if all things fail, I'm no worse off when I worked as a salaried manager of a motel. I can always go back to that trade.''

''Is that what you did?''

''Yup. Saved my money, borrowed to the hilt from friends, relatives, and anyone else I knew to make the down payment on my first motel. Then I did a couple of good trades and ended up with the Ocean Avenue baby. You guys financed that one. You set me up in business, and you made me one of the largest motel owners in this town. If I win, I'm big. If I lose, I'm no worse off than where I was.''

''You're making this sound like a crap game.''

''I certainly ain't playing this game with my money! It's your fault, and other banks, that we suffer from such overcapacity. It's killing us.''

''And I guess the Shore Motel Association will again come to our rescue on building statistics.''

''That's their business. You see, everything is based on the summer occupancy rate. It's all here in the figures. If the overall occupancy rate is above 90 percent for one year, then the expansion in the number of rooms will vary between a low of 5 percent to a high of 12 percent in terms of current capacity. If the summer occupancy has been above 80, but below 90, then the expansion in the number of units will vary from a low of 4 to a high of 10 percent. Below 80 percent occupancy, the rate of construction, if any, equals the number of rooms lost from motels being removed from the market.''

''How do motels get removed from the market?''

''Land values mostly. Older motels may be sitting on desirable pieces of property for, say, a site for a shopping center. The motel ain't worth nothing because the building is old and business is bad, but the land sure is. Some motels get converted to apartments for single people. Others burn to the ground— sometimes by accident, and sometimes to collect on the insurance policy. One way or the other, they go. When occupancy during the summer months is below 70 percent, the net shrinkage in the number of rooms varies between 2 and 5 percent. You got the numbers?''

''Wait a minute.''

OCCUPANCY RATE ALL MOTELS	ROOM EXPANSION/ CONTRACTION	
	LOW	HIGH
90% OR MORE	5	12
80–90%	4	10
70–80%	0	0
70% OR LESS	−2	−5

''Now remember that it takes two years for a motel to be built and made ready for business. So as long as occupancy hangs in at a high number, the supply of new rooms hits the market as a flood tide two years after the fact. And then as the occupancy rate declines, so do rates. There may even be more tourists down here, but that is not the key. The key is not the number of tourists, which affect rates, but the occupancy rate. We can only raise rates through the ceiling when there are essentially no spare rooms. When there are empty rooms, we compete for the available tourists, which drives down room rates. That's the free market at work, wouldn't you say?''

''It keeps us all hopping.''

''When those motels still in the pipeline of being built are completed, the surplus becomes a glut, and this wipes out what little remains of the rate structure for motel rooms.''

''So the expansion figures you gave me are the units started, not the units completed.''

''Yes. You have to incorporate that in your analysis. As you can see from the data, the shrinkage numbers are applied against current capacity. But there is a two-year delay in expansion. The expansion numbers are really new motels in the building permit stage.''

''I think I understand . . .''

''So in a nutshell, this is what we have. When times are good, rates are such that the gross income can pay off the motel in a relatively few years. Then everyone rushes in to build a new motel. Problem is that too many people are thinking the same thing. Then it becomes emotional with everyone trying to beat everyone else to the punch. And the banks aid the problem by making it financially possible to build motels with very little upfront cash. All you need is 5 or 10 percent of the building cost in cash, and you have to beat the bankers away from your door. Just look at me. I asked for money to build one, and you gave me the money to build three.''

''That may stop as a result of this study.''

''I doubt that. I doubt that very strongly.''

''Why do you say that?''

''Even if this bank should get religion, what good will it do? When your competitors are out there offering 90 percent financing, and you are offering 50 percent financing, how many loans are you going to book? And if you don't book any loans, how do you advance in the organization? Bankers advance in position by making loans, not by rejecting loans. It's all part of the Deluge Theory.''

''What's the Deluge Theory?''

''The Deluge Theory states that the organization man will do whatever he has to do for his personal advancement even if it is to the detriment of the organization—for instance, making excessive loans to the motel operators. Suppose that a lending officer books a huge quantity of loans when times are good and hopes for a personal advancement because of his outstanding performance. That advancement also keeps him one step ahead of the deluge of problems he is creating in order to be able to advance in the organization in the first place. Sooner or later, the advancement stops, but the deluge of problems created to promote that advancement are still right behind him. Then he finds he can't get out of the way of the breaking tidal wave of his own doing and he is swept away in the deluge. Like your boss. Trapped by his own . . .''

''I hardly think so . . .''

''Well, we'll see.''

''So you are saying that I am wasting my time doing this exercise.''

''In light of how this bank will react to the motel operators when the good times return? Absolutely. No criticism to you, personally; you are not bankers, but money salesmen. You act as though you get a commission on what you do.''

''Well, anyway, to finish this exercise, I take it that there are no new motels ordered when occupancy is less than 80 percent?''

''Look at the figures. At 75 percent occupancy, you take 75 percent of fifty rooms times $50 per day per room for ninety days, and what do you have?''

''Looks like $168,750.''

''Less $20 per day per room for operating costs, for ninety days; that's

$90,000 in gross operating costs. Subtract that from gross revenue and that is the gross income. What is that?''

"Looks like $78,750.''

"There isn't enough cash flow to support running to a bank for a loan. The interest alone on the cost of a new motel at 12 percent of $1 million is $120,000.''

"That means no construction of new motels.''

"Absolutely, no motel operator has $1 million in cash lying around to build one of these babies.''

"Do you have anything more for me?''

"Yes, the present situation.''

"And that is?''

"The present capacity of motel rooms is 20,000 for the Shore Area. Counting only the summer season of 90 days, we have a total capacity of 1.8 million room-days. Looks like this year is going to be a real bummer of 1.2 million room-days.''

"I really don't know what to do with all this data. From what you have given me, I can obtain an average growth rate of the tourist trade. I can apply this to the current 1.2 million room-days and extrapolate the demand curve out into the future. I can take the current 1.8 million room-days of capacity and let that decrease at about 3 percent per year. By comparing the relationship between the projected supply and projected demand for motel room-days, I can estimate when capacity reaches, say, 80 percent. This probably would be the point where you can start generating enough money to service your mortgages.''

"I have done that with your boss. That's why I still have the motels. He, himself, is convinced that better days are not that far off. Then I can get current in both principal and interest payments from any excess cash that I generate.''

"I can see that better days will come as long as nothing disturbs the long-term trend lines. We know that the pollution problems up north are driving the tourists to our beaches. It is a matter of time and patience.''

"My gamble is that I don't run out of time before you run out of patience.''

"All this is nice in that it helps us to estimate when you are earning enough money to start repaying, but it doesn't answer the question of what is a reasonable support level for financing motels. Obviously, 90 percent is too high and 20 percent is too low. What is the right number?''

"Isn't that your problem? I'm here to describe to you the facts of the business. It's up to you to come up with the answer.''

"Yes, you're right. That is my problem, but I am at a loss as to how to proceed.''

A POSSIBLE SOLUTION TO THE PROBLEM

The assistant to the lending officer is probably not a programmer nor versed in simulation. However, with a calculator, and a bag containing one hundred numbered ping-pong balls, and a great deal of patience that transcends understanding, he could perform the following steps. However, to make life easier for the assistant, suppose that he has a random number generator. When he punches a key, the generator will produce a random number whose value is between 0 and 1. The assistant starts the process by noting that the current demand for room-days is 1.2 million and the current supply of room-days is 1.8 million. No motel rooms are under construction. Over some multiyear period, the assistant is going to perform the following steps.

1. At the start of each year, he is going to decide whether it is an up-year or a down-year. He will do this by punching the random number generator and looking at the result. If the random number is 0.45 or above, the assistant will assume that the number of tourists, or room-days, will be better than the previous year. This models the statistician's observation that 55 percent of all years show an improvement from the previous year's level of demand for room-days. Obviously, if this condition is not satisfied, the demand for room-days is less than the previous year's level.

2. If it is an up-year, the assistant then punches the random number generator and obtains another random number between 0 and 1. He then multiplies the number drawn from the random number generator by 15 percent. This will generate the percentage of growth for the up-year that will vary between zero and 15 percent. Each percentage will have equal probabilities with any other percentage of growth. If the statistician's analysis of the Shore Motel Association's data was in sufficient detail, then the CUMDIST program could be put to use to better model the relative improbability of having growth as low as zero percent or as high as 15 percent. In a similar fashion, the percentage decline for a down-year can be determined.

3. The next thing the assistant has to do is adjust current capacity for any new motel construction that had started two years previous to the present year. This models the two-year lag between the motel owners' deciding to build new motels and the motels opening for business. Rental rates for motels are influenced by the number of existing motels, not by those under construction.

4. Then the assistant examines the occupancy rate, which is obtained by dividing the demand for motel rooms (determined in step 2) by the supply of motel rooms (determined in step 3).

5. The resulting occupancy rate allows the assistant to determine the daily rental rates and the factors influencing the future supply of motel capacity by entering the following table of events for the applicable occupancy rate.

   A. If the occupancy rate is above 90 percent, room rates will be $85 per day, and the motel owners will start the construction of motels that will expand capacity by 5 to 12 percent. This capacity will not hit the market until two years after the motel owners have made the decision to proceed with the expansion. The assistant will determine the actual growth by punching the random number generator and multiplying the result by the difference between the high and low estimates, which is 7 percent. He then adds this to the low estimate of 5 percent. The results will be a growth rate that varies between 5 and 12 percent. He then multiplies this by the current capacity, and this becomes the additional capacity which will be added to the capacity of room-days two years hence.

B. If the occupancy rate is between 80 and 90 percent, the rental rate is $60 per day, and expansion will vary between 4 and 10 percent of present capacity. The expansion of capacity two years in the future is calculated the same way except for the different high and low estimates on potential growth.

C. If the occupancy rate is between 70 and 80 percent, daily rates are $50 per day, and there will be no net expansion or contraction of capacity two years in the future. This is equivalent to saying that expansion of motels will be essentially of the same magnitude as those that are removed from the market two years in the future.

D. If the occupancy rate is below 70 percent, daily rental rates are $45 per day, and there will be a net shrinkage in the order of 2 and 5 percent. There is no time delay associated with shrinkage. Shrinkage represents motels going out of business for any number of reasons.

6. The assistant figures up the gross revenue during the summer season by multiplying the room rental by the ninety-day summer season and by the fifty units of an average sized motel and by the occupancy rate. The gross operating cost is the $20 per room per day multiplied by ninety days and by fifty rooms per motel, or $90,000 during the summer season, regardless of the occupancy rate. The gross income is determined by subtracting the gross operating cost from the gross revenue. The gross income supports the mortgage payments. Taxes are of no real concern because the interest is a tax deductible expense, and the principle payments are essentially shielded from taxation by depreciation. Taxes are paid by owners when the gross income begins to exceed the mortgage servicing obligations. This may be of concern to the owners, but not to the bank holding the mortgage.

7. The assistant would record the gross income for the year and proceed to the next over the multiyear period he is considering.

8. Then he might repeat the entire exercise, if he were a glutton for punishment.

9. His final step would be to look at the times when the motel owner would be making various levels of gross incomes. This would provide him with the probability distribution of gross income and the input required for assessing the risk of a bank supporting various sized mortgages.

The accompanying appendix contains the computer instructions for performing each of these steps. If an evaluation of a situation can be translated into simple arithmetic calculations and simple logical comparisons of one number being larger, smaller, or equal to another, the evaluation can be programmed on a computer. The program in the appendix contains only thirty-one lines. It could be expanded to model the daily rental rates with more numerous increments of occupancy rates. The CUMDIST program could also be brought into the picture to better model the growth factors related to up- and down-years, and to the expansion or contraction of the number of motel rooms. This would provide a more refined output. The point is that the simulation is not a large-sized program requiring the efforts of huge support staff. Much more effort would be expended in collecting the data than in writing the program and performing the analysis.

The program in the appendix performs the same aforementioned steps the assistant would have had to do manually, only the computer performs the task somewhat quicker and removes some degree of tedium from the life of the assistant if he were to do the task. And assuming a big "if" in that there are no programming bugs, the computer would not make the arithmetic errors we humans are prone to do.

Each simulation covers a period of one hundred years starting from the present supply/demand relationship of room-days. The results of running the simulation 1,000 times, which represents an aggregate of 100,000 years of motel business, are summarized as follows in terms of the probability distribution associated with the specified range of annual gross incomes. The expected value calculation for the annual gross income is the summation of the probability of occurrence multiplied by the midpoint value of the corresponding range of gross income.

RANGE OF GROSS INCOME BEFORE SERVICING MORTGAGE		PERCENTAGE PROBABILITY OF OCCURRENCE (NEAREST 0.1%)	MID-POINT OF RANGE	EXPECTED VALUE
$-10,000	0	Negligible	$ -5,000	$ 0
0	10,000	0.1	5,000	5
10,000	20,000	0.6	15,000	90
20,000	30,000	2.5	25,000	625
30,000	40,000	8.3	35,000	2,905
40,000	50,000	16.0	45,000	7,200
50,000	60,000	2.3	55,000	1,265
60,000	70,000	5.0	65,000	3,250
70,000	80,000	18.4	75,000	13,800
80,000	90,000	16.4	85,000	13,940
90,000	100,000	0	95,000	0
100,000	110,000	0	105,000	0
110,000	120,000	0	115,000	0
120,000	130,000	5.7	125,000	7,125
130,000	140,000	8.5	135,000	11,475
140,000	150,000	6.5	145,000	9,425
150,000	160,000	1.3	155,000	2,015
160,000	170,000	0	165,000	0
170,000	180,000	0	175,000	0
180,000	190,000	0	185,000	0
190,000	200,000	0	195,000	0
200,000	210,000	0	205,000	0
210,000	220,000	0	215,000	0
220,000	230,000	0	225,000	0
230,000	240,000	0	235,000	0
240,000	250,000	0	245,000	0
250,000	260,000	2.7	255,000	6,885
260,000	270,000	2.3	265,000	6,095
270,000	280,000	1.5	275,000	4,125
280,000	292,500*	1.9	286,250	5,440
TOTAL		100.0		$95,665

*$292,500 represents the maximum gross margin at 100 percent capacity. This occurred in about 1 percent of all runs.

THE AFTERMATH

"By golly, didn't I tell you!? You can make a fortune in this business. At $250,000, or $290,000 per year, you can pay off a motel in about four years of operation. What did I tell you? It's the best business there is!"

"It doesn't happen very often. Maybe this [Exhibit 11.1] will throw a little light on the subject."

"I know, but when it does, bingo!"

"Bingo, is right. The total probability of your earning that kind of money is 8.4 percent. That is 8.4 years in a century. Throw in a thirty-year life on a motel from the time you build it until you sell it for a parking lot, it happens in two or three years of operation."

"Is that so?"

"Yes, that's so. There is an 8.4 percent chance of earning that kind of money. In a thirty-year period of time, that works out to 2.5 years with that kind of income."

"Well that is what ownership is all about."

"Yes, but that is not what banking is all about."

"Look, I know it's infrequent, but when it occurs, it's wonderful."

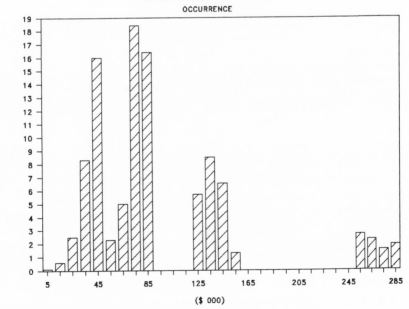

PROBABILITY OF
OCCURRENCE

Exhibit 11.1.
Probability of Occurrence

"I know that and I know that is what keeps you guys in the motel business. The hope for the killing. The problem is that the killing only occurs from time to time. Both you and I are living with the fact that it does not occur often enough. Let's look at this not from your point of view as an owner, but from my point of view as a lender. For this scenario that we have created to approximate reality, what can we, as lenders, expect you to earn over the life of the mortgage?"

"You are always a pessimistic lot. You focus on the low end of the scale."

"No, we're not always pessimistic. Not when you look at how we have financed you! But you are right in one respect. We are all highly sensitive to the gross income. You focus your attention on the potential for making a killing— the high end of the spectrum of possible incomes. That represents the reward of an investment. We focus our attention on the low end of the spectrum where you might not be able to make your mortgage payments. That represents our risk of holding your mortgage. Nevertheless, both of us, as owner or lender, have our hopes on the return of, and on, an investment. We both have our destinies bound to the nature of the same cash flow stream."

"Why—are there gaps in your income figures?"

"Yes. It is caused by the nature of the way the daily rates step up with occupancy rates. For instance, as a consequence of the modeling, there is no time in 100,000 years of operation that you will earn between $90,000 and $120,000. Maybe more discrete steps between occupancy rates and daily rates would take care of it by filling in the gaps. But peaks would remain because daily rental rates for rooms jump as the motel occupancy rate climbs nears 90 percent. In other words, the simulation is telling us what we already know: The motel business is highly volatile. It is either great or lousy and seldom in between."

"That's the name of the game."

"Unfortunately for all of us, there is that gap between $90,000 and $120,000."

"Yes, makes my mortgage payments look pretty bad, doesn't it?"

"It is not the fact that your financing charges happen to fall into a range that will never occur. The problem is that your financing charges exceed the expected gross income of $95,655 or, say, $96,000."

"What does that mean?"

"The expected gross income of $96,000 means, from our point of view as lenders, that it is guaranteed that the mortgagee will not be able to make his payments over the life of the mortgage if his annual payments exceed that amount. Another way of saying this is that we guarantee our position of becoming the largest motel owner in the county if we give mortgages to owners of fifty-unit motels whose annual payments exceed $96,000. That is not our purpose in life."

"Hmm."

"Look at what we have done with you. The average cost of construction of a fifty-unit motel is $1 million—such as yours. We financed it at 90 percent of cost. That means we gave you a $900,000 mortgage in round terms. At 11⅝ percent interest, you are paying a monthly rate on your twenty-year mortgage of

1.075 percent, or .01075 times $900,000, or $9,675. Times that by twelve, and your annual mortgage service payments are $116,100. Do you know what that means?''

"You are going to end up with a twenty-five-year or more mortgage.''

"That's right. It is virtually impossible for you to pay off the mortgage in twenty years. It has to be extended to lower the effective payments to $96,000. Which, in effect, is what we are doing right now. Either that or we end up owning your motel. Our mortgage payments exceed your expected income.''

"Or good times come more often than what you expect.''

"If we have to look to good times for repayment, we really aren't debt holders anymore, are we? If higher than expected good times is what is needed to liquidate the debt, we are owners, not lenders. Furthermore, if this model has any validity, the chances of your earning more than $96,000 per year is only 30.4 percent. Do you know what the implication of that is? In a twenty-year mortgage, you are earning your keep, so to speak, during six years of operation. Of the remaining fourteen years, your gross income is insufficient to make your mortgage payments. I don't think we did a very good job with our homework, do you?''

"You made the offer, and if you didn't, I would have done the deal with First Savings.''

"And today, First Savings would have this problem, not us. Your mortgages aren't even worth 50 cents on the dollar today. We should have let First Savings do the deal.''

"And my problem today would have been with one, maybe two, new motels, not three. I might have been able to survive with one motel in trouble, but not three. But then again, it really is your money at this point. You can bankrupt me three times over, and you're still stuck with the motels. Anyway, I still feel we can work ourselves out of this mess. But you have to have the patience and give me the time for the tourist trade to expand to the point that the occupancy will drive up the rental rates.''

"You know that bankers can run out of patience. It has happened before. Anyway, let's continue. Even if we limit the mortgage payments to $90,000, the motel owner is going to have difficulty making his payments in fourteen years of a twenty-year mortgage. That is some figure: 70 percent of the time he will be short in generating sufficient cash to make his payments to us.''

"Well, you are being far too pessimistic. Ninety thousand dollars is below the expected annual gross income of $96,000. So that he will, over the term of the mortgage, make enough money to service the debt. From your point of view, the 30 percent of good years will outweigh the 70 percent of bad years. For those years that there is a shortfall, you would only have a problem if he has insufficient cash reserves generated from the better years.''

"Well, we do take care of that by getting a personal guarantee on the loan from the motel owner.''

"Furthermore, I would say that shortfalls occurring in the latter half of the mortgage period are not so risky as those that occur during the first half of the mortgage period. During the latter half of the mortgage period, the chances are that the asset value of the motel exceeds the amount owed under the mortgage. A simple refinancing of the loan can easily take care of the problem without the bank assuming any real risk as long as the asset value of the motel exceeds the mortgage amount by a comfortable margin. That really cuts your risk in half over the course of the mortgage.''

"True, the real risk to us is during the first ten years of the mortgage. In that respect, you're right. But, I guess, the real point is that we finally have a tool that can be refined and updated, which gives us the probability, or the number of years, we can expect some difficulty from a mortgage holder if we finance him for various amounts. For instance, in your case, we now know that we offered you financing that was beyond your capacity to repay over the term of the mortgage. Therefore, these meetings with you now were a foregone conclusion on the day we signed the documentation of the mortgages. We have a clearly impossible position with you that is going to take an awful lot of papering over.''

"What do you intend to do now?''

"Recommend pulling the plug on you.''

"What?''

"Sure, the situation is clearly impossible. Your expected income is less than the mortgage payments. We have, de facto, become owners. We also must look for a premature arrival of good times to get out of this mess. Therefore, we might as well derive the benefits of being owners when the good times come. We are certainly deriving no benefit having you as an owner. We can hire a good motel operator. Maybe you can apply for the job. I am also recommending that we close down one or more of the motels until the level of business improves. Of course, if you can come up with more equity—and that is what it is going to take for you to keep the motels—you can salvage the situation. The days of your telling us that it is our problem are over as far as I'm concerned.''

"I don't have any money to put into these albatrosses.''

"Well, maybe you don't, but you might have friends or relatives who are eager to pick up a half interest in four motels, which cost several million to build, for a few hundred thousand dollars. Go back to the same people who got you going in this business, only give them some ownership interest in the motels for the risk that they are taking in backing you. Maybe it is about time we do a little de-concentrating of wealth. Debt concentrates wealth to those who have access to it. And maybe it is time we start acting as bankers instead of money salesmen. Maybe it is time we should start listening to you.''

Appendix to Chapter 11

FINANCIAL STRATEGIC PLANNING SIMULATION

The results of the simulation are stored in the array M(1000), which is set to a zero value at the start of the program in statement 30. The number of one-hundred-year simulations is entered in statement 40. Statement 60 sets up the program with a current supply of 1,200 room-days and a current capacity of 1,800 room-days. Current motel rooms under construction to be completed this year (Z1) and next (Z2) are set to zero.

For a century of time (statement 70), whether or not a year is an up-year, or a down-year, and its impact on demand, is determined in statements 90–110. As each year of the simulation progresses, statement 120 transfers building activity to building completions by adding Z1 to capacity C. Z1 then assumes the value assigned to Z2, and Z2 is set equal to zero. This simulates the lag associated with building and completing new motel capacity.

The resulting occupancy rate for each year is determined in statement 130. Statement 140 merely prevents occupancy from going over a value of 100 percent. Statements 150–220 determine the daily rental rate and the expansion in capacity that will take place two years hence (Z2). Shrinkage occurs without any delay (statement 220). Gross income is calculated in statement 230 and stored in statement 240 as V in the array M(V). In this method of storing results, there can be no negative numbers assigned to V in the array M(V). If V took on a negative value, the program would stop.

The most negative gross margin would result for the case of zero occupancy. In this case, the resulting gross income would be −$90,000, or −90. Adding 100 to the value V ensures that no reference would be made to M(V) with V having a negative value. The 100 is subsequently removed in the printout of the expected value in statement 260 and in the printout of the probability distribution in statement 300.

Adding the statement, 55 PRINT K, keeps track of the progress of the simulation. The internal workings were checked by the statement: 235 PRINT C;R;U,P,Z1,Z2:INPUT Z$

```
10 REM NAME OF THIS PROGRAM IS ·MOTEL
20 DIM M(1000)
30 FOR I=1 TO 1000:M(I)=0:NEXT
40 PRINT:INPUT "NUMBER OF SIMULATIONS: ";S
50 FOR K=1 TO S
60 R=1200:C=1800:Z1=0:Z2=0
70 FOR I=1 TO 100
80 X=RND(X)
90 IF X>.45 THEN 100 ELSE 110
100 X=RND(X):G=X*.15:R=(1+G)*R:GOTO 120
110 X=RND(X):G=X*.12:R=(1-G)*R
```

```
120 C=C+Z1:Z1=Z2:Z2=0:R=INT(R+.5)
130 U=100*R/C:IF U<100 THEN 150 ELSE 140
140 U=100
150 IF U>90 THEN 190
160 IF U>80 THEN 200
170 IF U>70 THEN 210
180 GOTO 220
190 P=85:X=RND(X):G=5+X*(12-5):Z2=INT(C*G/100):GOTO 230
200 P=60:X=RND(X):G=4+X*(10-4):Z2=INT(C*G/100):GOTO 230
210 P=50:Z2=0:GOTO 230
220 P=45:X=RND(X):G=2+X*(5-2):Z2=0:C=C-INT(C*G/100)
230 V=P*90*50*U/100-20*50*90
240 V=100+INT(V/1000+.5):M(V)=M(V)+1:NEXT:NEXT
250 A=0:FOR I=1 TO 1000:A=A+I*M(I)/(100*S):NEXT
260 PRINT:PRINT "EXPECTED GROSS INCOME: ";A-100:PRINT
270 PRINT "% PROB","GROSS INCOME"
280 FOR I=1 TO 1000
290 IF M(I)=0 THEN 310
300 PRINT M(I)/S,I-100:INPUT Z$
310 NEXT:END
```

12

Investment Planning

SYNOPSIS

The planning associated with investment decision making usually takes the form of a projection of the anticipated cash flow. This can then be compared to the amount of the investment to gauge the magnitude of the return. Alternative projects can be weighed on the same scale of economic justice to select the one with the highest return. This would be one aspect of making a decision with regard to investments. Risk and strategic considerations are other aspects.

The two principal methods of evaluating the return of, and on, an investment are the net present value and the internal rate of return. Payback is another method of evaluating the return on an investment. If risk and strategic considerations are the same for two investment alternatives, then an investor would presumably select the alternative with the higher return. The net present value and the internal rate of return are means to evaluate the return on a projected cash flow stream taking into consideration both the timing and magnitude of each year's earnings.

This chapter incorporates simulation in the investment planning process utilizing the internal rate of return method of evaluating investment alternatives. Simulation is not another solution to an age-old problem of where to invest one's money, nor does it change the heart of the internal rate of return methodology of obtaining a comparative evaluation on the relative merits of one project over another. Simulation does add another dimension in viewing the results of an internal rate of return evaluation of a prospective investment.

Simulation provides a kaleidoscopic or ever-changing view of the uncertainties associated with the assessments of future values. The results of a simulation—the expected rate of return and the probability distribution of the range of possible rates of return—are sensitive to changes in the uncertainties surrounding the various assessments pertinent to an investment decision. In this world of shifting perceptions, with an ever-changing economic and political environment, man's best judgment on critical variables concerning an investment decision is as stable as the ebb and flow of the tide. Simulation can show which variables are most critical for evaluating a situation. Simulation can also measure the impact of changes in assessments of critical variables on the return of an investment opportunity.

All of this is very pertinent up to the moment that the investment is made.

Neither the net present value or the internal rate of return, with or without simulation, can prevent bad investments. An investment always looks promising at the time one decides to proceed with the investment. Unfortunately, a promising investment can turn sour. A perception of the future, and the unfolding of events that gives form and substance to the future, are not one and the same thing. Mortals are given the power to think about the future, to make judgments about the future, and to make decisions based on these judgments. And that's where the power stops. Mortals have not been given the power to peer into the future and see what will transpire. If that were possible, then there would be little in the way of a decision making process concerning investments. Not much thought has to be given as to what stocks to buy if one has a copy of next week's *Wall Street Journal*.

As long as the future cannot be penetrated, and today's perceptions of tomorrow's world are not always correct, then the best-laid plans of mice and men will go astray. One way to deal with uncertainty is to pin investment alternatives on a wall, turn out the lights, and throw a dart at the wall. Flicking on the lights takes care of the investment decision process. Even if this method is effective, rational man does not like to think that his powers of reason are to no avail. As long as there is uncertainty to contend with, then some thought has to be given as to the best investment. Simulation is one way to quantify the uncertainty of an investment as perceived in an investor's mind.

The illustration of simulation in investment planning will be built around a scenario of investing in an existing oil well. Other investment vehicles, such as real estate, could have been selected. The purpose of selecting any investment medium is to illustrate the two principal means of investment evaluation including the incorporation of simulation into the process of investment decision making. As will be demonstrated in this chapter, simulation can be formed and molded to the essential features of a given situation and tailored to fit its lines and contours. Pottery makers and tailors are sources of inspiration for a simulation model builder.

THE INVESTMENT VEHICLE

In 1988, and for a number of years before 1988, there had been trouble in the oil patch. The problem was that investments were made on the basis of $35 per barrel of oil and that the 1988 price for oil was $16 per barrel. With revenue at half of what was assumed when the debts were originally booked, it was no wonder that firms were having difficulties satisfying the interest and amortization payments. Many small companies in the oil patch had either collapsed or were consolidated with other firms possessing greater financial wherewithal or were absorbed into larger firms.

To illustrate the magnitude of the financial difficulties of the oil patch economy, suppose that an oil operator approached his banker in 1982 with the proposal to drill a well that was expected to have an average production of 100 barrels per

week with direct operating costs of $12 per barrel. His proposal for a loan would
have contained the following cash flow projection.

PROJECTED CASH FLOW
MADE IN 1982

YEAR	BARRELS PER WEEK	REVENUE $35/BBL	OPCOSTS $12/BBL	WEEKLY GROSS INCOME	ANNUAL (50 WEEK) GROSS INCOME BEFORE TAXES & FINANCING COSTS
1982	100	$3,500	$1,200	$2,300	$115,000
1983	100	3,500	1,200	2,300	115,000
1984	100	3,500	1,200	2,300	115,000
1985	100	3,500	1,200	2,300	115,000
1986	100	3,500	1,200	2,300	115,000
1987	100	3,500	1,200	2,300	115,000
1988	100	3,500	1,200	2,300	115,000
1989	100	3,500	1,200	2,300	115,000
1990	100	3,500	1,200	2,300	115,000
1991	100	3,500	1,200	2,300	115,000

What would a banker be willing to lend on this cash flow stream? If the terms
for a loan were 12 percent interest with repayment over ten years, the borrower
would have to repay his loan on the basis of an annual capital recovery factor of
17.2 percent. This recovery factor generates sufficient funds to pay 12 percent
interest on the outstanding balance of the loan and repay the entire loan in ten
years. If the banker were extremely confident that the new well would produce
100 barrels per week, and if he were extremely confident that the price of oil
would forever remain at $35 per barrel, the most he would lend is just under
$670,000. This amount of a loan, when multiplied by the required annual capital
recovery factor of 17.2 percent, would be about equal to the excess cash flow of
$115,000 being generated by the new well.

Even in the exuberance of the best of good times, a banker would not lend to
the full limit of the gross income—at least, not a prudent banker. After all, there
is no assurance that the future cash flow will materialize. The new well may not
generate the anticipated volume of oil, or the price of oil may not generate the
anticipated cash flow. The banker would apply some factor against the projected
cash flow to compensate for his assessment of risk. Suppose that his assessment
of risk was translated into a policy of not lending an amount of money whose
repayment would absorb more than two-thirds of the projected cash flow. Under
these circumstances, the maximum amount that he would lend would be two-
thirds of $670,000, or a little under $450,000. And, of course, the banker would
examine the use of the proceeds of the loan, the cost of the new well, the cash
reserves of the company, its earnings potential, and other aspects of judging the
creditworthiness of the borrower.

At $35 per barrel for oil, the loan would have been considered a good loan (all
loans are good loans on the day the documents are signed), and the proceeds for
drilling another oil well would have been considered a good use of the funds. By

1988, the price of oil had sunk to $16 per barrel. At $16 per barrel, it did not matter how conservative the banker might have been in evaluating the loan proposal, or how good he might have felt about making the loan. The lender and borrower were in trouble with this loan. The banker rued the day when the loan documents were signed. The borrower was sorry he had drilled another well. This could be seen in the projected cash flow starting in 1988 assuming that the borrower had hit his mark with regard to his production output and operating cost targets.

```
PROJECTED CASH FLOW
MADE IN 1988
                                               ANNUAL (50 WEEK)
                                      WEEKLY   GROSS INCOME
          BARRELS   REVENUE   OPCOSTS  GROSS    BEFORE TAXES &
YEAR      PER WEEK  $16/BBL   $12/BBL  INCOME   FINANCING COSTS

1988      100       $1,600    $1,200   $400     $20,000
1989      100        1,600     1,200    400      20,000
1990      100        1,600     1,200    400      20,000
1991      100        1,600     1,200    400      20,000
1992      100        1,600     1,200    400      20,000
1993      100        1,600     1,200    400      20,000
1994      100        1,600     1,200    400      20,000
1995      100        1,600     1,200    400      20,000
1996      100        1,600     1,200    400      20,000
1997      100        1,600     1,200    400      20,000
```

A cash flow of $20,000 per year would support a loan of about $116,000, an amount much less than what was probably borrowed in 1982. By 1988, the borrower had already pleaded with the banker that better days were ahead. The banker had already retorted that the story line had a hollow ring, that he had heard it too many times, that his patience for enduring an even longer streak of bad days had been exhausted. Furthermore, the banker had stated that he was afraid that things would get worse before they got better.

The borrower cringed when he heard these words because he realized that this was the prelude to the announcement of the decision that the well was about to be placed on the auction block. The banker had decided to hedge his bets by forcing the sale of some wells. The sale of some of the assets would protect the banker's interests in case there was a further decline in the price of oil. The borrower might protest vigorously, but the decision was essentially out of his control. He was in default of his debts.

The loan linked a borrower and lender together in the same transaction, but their expectations, and differences in outlook, were worlds apart. The borrower was interested in expanding his asset base. Maximizing the acquisition of assets was foremost in his mind. The lender was interested in using the assets as collateral to ensure the repayment of a loan. Minimizing the risk of loss, and the degree of loss, was foremost in his mind.

A lender wanted to sell a well in a depressed market to try to minimize his loss week with direct operating costs of $12 per barrel. His proposal for a loan would have contained the following cash flow projection.

PROJECTED CASH FLOW
MADE IN 1982

YEAR	BARRELS PER WEEK	REVENUE $35/BBL	OPCOSTS $12/BBL	WEEKLY GROSS INCOME	ANNUAL (50 WEEK) GROSS INCOME BEFORE TAXES & FINANCING COSTS
1982	100	$3,500	$1,200	$2,300	$115,000
1983	100	3,500	1,200	2,300	115,000
1984	100	3,500	1,200	2,300	115,000
1985	100	3,500	1,200	2,300	115,000
1986	100	3,500	1,200	2,300	115,000
1987	100	3,500	1,200	2,300	115,000
1988	100	3,500	1,200	2,300	115,000
1989	100	3,500	1,200	2,300	115,000
1990	100	3,500	1,200	2,300	115,000
1991	100	3,500	1,200	2,300	115,000

What would a banker be willing to lend on this cash flow stream? If the terms for a loan were 12 percent interest with repayment over ten years, the borrower would have to repay his loan on the basis of an annual capital recovery factor of 17.2 percent. This recovery factor generates sufficient funds to pay 12 percent interest on the outstanding balance of the loan and repay the entire loan in ten years. If the banker were extremely confident that the new well would produce 100 barrels per week, and if he were extremely confident that the price of oil would forever remain at $35 per barrel, the most he would lend is just under $670,000. This amount of a loan, when multiplied by the required annual capital recovery factor of 17.2 percent, would be about equal to the excess cash flow of $115,000 being generated by the new well.

Even in the exuberance of the best of good times, a banker would not lend to the full limit of the gross income—at least, not a prudent banker. After all, there is no assurance that the future cash flow will materialize. The new well may not generate the anticipated volume of oil, or the price of oil may not generate the anticipated cash flow. The banker would apply some factor against the projected cash flow to compensate for his assessment of risk. Suppose that his assessment of risk was translated into a policy of not lending an amount of money whose repayment would absorb more than two-thirds of the projected cash flow. Under these circumstances, the maximum amount that he would lend would be two-thirds of $670,000, or a little under $450,000. And, of course, the banker would examine the use of the proceeds of the loan, the cost of the new well, the cash reserves of the company, its earnings potential, and other aspects of judging the creditworthiness of the borrower.

At $35 per barrel for oil, the loan would have been considered a good loan (all loans are good loans on the day the documents are signed), and the proceeds for drilling another oil well would have been considered a good use of the funds. By

1988, the price of oil had sunk to $16 per barrel. At $16 per barrel, it did not matter how conservative the banker might have been in evaluating the loan proposal, or how good he might have felt about making the loan. The lender and borrower were in trouble with this loan. The banker rued the day when the loan documents were signed. The borrower was sorry he had drilled another well. This could be seen in the projected cash flow starting in 1988 assuming that the borrower had hit his mark with regard to his production output and operating cost targets.

PROJECTED CASH FLOW
MADE IN 1988

YEAR	BARRELS PER WEEK	REVENUE $16/BBL	OPCOSTS $12/BBL	WEEKLY GROSS INCOME	ANNUAL (50 WEEK) GROSS INCOME BEFORE TAXES & FINANCING COSTS
1988	100	$1,600	$1,200	$400	$20,000
1989	100	1,600	1,200	400	20,000
1990	100	1,600	1,200	400	20,000
1991	100	1,600	1,200	400	20,000
1992	100	1,600	1,200	400	20,000
1993	100	1,600	1,200	400	20,000
1994	100	1,600	1,200	400	20,000
1995	100	1,600	1,200	400	20,000
1996	100	1,600	1,200	400	20,000
1997	100	1,600	1,200	400	20,000

A cash flow of $20,000 per year would support a loan of about $116,000, an amount much less than what was probably borrowed in 1982. By 1988, the borrower had already pleaded with the banker that better days were ahead. The banker had already retorted that the story line had a hollow ring, that he had heard it too many times, that his patience for enduring an even longer streak of bad days had been exhausted. Furthermore, the banker had stated that he was afraid that things would get worse before they got better.

The borrower cringed when he heard these words because he realized that this was the prelude to the announcement of the decision that the well was about to be placed on the auction block. The banker had decided to hedge his bets by forcing the sale of some wells. The sale of some of the assets would protect the banker's interests in case there was a further decline in the price of oil. The borrower might protest vigorously, but the decision was essentially out of his control. He was in default of his debts.

The loan linked a borrower and lender together in the same transaction, but their expectations, and differences in outlook, were worlds apart. The borrower was interested in expanding his asset base. Maximizing the acquisition of assets was foremost in his mind. The lender was interested in using the assets as collateral to ensure the repayment of a loan. Minimizing the risk of loss, and the degree of loss, was foremost in his mind.

A lender wanted to sell a well in a depressed market to try to minimize his loss in case there was a further decline in the price of oil. The borrower viewed the idea in absolute dismay because the sale of the well would forever destroy any opportunity for him to recoup his original investment.

How much could a banker expect to obtain when selling an oil well in a depressed market? The answer was not much. There was a mismatch between the number of adventuresome souls, as buyers, and desperate bankers as sellers. Recovery in oil prices did not seem imminent. Recovery could take longer than anticipated; and worst of all, the price of oil might decline further before it recovered. This was not the makings of a strong case for anyone to buy oil wells. Nevertheless, the well was producing $20,000 per year in excess cash flow even at 1988 oil prices. What could the banker hope to receive in forcing the sale of the well?

Many investors would pay $20,000 for the well and recoup their entire investment in one year as long as the price of oil did not decline further. Not quite as many investors would pay $40,000 for the well because some investors might not be willing to accept a risk of a payback period of two years for their money. On the other side of the transaction, the banker would not be willing to sell the well for $20,000 or $40,000 because the future loss of income was not commensurate with the proceeds from the sale.

As the proposed price of the well increases beyond $40,000, the willingness of investors to purchase the well declines as the willingness of the seller to dispose of the well grows. A point would eventually be reached resulting in the consummation of the transaction where one side of the transaction would not be willing to pay more, and the other side would not be willing to accept less. That transaction becomes a data point in establishing the market valuation of an oil well.

Suppose that in 1988 the market for wells that had a ten-year remaining life was five times current annual earnings before taxes. That would generate a market valuation of $100,000 for the well under consideration, which probably represented a fraction of its original cost to the borrower.

From the point of view of a potential investor, he was not interested in the borrower's, or in the lender's, predicament. He saw a relatively new oil well available for about $100,000. He realized that the cost of drilling a new well was some multiple of this amount. Parenthetically, this inducement to buy the well on the basis that it was being sold for a fraction of its replacement cost is a red herring. No one in this right mind would drill a new well of this cost and production output because the economics of $16 per barrel mitigate against anyone making such an investment. Yet, it is a frequently heard argument when one is rummaging around the second-hand market.

The potential buyer would note that he had to pay taxes. Although the buyer would do all he could to obtain the well for less than $100,000, the market valuation meant that he would probably have to pay close to that amount. If he did pay $100,000 for the well, he would be able to depreciate the well at $10,000 per year over the remaining ten years of life of the well. The potential investor would evaluate the investment by continuing the cash flow projection as shown in the following table.

YEAR	GROSS INCOME	DEPRECIATION	BEFORE TAX PROFITS	TAXES (34%)	NET CASH FLOW
1988	$20,000	$10,000	$10,000	$3,400	$16,600
1989	20,000	10,000	10,000	3,400	16,600
1990	20,000	10,000	10,000	3,400	16,600
1991	20,000	10,000	10,000	3,400	16,600
1992	20,000	10,000	10,000	3,400	16,600
1993	20,000	10,000	10,000	3,400	16,600
1994	20,000	10,000	10,000	3,400	16,600
1995	20,000	10,000	10,000	3,400	16,600
1996	20,000	10,000	10,000	3,400	16,600
1997	20,000	10,000	10,000	3,400	16,600

NET PRESENT VALUE METHOD OF EVALUATION

The net present value method of evaluation requires the selection of an appropriate discount factor. The discount factor can be selected on the basis of the returns on alternative investments of comparable risk. Ninety-day Treasury bills provide the safest investment with the surest liquidity. Their yield in 1988, around the time of making the investment decision, was between 7 and 8 percent. This was not a comparable investment to an oil well that could have operational problems or might suffer from a further decline in the price of oil. The projected payback period for the oil well was six years (six times $16,600 is close to the original investment of $100,000) assuming no further decline in the price of oil. This did not match the ninety-day maturity of the Treasury bills. Ten-year high-grade corporate bonds were yielding 10 percent, and junk bonds were as high as 15 percent in yield. Both of these were before-tax returns. After-tax returns would be between 7 and 10 percent.

With these as alternatives, a potential investor in 1988 might have selected 12 percent as the appropriate discount factor for the after-tax cash flow on the oil well. This would reflect that the payment of interest on a junk bond, at least superficially, was more dependable than the cash flow stream from an oil well operating in a volatile oil market. Some investors might take issue with that observation and would consider an investment in an operating oil well with oil at $16 per barrel more secure than holding junk bonds. Whatever the case, the selection of an appropriate discount factor is one of personal choice. For these circumstances, the choice of the appropriate discount factor for most investors would probably fall in a range between 10 and 15 percent.

The net present value for a ten-year cash stream of $16,600, assuming no residual value for the well at the end of the tenth year, discounted at 12 percent, and at 15 percent, is calculated as follows.

YEAR	NET CASH FLOW	DISCOUNT FACTOR (12%)	DISCOUNTED CASH FLOW	DISCOUNT FACTOR (15%)	DISCOUNTED CASH FLOW
1988	$16,600	1.00	$16,600	1.00	$16,600
1989	16,600	1.12	14,820	1.15	14,430
1990	16,600	1.25	13,280	1.32	12,580
1991	16,600	1.40	11,860	1.53	10,850
1992	16,600	1.57	10,570	1.75	9,490
1993	16,600	1.76	9,430	2.01	8,260
1994	16,600	1.97	8,430	2.31	7,190
1995	16,600	2.21	7,510	2.66	6,240
1996	16,600	2.48	6,690	3.06	5,420
1997	16,600	2.77	5,990	3.52	4,720

NET PRESENT VALUE AT 12%: $105,180

NET PRESENT VALUE AT 15%: $95,780

Discounting takes into account the time value of money. Using the 12 percent discounted cash flow column as an example, $14,820 placed in an investment medium with an after-tax return of 12 percent would be equal to $16,600 one year from now. Therefore, $16,600 flowing into the investor's coffers one year from now has a discounted present value, at 12 percent after-tax return, of $14,820. Similarly, $13,280 invested at 12 percent after tax is worth $16,600 two years from now. Therefore, $13,280 is equivalent to receiving $16,600 two years in the future. Dropping down to the bottom of the column, $5,990 deposited in an investment which bears 12 percent after tax will grow to $16,600 in ten years. Therefore, the present value of receiving $16,600 ten years from now is equivalent to placing $5,990 in an escrow account today bearing a 12 percent after-tax return. The projected cash flow for each year is stated in terms of its present value. The total of the discounted cash flow for each year is called the net present value.

If an investor's discount factor is 12 percent, he would purchase the oil well for $100,000 because the net present value of the cash flow stream of $105,180 exceeds what he is paying for the investment. If his discount factor is 15 percent, he would not pay $100,000 for a cash flow stream whose net present value is $95,780.

THE INTERNAL RATE OF RETURN METHOD OF EVALUATION

This method of evaluation takes the process one step further. What is the discount factor where the net present value of the projected cash flow stream is exactly equal to the investment of $100,000? This is the internal rate of return. From the previous discussion, the internal rate of return is somewhere between 12 and 15 percent because the net present value for 12 percent is above $100,000 and the net present value for 15 percent is below $100,000. One can experiment with various discount factors between 12 and 15 percent until one stumbles onto the internal rate of return where the discounted value of the future cash flow stream is exactly equal to the investment.

An equivalent way to handle the situation is to subtract the investment of $100,000 from the net present value of the discounted cash flow stream. For the 12 percent discount factor, the net present value of $105,180 less the investment of $100,000 is $5,180. For the 15 percent discount factor, the net present value of $95,780 less the investment of $100,000 is −$4,220. Plotting these points on a graph enables one to pick off the discount factor where the net present value is equal to the investment. This is the zero line in Exhibit 12.1. The internal rate of return of about 13.8 percent is the point where the net present value of the future cash flow stream is equal to the amount of the investment.

The internal rate of return is useful in that investments of differing amounts can be compared without reference to the size of the investment. For instance, suppose that the internal rate of return for an investment of $125,000 in an oil well is 18 percent. Another oil well can be purchased for $150,000 and its internal rate of return is 21 percent. Which is preferable? Presumably the latter investment because of its higher internal rate of return. The fact that the former investment is $125,000 and the latter is $150,000 is not critical in deciding where

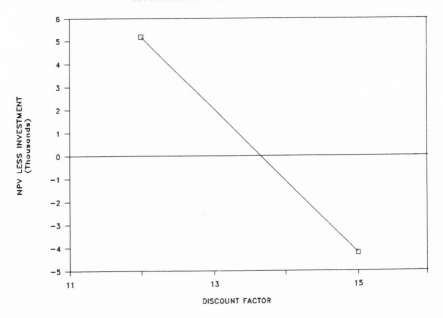

Exhibit 12.1.
Internal Rate of Return

to place one's money. This is not true for the net present value method of evaluating alternative investments. A little experimenting with vastly different sized investments can lead one to a situation where the stipulated discount factor may cause one to invest in the larger project even though the smaller project has a higher internal rate of return. This would not happen if one were making decisions on the basis of the internal rate of return. One caveat to this methodology is that the internal rate of return presumes that the cash flow is being reinvested at the same rate being generated by the investment itself. This may not be possible for investments with very high internal rates of return.

EVALUATING THE POTENTIAL INVESTMENT

One criticism for both the 1982 and 1988 cash flow projections is the fact that the price for oil is held constant throughout the projection period. It is understandable why this is done. The $35 per barrel in 1982 and the $16 per barrel in 1988 were the values for oil at the time the loan was being arranged and at the time it was being liquidated. No one can argue with the present price. The criticism is holding the value unchanged for ten years. This issue can be neatly sidestepped by those who make up projections by their saying that the current price of oil will be the average price of oil over the projection period. It is hard to argue with that.

The point is that no one knows what the price of oil will be over the next ten years. However, there are experts who do peer into the future and who are bold enough to venture their opinions as to the future price of crude oil. In 1988, the promoters for buying oil wells at $16 per barrel might borrow from these pundits and put together a presentation that would go something like this.

The United States is a major world consumer of oil. The cost of drilling and getting a well into production requires at least $25 per barrel to economically justify the investment. As long as oil is below $25 per barrel, domestic production will continue to decline. In a presentation to potential investors, slide one showing U.S. domestic production over the last decade would be flashed on the screen. Lo and behold, domestic oil production looks a bit anemic, although the slide would not be too convincing that the bottom is falling out of domestic production. However, throwing on slide two, which is U.S. consumption, and slide three, which is the difference between the domestic consumption and domestic production, would demonstrate the sharply rising level of U.S. imports in the years preceding 1988. Thus it becomes simply a matter of time before U.S. oil imports rise to such an extreme level that the early 1970s explosion in the price of oil will occur again. Slide four is a comparison of U.S. imports and the price of oil year by year since 1968. This would cinch the argument that the level of U.S. imports is key to understanding the future price of oil.

In answer to the question from a potential investor as to when will be the timing of an explosion in price, a safe response would be two to four years in the future. No one can be taken to court for saying that. How much of a price rise would take place when the United States is consuming much of the production capacity of the oil exporting nations? The answer to that query depends on how successful OPEC is in maintaining a pricing structure. The success of OPEC in controlling the world price for oil depends on both the ability of OPEC to attract the non-OPEC oil exporters into its fold and its ability to enforce production quotas on its members. Certainly, these are major imponderables that have to be weighed in order to evaluate the investment.

A potential investor is sure to ask what would happen if the price increase takes longer than four years considering the ten-year remaining life of the well. If an investor does not ask this question, the promoter will do so rhetorically.

As the well is currently in production to make some feeble attempt to pay interest on existing debt, and since the well is being purchased only with equity funds, the well will be shut down and mothballed until oil prices start heading for $20 per barrel. Since higher oil prices are inevitable, and since there is at least ten years of life left in the well, the investors are sure to get their money back, although there may be a question of timing if the anticipated price hikes take longer than expected.

Slide five is the oil price projections by various pundits. The range in oil prices is based on a strong and on a weak OPEC control of the market. A summary of their predictions follows with oil prices expressed in current dollars.

PRICE OF OIL IN $/BARREL

	LOW END OF RANGE WEAK OPEC COHESION	HIGH END OF RANGE STRONG OPEC COHESION
1989	$13	$17
1990	12	16
1991	14	18
1992	18	22
1993	22	25
1994	24	30
1995	26	32
1996	28	35
1997	30	38
1998	28	35
1999	25	30
2000	20	25
2001	20	25

The fall-off in the latter years is the self-correcting mechanism of the market place. As oil moves above $25 per barrel, economic justification returns for developing comparably higher cost oil fields in the United States and elsewhere, which, with some suitable time lapse, reduces imports from OPEC nations. Reduced oil imports encourage dissension within OPEC ranks. The ultimate result of their squabbling over who has to cut production by how much is price erosion. This discourages further development of higher cost U.S. production. After a few years of stagnation in exploring and developing new oil finds, oil imports into the United States begin to rise and the cycle repeats itself.

Operating costs are expected to be a function of the output of the well, which, in turn, will be related to the market price of oil. The following table indicates the intention of management for maximizing the revenue generation of the well by adjusting production to market price. The experts for the data contained in the table are the managers of the operating company.

PRICE OF OIL	WELL OUTPUT (BARRELS/WEEK)	OPERATING COST $/BARREL	
		LOW ESTIMATE	HIGH ESTIMATE
LESS THAN $25	90	10	13
$25-$30	100	11	14
MORE THAN $30	120	14	18

The promoters feel that higher taxes are going to be imposed on the American people regardless of the political party in power. One political party may hit the business community harder than the other party with regard to taxes. Nevertheless, polling the pundits of the tax scene created the following table.

	EFFECTIVE TAX RATES	
	LOW	HIGH
1989	34%	34%
1990-1995	34	38
After 1995	36	42

For the particular well in question, the net of tax residual value is assumed to be somewhere between zero to 5 percent of the investment of $100,000. The promoters expect very little residual value after ten years of operation.

The usual way for assessing this investment is to calculate three internal rates of return. One is for the best of all possible worlds where everything goes in favor of the investor: the highest price of oil, the lowest cost of operation, the lowest tax rates, and the highest residual value. The second covers the worst of all possible worlds with the lowest price of oil coupled with the highest cost of operation, the highest tax rates, and the lowest residual value. The third would be the most middling of all possible worlds where all the variables assume average values between their upper and lower bounds.

Actually, it would be highly unlikely for the two extreme cases to occur. There is no reason why the highest price on oil would be coupled with the lowest cost of operation and why this would occur each and every year of operation. Second, the middle of the oil price range may not be very probable. If 1992 is considered a key year for OPEC to have its act together, there is more reason for the price of oil to be closer to the extremes of the range than to be in the middle range. Having oil prices closer to the extremes of their projected ranges would reflect the cohesiveness of OPEC to control the market. If, after 1992, OPEC cannot exert tight control over the market either by internal leadership for members to abide by their production quotas, or if the non-OPEC member nations have significant production capacity to thwart OPEC objectives to control prices through production quotas, then the price of oil would most probably remain in the lower half of the range. If OPEC is weak as a controlling force on prices in 1992, this condition would most likely remain that way in succeeding years. This condition can be modeled by making it highly probable that the price of oil in succeeding years will also be in the lower half of the range.

Similarly, if the price of oil is in the upper half of the range of values in 1992, then it is highly probable that OPEC can continue to dominate the market, price-wise, in succeeding years. This can be accomplished by the same mechanism that kept prices in the lower half of the range. On the other hand, it is possible for a weak OPEC in 1992 to become a strong OPEC in later years, and vice versa. This, too, can be incorporated in the model by having some small probability in any given year that OPEC will traverse the barrier between cohesive, and non-cohesive, control over the pricing structure. This, in effect, is modeling the economic repercussions of a political situation.

The simulation that incorporates the anticipated performance of the oil well, the predictions of experts of the future price of oil and tax rates, and the political cohesiveness of OPEC from the point of view of price maintenance is contained in the appendix to this chapter. The program calculates the expected internal rate of return of this investment and the probability distribution for all generated values of the internal rate of return. The program also generates the internal rate of return for the worst case, the best case, and the average case.

The worst case is the calculation of the internal rate of return with the lowest possible oil prices and the highest possible operating costs and tax rates. The best case is the calculation of the internal rate of return with the highest possible oil prices and the lowest possible operating costs and tax rates. The average case is calculated using the mean value between the highest and lowest values of oil prices, operating costs, and tax rates. All three of these calculations can be performed by hand with the assistance of a calculator. They could be presented to potential investors in the form of a sixth slide.

SCENARIO	IRR
ABSOLUTE WORST	17%
AVERAGE	23
ABSOLUTE BEST	28

The simulation in the appendix selects random values for the key variables within their respective permissible ranges. There is an additional proviso that once in the lower half, or the upper half, of the oil price range, the probability that the oil price will remain in the same half of the range in the following year is 95 percent. The result of 1,000 simulations provides an expected return of 22.7

percent, which is quite close to the simple calculation using average values for all the variables. The probability distribution for various internal rates of return is as follows.

INTERNAL RATE OF RETURN	PERCENTAGE PROBABILITY
20	3.4%
21	23.9
22	17.5
23	14.6
24	31.1
25	9.4
26	0.1

The distribution is bimodal reflecting the point that the price of oil is more apt to be at either extreme of its range than in the middle. This can be seen in Exhibit 12.2.

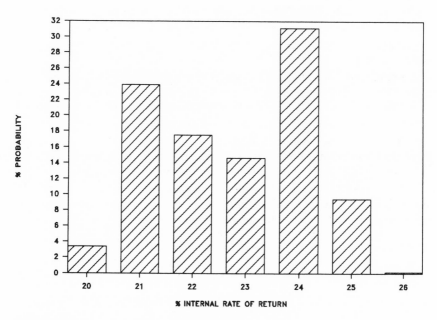

Exhibit 12.2.
Internal Rate of Return (probability distribution)

What has been gained by all this? One point is that the chance of the absolute worst and best cases actually occurring is something less than nil. As a matter of fact, they are misleading indicators of performance. Simulation provides a better description of the possible outcomes showing a bimodal distribution about the expected outcome of 22.7 percent. With a little effort, the simulation program can be made more user friendly and permit alternative investments in oil wells to be investigated. The program could ask the operator for the amount of the investment and the interplay between production output and operating costs. The assessment on oil prices and tax rates would remain the same. The output for the internal rate of return should probably be in tenths of a percent rather than the next higher integer value as presently built into the program.

Nevertheless, whether an individual investor would desire this insight into the potential result of an investment in an oil well in the form of a sixth slide is a matter of personal preference. Regardless of the choice, both methods depend on the assessments of experts being essentially correct. The history of investments shows that the experts have been dumbfounded time and time again. The world's roster of bad investments is a brilliant indictment against man's perceptive abilities to see into the future. The best-laid plans of mice and men often, if not nearly always, go astray.

Having said that, the point to bear in mind is that people have money that they desire to invest. If an investor were interested in oil wells in 1988 with ten years of remaining reserves, and if management's assessments on the operational aspects of the well had any validity, and if the experts' opinions on the future price of oil, and tax rates, were to be taken seriously, and if one wondered about the impact of the cohesiveness of OPEC in maintaining a pricing structure, what was the investor to do?

If an investor wants to give the slightest forethought as to where his money is to be invested, then some thought has to be given to the key variables that will affect the return on that investment. And if an investor is going to expend some effort in thinking about the future, or if he wants to weigh the potential return of one investment against another, simulation can be a better aid in making up his mind than blindly throwing darts at a wall. However, in saying all this, the responsibility for making the investment decision rests solely in the hands of the investor. The investor must live with the repercussions of decisions made with regard to investments as events unfold with the passing of time. The analyst, or the simulation model builder, certainly doesn't.

Appendix to Chapter 12

INTERNAL RATE OF RETURN SIMULATION

This program is used in the simulation of the internal rate of return. The internal rate of return (IRR) is calculated on the basis that the well will be shut down from 1989 to 1991 and will start in operation in 1992.

STATEMENTS	PURPOSE
30–90	Data base for low, medium, and high oil prices and low and high tax rates over the next thirteen years.
100	Depreciation schedule starting in 1992.
110–220	Worst case IRR calculation.
230–340	Average case IRR calculation.
350–460	Best case IRR calculation.
470	Input of the number of simulations.
480	Marks the start of each simulation.
490	50/50 chance of the price of oil in 1992 being in the lower or upper half of the permissible price range.
500–600	Oil prices are determined for the following nine years based on a 95 percent probability that the price will be in the same half of the permissible range as in the previous year.
610–650	Calculates the cash flow projection and evaluates the resulting IRR in subroutine 900.
660	Stores resulting IRR at end of individual simulation.
670–680	At end of all simulations, calculates and prints expected value of the IRR.
690–730	Printout of all IRRs and their associated probabilities of occurrence.

```
10 REM NAME OF PROGRAM IS IRR
20 DIM P(3,20):DIM T(2,20):DIM C(20):DIM Q(20)
25 DIM R(20):DIM D(20):DIM E(20):DIM O(20):DIM S(100)
30 FOR I=1 TO 3:FOR J=1 TO 13:READ P(I,J):NEXT:NEXT
40 DATA 0,0,0,18,22,24,26,28,30,28,25,20,20
50 DATA 0,0,0,20,23.5,27,29,31.5,34,31.5,27.5,22.5,22.5
```

```
60  DATA  0,0,0,22,25,30,32,35,38,35,30,25,25
70  FOR  I=1  TO  2:FOR  J=1  TO  13:READ  T(I,J):NEXT:NEXT
80  DATA  0,0,0,.34,.34,.34,.34,.34,.34,.34,.36,.36,.36
90  DATA  0,0,0,.34,.38,.38,.38,.38,.38,.38,.42,.42,.42
100 V=100:FOR  I=4  TO  13:D(I)=V/10:NEXT
110 FOR  I=4  TO  13
120 P=P(1,I):GOSUB  800
130 IF  P<25  THEN  160
140 IF  P<30  THEN  170
150 GOTO  180
160 O(I)=13*90*50/1000:GOTO  190
170 O(I)=14*100*50/1000:GOTO  190
180 O(I)=18*120*50/1000
190 E(I)=(R(I)-O(I)-D(I))*T(2,I)
200 C(I)=R(I)-O(I)-E(I)
210 NEXT:C(13)=C(13)+0*V:GOSUB  900
220 PRINT:PRINT "MINIMUM IRR PERCENT: ";R*100
230 FOR  I=4  TO  13
240 P=P(2,I):GOSUB  800
250 IF  P<25  THEN  280
260 IF  P<30  THEN  290
270 GOTO  300
280 O(I)=11.5*90*50/1000:GOTO  310
290 O(I)=12.5*100*50/1000:GOTO  310
300 O(I)=16*120*50/1000
310 E(I)=(R(I)-O(I)-D(I))*(T(1,I)+T(2,I))/2
320 C(I)=R(I)-O(I)-E(I)
330 NEXT:C(13)=C(13)+.025*V:GOSUB  900
340 PRINT:PRINT "AVERAGE IRR PERCENT: ";R*100
350 FOR  I=4  TO  13
360 P=P(3,I):GOSUB  800
370 IF  P<25  THEN  400
380 IF  P<30  THEN  410
390 GOTO  420
400 O(I)=10*90*50/1000:GOTO  430
410 O(I)=11*100*50/1000:GOTO  430
420 O(I)=14*120*50/1000
430 E(I)=(R(I)-O(I)-D(I))*T(1,I)
440 C(I)=R(I)-O(I)-E(I)
450 NEXT:C(13)=C(13)+.05*V:GOSUB  900
460 PRINT:PRINT "MAXIMUM IRR PERCENT: ";R*100
470 PRINT:INPUT "NUMBER OF SIMULATIONS: ";S:PRINT
480 FOR  L=1  TO  S
490 X=RND(X):Q(4)=P(1,4)+X*(P(3,4)-P(1,4))
500 FOR  I=5  TO  13
510 IF  Q(I-1)<P(2,I-1)  THEN  520  ELSE  540
520 X=RND(X)
```

```
530 IF X<.95 THEN 590 ELSE 580
540 X=RND(X)
550 IF X<.95 THEN 580 ELSE 590
580 X=RND(X):Q(I)=P(2,I)+X*(P(3,I)-P(2,I)):GOTO 600
590 X=RND(X):Q(I)=P(1,I)+X*(P(2,I)-P(1,I))
600 NEXT
610 FOR I=4 TO 13
620 P=Q(I):GOSUB 800
630 X=RND(X):E(I)=(R(I)-O(I)-D(I))*(T(1,I)+X*(T(2,I)-T(1,I)))
640 C(I)=R(I)-O(I)-E(I)
650 NEXT:X=RND(X):C(13)=C(13)+X*.05*V:GOSUB 900
660 R=100*R:S(R)=S(R)+1:NEXT
670 A=0:FOR I=1 TO 100:A=A+I*S(I)/S:NEXT
680 PRINT "EXPECTED IRR: ";A:PRINT
690 PRINT "PERCENT":PRINT "PROBABILITY","IRR":PRINT
700 FOR I=1 TO 100
710 IF S(I)=0 THEN 730
720 PRINT 100*S(I)/S,I:INPUT Z$
730 NEXT:END
800 X=RND(X):IF P<25 THEN 830
810 IF P<30 THEN 840
820 GOTO 850
830 R(I)=P*90*50:O(I)=(10+X*3)*90*50:GOTO 860
840 R(I)=P*100*50:O(I)=(11+X*3)*100*50:GOTO 860
850 R(I)=P*120*50:O(I)=(14+X*4)*120*50
860 R(I)=R(I)/1000:O(I)=O(I)/1000:RETURN
900 FOR I=1 TO 3:C(I)=0:NEXT
910 FOR K=1 TO 100:R=K/100
920 A=0:FOR I=4 TO 13:A=A+C(I)/((1+R)^(I)):NEXT
930 A=A-V:IF A>0 THEN 950
940 K=500
950 NEXT:RETURN
```

13

Portfolio Management Planning

SYNOPSIS

The reader should be sufficiently forewarned by the observation that the thirteenth chapter of this book is dedicated to the utilization of simulation in the management of a portfolio of stocks. Let the reader beware!

The classical approach to buying and selling stocks is to buy and hold VALUE. Selling really is not part of this strategy. VALUE is defined as a company that is firmly established in its market. Its product line is widely used and is of a nature where the risk of technological obsolescence is nil. Moreover, the company leads its industry in keeping its product line up-to-date through a vigorous research and development effort. The management is considered by all to be wise and omniscient. The capitalization of the company has little in the way of debt; its liquidity and creditworthiness are sufficient to weather the worst of economic storms; and its history of earnings and dividend growth expands the better part of a century.

There is nothing wrong with this approach other than the possibility that VALUE investments made on this basis in the 1950s, and still held in the 1980s, might consist of a portfolio of steel and railroad, rather than computer and airline, stocks. Simulation does not have much of a role to play in the buy and hold VALUE approach to investing. The effort might be better placed trying to identify the companies of VALUE, which will still be companies of VALUE decades into the future.

Another investment strategy is to explore the new issue and over-the-counter markets in search for Xerox when it was known as Haloid. The chances of discovering such companies are small, but the payoffs are large. Simulation is of little use in this market. The effort can be better expended understanding the nature of the company's product, its prospects for success, the depth of management, the technical expertise to make a reality out of a dream, and the financial resources to get from here to there.

There is another approach to investing that has deep roots in the past. That is to anticipate that a commodity, such as copper, will fluctuate in price with respect to the business cycle. Copper does fluctuate in price and, like all things, in an unpredictable manner. However, the price of copper is not entirely unpredictable. When there is too much copper being mined, and copper inventories are piled to the warehouse ceiling, one can predict a low price for copper with a fair degree of confidence. In fact, under these conditions, it will already be low.

Likewise, when copper production, and inventory levels, are insufficient to satisfy market demand, one can safely predict that the price of copper will not be low.

There are investors who accumulate holdings in copper mining companies during depressed times in the copper industry. Their concept of VALUE is selecting companies that are going to survive the bad times in the copper business. The investors have no idea when the market will turn. In some respects, they may not even care. With the patience of Job, they await the inevitable, continuing to accumulate copper stocks in a weak market environment, weakened all the more by most Wall Street–smart analysts telling their clients to shun an industry with such dismal prospects.

As any economist will tell you, the depressed price of copper will force privately owned companies to cut back on production. However, recent experience has shown that low copper prices do not always affect production of state-owned copper mining companies. Nevertheless, reduced copper production eventually leads to the draw down of the stockpiles of copper. Sooner or later, the price of copper begins to increase. As the price of copper begins to climb, so does the price of copper mining companies. At some point, these investors cease their accumulation of copper stocks.

The copper mining companies may be a bit slow to increase production to a commensurate degree with the growth in demand and the shrinkage of inventories. As inventories are being drawn down in the normal course of business, copper users decide to hedge against a potential shortfall of copper and sharply increase their private holdings. The herd instinct brings about what was feared most. Copper inventories in the public domain are nearly exhausted, shortfalls begin to appear in the form of unfilled orders, and the price of copper soars. For reasons that can best be described as perverse, copper stocks begin to be touted by the Wall Street–smart stock analysts giving further impetus to rising prices for copper mining stocks. The public is buying copper mining stocks. That means someone is selling them to complete the transaction. Could it be those who were accumulating shares when the price of copper was in the basement? Heaven forbid.

This is the contrarian approach to investing. Buy low, sell high. As simple as this sounds, it is actually difficult to do. It means buying something that no one wants and selling something that everyone wants. It requires a rare virtue called patience. This is the model that will be explored in this chapter. However, this same model can be used to evaluate other strategies to investing such as buying as the market moves up and selling as the market moves down. This chapter explores the possibility of evaluating various portfolio buy and sell decision rules using simulation as a bloodless experiment to select an optimal investment strategy.

Every investor in the stock market has, at some point in his life, been swept away by Wall Street fever. The fever has two distinctive phases. One phase is to remain out of the market as the market proceeds higher after a severe decline in stock prices. In retrospect, it is easy to identify the period of time when the bear apparently died giving way to the birth of the bull. Nevertheless, in living through this period of transition, it is difficult, in the weekly ups and downs of the stock market, to sense an emerging upturn in stock prices after suffering through the bruising experience of a severe downturn. New bull markets are greeted with disbelief. The new bull market slowly generates converts from the host of disbelievers with successive advances and retreats ending at ever higher levels. However, the bruised and battered erstwhile investor from the previous bear market slaughter may find himself waiting for a retrenchment in stock prices to a particular level before he commits his funds. The devil on Wall Street makes sure that the market does not reach that level, and the investor finds himself locked into a cash position as the bull market surges forward.

In retrospect, and only in retrospect, the bear market has changed into a bull market. Unfortunately for the hapless investor, he is not confident that this is happening. He fears that the recovery is a bear market trap, when, in fact, it is not. Nevertheless, if stocks would retreat near the previous lows of the bear market, he might start buying stocks. Although the market does have its normal corrections, it never reaches the investor's mental buy point. As the market keeps hitting successive highs, the investor keeps moving up his buy level. The market simply does not cooperate in retreating to that point. The investor is out in the cold. In total frustration he commits his money to the market. Naturally, this is close to the peak of the bull market.

The second phase starts some time later as the bull begins his transformation into a bear. After the first broad retreat of the market, the investor hangs in fully invested waiting for a new all-time peak to occur. He has the bull market mentality and cannot bring himself around to the point that the all-time market peak for this cycle is already history. Eventually, the market declines to a level that begins to worry the investor. Maybe the bull market is over. He then begins establishing recovery points at which time he will start selling his holdings. The first recovery point that would trigger the selling of his holdings might be where he can break even on his investment. The devil on Wall Street is not cooperative. Then the investor lowers his selling point to where his losses are about 5 percent of his investment. The market never quite recovers to that point. Each decline is worse than the one before; each recovery does not reach the level of the previous one. The investor feels locked into his stock position. The market continues to deteriorate. He is immobilized with fear. Then the market moves into a severe retreat. Finally he can't take it anymore and sells out during the worst of the carnage. One does not need to be told that this is usually close to the end of the bear market.

The investor is ready to repeat the cycle of being whipsawed to buy high and sell low unless he changes his ways. Once he has been whipsawed once, or twice, by the devil on Wall Street, he is ready to explore other alternatives to investing. Any alternative will do as long as he can remove himself from the emotional trauma of being immobilized to take corrective action at the right time.

The investor could buy and hold VALUE. In today's world, a company whose product line is in every household may be fighting for its life against foreign imports and may be up to its ears in debt. A company in the forefront of technological change doesn't have the history of earnings and dividend growth to qualify as VALUE. The concept of VALUE is more amenable to a world where technological change proceeds at a slower pace. VALUE might be obvious in previous decades, but the accelerating rate of change of technology, the globalization of production, and the increasing fickleness of consumer tastes can make the product line of a VALUE company, even with its commitment to research and development, obsolete or non-competitive in a relatively short period of time.

He could explore the high infant mortality world of new issues. Unless one's occupation, or preoccupation, lends itself to understanding what BIONUCOM-PUTECHTRONIX means in terms of products, market, competition, management, and financial resources, it might be preferable to go back to the old habit of being whipsawed by the devil.

The investor could subscribe to a stock advisory service. There is no better way to assess this domain of assistance than by obtaining one issue of a stock advisory service that does nothing but survey what the other advisory services are saying. One can read the summary of one advisor telling his clientele that the market is about to burst into the stratosphere and that any hesitation in the market between now and take-off time is an opportunity to buy, buy, and buy. There, right next to this one, is the summary of another advisor telling his clientele that the market is poised for a descent that will rival the *Titanic's,* and any hesitation in the market between now and doomsday is an opportunity to sell, sell, and sell. And to complete the picture, both scenarios will be surrounded by advisors telling their clients that the market may go up if it doesn't go down, or that it may go down, if it doesn't go up. Therefore, the best course of action is to be half in cash and half in VALUE stocks.

The pitiful thing about all this is that one of these advisors is correct. It is just a matter of selecting which one. Even if the right one is selected, it still doesn't mean that he will be correct the next time around. Studies have been done on this subject. Let's just say that it is a rare advisor who is consistently right.

The investor can leave the decision as to how his funds are invested to a professional portfolio manager. There are hundreds of professionally managed mutual funds listed daily in the financial papers. Being listed means one can measure performance. There are advisory services that do nothing but measure mutual fund performance. The results? About two-thirds of the fund managers, whose purpose in life is to maximize the value of a portfolio of stocks, cannot keep up with an unmanaged average such as the Dow Jones or the Standard & Poor's 500. Part of the reason is that the internal charges sop up some of the value of the portfolio—after all, fund managers are entitled to make a living. The primary reason is the perverse nature of the market. If the market is going up, the fund may be in stock groupings that are not participating fully in the market rally. The fund may be in the right stock groupings, but not in the particular stocks that are propelling the value of the group. Again, it is a rare fund manager who can consistently beat the market averages.

This is not to be critical of stock advisors and fund managers. They just happen to operate in a world where their advice, or performance, can be easily measured. If other occupations could be as easily evaluated as these two, the results would probably be quite similar.

One other investment mechanism should be mentioned. Investment decisions can be based on chart patterns of price versus time. The market average, a stock group average, or an individual stock may be in the process of completing a head-and-shoulders chart pattern. This, to a technical advisor, means a buy signal. Or is it a sell signal? Is the past stock price movement a prelude to its future movement? The chartists say yes. They would hardly do otherwise. They can point to many instances where their recommendations to buy, or sell, based on chart patterns were correct. The critics respond that this whole thing is a self-fulfilling prophecy. If the chartists have a large following, and they say buy, or sell, in unison, is it any wonder if the stock moves up, or down, accordingly.

The critic who did most to cast doubt on this profession was a professor named Malkiel who took a random walk down Wall Street. He managed to create every imaginable price pattern a chartist can dream up by simply reaching into a bag of random numbers to determine the daily change in the price of a stock. To Malkiel, past price movements were not a prelude to the future.

What is to be done? One can tack the financial pages on a wall and throw darts to select a stock. Some maintain that the results would not be that bad. In a broader perspective of the problem, one doesn't have to pick stocks. The investment problem is solved by just being able to identify the next broad stock market move. If an investor feels that the next market move is up, he should buy shares in a stock fund. If he feels it is going down, put everything in cash. This alone would beat the record of nearly every professional portfolio manager.

The point is that the investor, and the portfolio managers, do not know what the next major move of the stock market will be because they cannot peer into the future. This is the challenge of being a decision maker. An investor, as a decision maker, can contemplate the various factors that may affect the future level of stock prices, but he doesn't know what the future will bear.

From the point of view of investing in the stock market, an investor can investigate various decision rules and use simulation to evaluate the decision rule. This is a bloodless experiment in the sense that funds are not being exposed to risk of loss. If future market behavior with regard to volatility and general trends have similar characteristics with the past, and if one class of decision rule works better than others, perhaps something useful can be gleaned by such an exercise.

Then, again, perhaps not. The trading patterns of future markets may have nothing in common with past markets. A decision rule that may have worked well in the past market would then have no relevance as to its relative performance with other decision rules, or plans of action, for the future market.

Nevertheless, the simulation to evaluate various plans of action requires a model of a future market. The assumption is made that the future market will have similar characteristics with the past. Chartists may be useful at this point. They are in the best position to provide a history of general trends in the market. They, or statisticians or economists, or those possessing a modicum of analytical ability for that matter, can measure trends in the market both as to the monthly change in the market average and the duration of the trend. For illustrative purposes, suppose that their findings are of the following nature.

TREND DESCRIPTION	PERCENTAGE RANGE MONTHLY CHANGE IN MARKET AVERAGE	DURATION OF TREND IN MONTHS
STRONG BULL	-1.0% - 4.0%	1 - 15
MEDIUM BULL	-1.5 - 3.5	1 - 12
WEAK BULL	-2.0 - 3.0	1 - 10
NEUTRAL	-2.5 - 2.5	1 - 8
WEAK BEAR	-3.0 - 2.0	1 - 10
MEDIUM BEAR	-3.5 - 1.5	1 - 12
STRONG BEAR	-4.0 - 1.0	1 - 15

In this example, seven major trends have been established. For each trend, some poor soul has examined the range of monthly changes in the market and the duration of the market trend. As an example, weak bull markets can last from as short a period as one month to as long as ten months. During the period of what is termed a weak bull market, the range of monthly changes in stock prices were between −2 and +3 percent from the level of the previous month. At this point, someone of analytic ability can obtain the probability distribution of monthly changes. This may be a tedious task, but it is not difficult.

In examining the history of the stock market over the past ten or twenty years, one can obtain the probability of occurrence for each of the major trends. Suppose that the following is the summary of such an analysis. The average monthly change is the midpoint of the previously indicated range for each of the major trends.

TREND DESCRIPTION	PROBABILITY OF OCCURRENCE	AVERAGE MONTHLY CHANGE
STRONG BULL	5%	1.5%
MEDIUM BULL	10	1.0
WEAK BULL	15	0.5
NEUTRAL	40	0.0
WEAK BEAR	15	-0.5
MEDIUM BEAR	10	-1.0
STRONG BEAR	5	-1.5

The symmetry of the probabilities, the symmetry of the range of possible changes in the monthly market average, and the symmetry of the length of the trend for the corresponding bull and bear market movements should be convincing evidence that this is a no-win, no-lose market environment. If an investor stays in this market long enough, he will eventually find himself at his starting point. However, he might have traversed several mountain ranges and canyons along the way.

Suppose that an individual is interested in investing $100 per month and further suppose that he has limited himself to two options. One is a money market fund and the other is a no-load mutual fund that perfectly tracks the market average. The former will be called the cash fund and the latter the stock fund. He is free to set up any set of rules on buying and selling that he desires. He could also simply place all the money in the cash fund. This is the base from which to measure other investment alternatives. If a stock market investment strategy cannot beat putting money in the bank, then there really is no point in investing other than the excitement of being whipsawed to death.

The program in the appendix to this chapter creates a randomly generated market for 1,000 months from a starting value of 1000 using the aforementioned rules of stock market behavior. Although this is a no-lose, no-win market, an appropriate print statement, better yet, screen graphing, would permit one to observe what Malkiel has concluded: The random draw of numbers can create every conceivable market pattern one can possibly imagine.

Suppose that the individual has two plans of action in mind. For both, he desires that at least 10 percent of his total funds be committed to both the stock fund and to the cash fund.

	PLAN ONE	PLAN TWO
MINIMUM INVESTMENT OF TOTAL FUNDS		
CASH FUND	10%	10%
STOCK FUND	10	10

If he is at one of these limits, the investor will split his $100 contribution equally to both funds regardless of the state of the market. If more than 10 percent of his funds is in the cash fund, and more than 10 percent is in the stock fund, then he will invest his funds on the basis of the comparison between the average cost of acquisition of shares in the stock fund and the current market price of a share of the stock fund.

Each month, the investor looks at the average cost of acquisition for shares in the stock fund and compares that cost with the current price. If the current price of a share of the stock fund is lower than the average cost of the acquisition of the shares, he will invest the $100 per month as per the following rules.

If the stock price is between 95 and 100 percent of the average acquisition cost of the shares, the investor divides the $100 evenly between the two investment media.

STOCK PRICE BELOW COST OF ACQUISITION

	PLAN ONE	PLAN TWO
MARKET VALUE OF SHARE OF STOCK FUND		
BETWEEN 95% AND 100% OF AVERAGE COST OF ACQUISITION		
CASH FUND	$50	$50
STOCK FUND	50	50

If the market price of the shares continues to fall below the average cost of acquisition, the investor starts buying more shares of the stock fund. This lowers the average cost of acquisition of his shares.

	PLAN ONE	PLAN TWO
MARKET VALUE OF STOCK SHARES BETWEEN 90% AND 95% OF AVERAGE COST OF ACQUISITION		
CASH FUND	0	0
STOCK FUND	$100	$100

If the market continues to decline, the monthly contribution of $100 continues to be placed in the stock fund. In addition, funds are drawn out of the cash fund and invested in the stock fund. Divestment from the cash fund to the stock fund is as follows.

	PLAN ONE	PLAN TWO
MARKET VALUE OF FUND SHARES AS PERCENTAGE OF AVERAGE COST OF ACQUISITION		
70% – 90%	CONVERT 2% CASH TO STOCK	CONVERT 2% CASH TO STOCK
BELOW 70%	CONVERT 5% CASH TO STOCK	CONVERT 5% CASH TO STOCK

In any month where the market price of a share of the stock fund is between 70 and 90 percent of the average cost of acquisition, 2 percent of the total value of the cash fund is converted to shares in the stock fund in addition to investing the $100 monthly investment allotment in the stock fund. If the market declines further, such that the market price of a share of stock is below 70 percent of the average cost of acquisition, then 5 percent of the total value of the cash fund is converted to the stock fund along with the investing of the $100. The average cost of acquisition declines with each purchase of new fund shares.

This takes care of down markets where the market value of the stock fund is below the average cost of acquisition of the stock fund shares. The two plans of action for an up market where the value of the stock fund exceeds the average cost of acquisition are not identical. Plan One will be a mirror image of the rules which apply for a down market. Plan Two will contain what amounts to a far greater reluctance on the part of the investor to divest funds from the stock fund and place the proceeds into the cash fund.

STOCK PRICE ABOVE COST OF ACQUISITION

	PLAN ONE	PLAN TWO
MARKET VALUE OF SHARE OF STOCK FUND		
BETWEEN 100% AND 105% OF AVERAGE COST OF ACQUISITION		
CASH FUND	$50	
STOCK FUND	50	
BETWEEN 100% and 150% OF AVERAGE COST OF ACQUISITION		
CASH FUND		$50
STOCK FUND		50

As the market value of the stock fund moves up in relation to the average cost of acquisition, the $100 is placed in the cash fund. If the market value exceeds the average cost of acquisition by a sufficient degree, then divestment from stock to cash proceeds differently for the two plans of action. Divestment from stock to cash starts when the market value of a share of the stock fund exceeds the average cost of acquisition by 5 percent for Plan One. For Plan Two, divestment does not start until the market value exceeds the average cost of acquisition by 50 percent. Divestment of stock does not change the average cost of acquisition.

	PLAN ONE	PLAN TWO
MARKET VALUE OF STOCK SHARES AS PERCENTAGE OF AVERAGE COST OF ACQUISITION		
105% – 130%	CONVERT 2% STOCK TO CASH	
ABOVE 130%	CONVERT 5% STOCK TO CASH	
150% – 200%		CONVERT 1% STOCK TO CASH
ABOVE 200%		CONVERT 2% STOCK TO CASH

The pertinent rules for each plan of action were incorporated in the simulation program contained in the appendix to this chapter. No interest accrued to the money market, or cash fund, and no dividend return or inflationary compensation of equity ownership was built into the stock fund. As mentioned, one option is to place all money in the cash fund. One hundred dollars deposited monthly in an account for 1,000 months, with no interest, is $100,000. This is the base to measure the effectiveness of either plan of action from the point of view of even investing in the stock fund.

The simulation was run 1,000 times, each time creating an individual, random number generated, stock market history of 1,000 months. Both plans of action provided marginally better returns than depositing the $100 per month inflow of investment dollars into the cash fund. The expected value of the portfolio of stocks and the proceeds in the cash fund at the end of 1,000 months was $101,595 for Plan One and $105,574 for Plan Two. The probability distribution for various portfolio values of stock and cash is shown here.

PORTFOLIO VALUATION STOCK AND CASH	PERCENTAGE PROBABILITY OF OCCURRENCE PLAN ONE	PLAN TWO
$ 30,000 – 50,000	2.8%	5.0%
50,000 – 70,000	10.5	14.2
70,000 – 90,000	14.6	18.3
90,000 – 110,000	27.0	15.4
110,000 – 130,000	41.1	19.6
130,000 – 150,000	2.9	19.2
150,000 – 170,000	0.6	6.1
170,000 – 190,000	0.3	1.7
190,000 – 210,000	0.2	0.5

PORTFOLIO VALUE

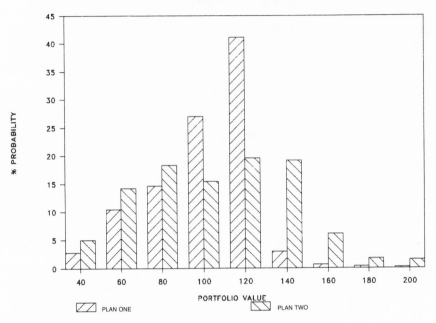

Exhibit 13.1.
Portfolio Value for Two Plans of Action

The comparative performance of these two plans of action can be seen in Exhibit 13.1.

The program listed in the appendix does not model the actual history of the stock market. Many of the market averages at the end of the 1,000-month simulation were between 500 and 1500, which seems reasonable considering a no-win, no-lose market starting out with an initial value of 1000. However, there were a fair number of occasions when the ending average of the market was outside this range. As an example, there were times when the end market value was less than 100. In far over a century of stock market history, a 90 percent decline happened only once (between 1929 and 1933). Thus the model of the stock market behavior is too severe on the down side when compared to reality. And equally so on the up side. The probability structure governing the trends in the model have to be amended to reflect actual market history. One way to do this is to enhance the probability of a neutral to bullish trend occurring as the market declines. And conversely, the probability of a neutral to bearish trend should also increase as the market moves to higher and higher ground. The final model of the stock market should have trends both in magnitude and length coupled with limits on the up side and down side that reasonably reflect the past history of the market plus any perceptions of a changing market environment.

For instance, the final model can incorporate more volatility than what has been observed in recent years. Surprise 10 or 20 percent rises, or drops, in the market can be thrown in by having a wild card, so to speak, buried among the random numbers.

The fact that Plan Two outperforms Plan One is immaterial to the discussion. The point is that the results for the two plans of action are different. That means one works better than the other. The evaluation of potential performance was done with a bloodless experiment—one that did not necessitate the actual investment of funds.

Once the final model of the stock market has been developed, far different sets of decision rules can be evaluated. One is buy when the market has recovered to a certain degree from a previous low, and sell when it has declined a certain degree from a previous high. This is the reverse of the contrarian strategy that is incorporated in the model. Who knows, maybe a conventional strategy is better than a contrarian one. The point is not whether the contrarian strategy is better or worse than the conventional strategy. The point is that simulation can help one decide which may be better. And the judgment can be made without risk of loss by not having to invest one's funds.

The model can be expanded to include various stock groupings. Stock groups usually follow the general movement of the market average, but some stock groups lag while others lead the market. The model could incorporate a mix of stock groups where those that lag and those that lead interchange with time. Another consideration may be to introduce gold as an alternative to the stock market along with a money fund. Whereas most stock groupings move in broad unison with the market average, gold has the potential to move in an opposite direction to the stock market. This may provide the opportunity to develop some interesting decision rules, or plans of action, for investment strategies involving gold, cash, and stocks.

Appendix to Chapter 13

PORTFOLIO MANAGEMENT PLANNING SIMULATION

In the simulation program for running Plan One, the number of simulations is entered in statement 30. Statement 50 sets the stock market averages at 1000 for the first month, and sets the amount of funds in the stock and cash funds at zero. Statements 60–260 create the stock market for the next thousand months. The variety of stock markets that can be created by a simple no-win, no-lose simulation can be viewed by insertion of the following statement (modifying the previous statement to refer to 265 rather than 270).

265   FOR I=1 TO 1000:PRINT I,S(I):NEXT

Screen graphing of the stock market would be a preferable way of viewing 1,000 simulations of eighty-plus years of stock market action.

The actual decision rules are contained in statements 310–420. The stock fund share price is assumed to be one hundredth of the value of the stock market ($10 per share when the market index is 1000). The insertion of the following statement permits one to view the end result of each simulation.

445   PRINT L;C,S(1000),S1,I

The evaluation of Plan Two was accomplished by editing statements 330, 340, 380, and 390.

```
10 REM NAME OF PROGRAM IS STOCK
20 DIM S(1000):DIM R(1000)
30 PRINT:INPUT "NUMBER OF SIMULATIONS: ";S
40 FOR L=1 TO S
50 P=1000:M=0:C=0:S(1)=1000:I=2
60 X=RND(X)
70 IF X<.05 THEN 140
80 IF X<.15 THEN 150
90 IF X<.3 THEN 160
100 IF X<.7 THEN 170
110 IF X<.85 THEN 180
120 IF X<.95 THEN 190
130 GOTO 200
140 X=RND(X):G1=-1:G2=4:N=1+INT(X*15):GOTO 210
150 X=RND(X):G1=-1.5:G2=3.5:N=1+INT(X*12):GOTO 210
160 X=RND(X):G1=-2:G2=3:N=1+INT(X*10):GOTO 210
```

```
170  X=RND(X):G1=-2.5:G2=2.5:N=1+INT(X*8):GOTO 210
180  X=RND(X):G1=-3:G2=2:N=1+INT(X*10):GOTO 210
190  X=RND(X):G1=-3.5:G2=1.5:N=1+INT(X*12):GOTO 210
200  X=RND(X):G1=-4:G2=1:N=1+INT(X*15)
210  IF I+N>1000 THEN 220 ELSE 230
220  A=I+N-1000:N=N-A
230  FOR J=I TO I+N
240  X=RND(X):G=G1+X*(G2-G1):G=G/100
250  S(J)=(1+G)*S(J-1)
260  NEXT:I=I+N:IF I=1000 THEN 270 ELSE 60
270  FOR I=1 TO 1000
280  IF I>1 THEN 300
290  C=50:V=S(1)/100:S1=50/V:M=50:GOTO 430
300  V=S(I)/100:A=M/S1
310  IF V*S1<.1*(C+V*S1) THEN 400
320  IF C<.1*(C+V*S1) THEN 400
330  IF V>1.3*A THEN 380
340  IF V>1.05*A THEN 390
350  IF V>.95*A THEN 400
360  IF V>.7*A THEN 410
370  GOTO 420
380  C=C+100+.05*S1*V:M=.95*M:S1=.95*S1:GOTO 430
390  C=C+100+.03*S1*V:M=.97*M:S1=.97*S1:GOTO 430
400  C=C+50:M=M+50:S1=S1+50/V:GOTO 430
410  C=.97*C:M=M+.03*C+100:S1=S1+(.03*C+100)/V:GOTO 430
420  C=.95*C:M=M+.05*C+100:S1=S1+(.05*C+100)/V
430  NEXT
440  I=INT((C+S(1000)*S1/100)/1000)
450  R(I)=R(I)+1:NEXT
460  A=0:FOR I=1 TO 1000:A=A+I*R(I)/S:NEXT
470  PRINT:PRINT "EXPECTED PORTFOLIO VALUE: ";A:PRINT
480  PRINT "PERCENT","PORTFOLIO"
490  PRINT "PROBABILITY","VALUE":PRINT
500  FOR I=1 TO 1000:IF R(I)=0 THEN 520
510  PRINT 100*R(I)/S,1000*I:INPUT Z$
520  NEXT:END
```

Index

About the Author

ROY L. NERSESIAN is Chair of the Management Department at Monmouth College, New Jersey. His previous book *Ships and Shipping: A Comprehensive Guide* reflects extensive planning experience in the maritime industry.